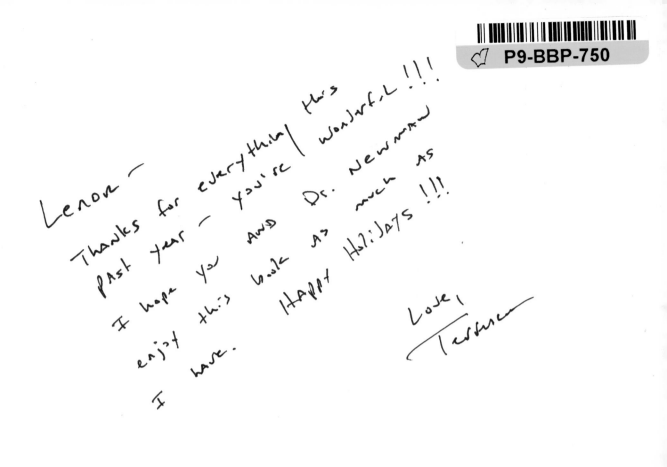

Lenore —
Thanks for everything this
past year — you're wonderful !!!
I hope you AND Dr. Newman
enjoy this book as much as
I have.   HAPPY Holidays !!!

Love,
Tessica

The NEW YORK RESTAURANT COOKBOOK

The NEW YORK RESTAURANT COOKBOOK

Recipes from the Dining Capital of the World

FLORENCE FABRICANT

NYC
& COMPANY
www.nycvisit.com

RIZZOLI
NEW YORK

First published in the United States of America in 2003
by Rizzoli International Publications, Inc.
300 Park Avenue South
New York, NY 10010
www.rizzoliusa.com

2003 2004 2005 2006 2007 / 10 9 8 7 6 5 4 3 2 1

Distributed in the U.S. trade by St. Martin's Press, New York

Printed in the United States of America

Designed by Patricia Fabricant

ISBN: 0-8478-2575-2

Library of Congress Control Number: 2003104980

THIS BOOK IS DEDICATED TO NEW YORK CITY'S
RESTAURANT COMMUNITY AND TO ALL THE
NEW YORKERS AND VISITORS WHO ENJOY THE
FINEST DINING IN THE WORLD.

CONTENTS

PREFACE

JONATHAN M. TISCH AND CRISTYNE L. NICHOLAS,
NYC & COMPANY

WHETHER YOU ARE A NEW YORKER, a lover of New York, or just a lover of great food and restaurants, this wonderful book is for you. These pages provide an insider's look, behind the scenes, at a wide variety of New York City restaurants and the outstanding food they serve.

New York City is big, brash, even overwhelming to some, but at its core, it is really a collection of unique neighborhoods. And in every neighborhood, there is great food. From the city's earliest days, food has brought people together. Gathering at "public tables" has been the center of our local life. Today, New York City offers the most internationally diverse dining experiences of any city in the world. At last count, there were more than 17,000 licensed eating establishments, representing everything from corner delis to four-star culinary palaces.

So if you are visiting New York City for pleasure or business, returning home from a visit here, or just living in the world's most dynamic city, remember to make reservations, wander in somewhere for a memorable meal, or, with the help of this book, make your own great meal at home. And by purchasing this book, you help support the NYC & Company Foundation, a charitable and educational organization whose mission is to support and promote New York City by encouraging tourism and the organizations that make visiting New York a special and exciting experience.

Let this book be your guide to the culinary pleasures of New York City. And as they say in the restaurants, "Enjoy!"

FOREWORD

DANNY MEYER

I AM ENORMOUSLY PROUD to be a member of New York's hospitality community. It is world-class in every way.

I did not set out, initially, to parlay my political science degree into a career in the restaurant business. But because my father's business had to do with tourism in France and Italy, I grew up with the privilege of traveling, experiencing wonderful restaurants, and even working as a tour guide in Rome by the time I was 20. I developed a passion for the hospitality business, for wanting to make people happy. I discovered that I was good at it. I believe it's in my genes. By the time I was 27, I had opened Union Square Cafe in Manhattan. There you have the seeds of my career.

There is probably no greater stage for a restaurateur than New York. As an adjunct to an art program, I opened a hot dog stand in the middle of Madison Square Park and before I knew it the national press had noticed. There is a voracious audience for both food and news about food, and if you have something to add to the culinary dialogue your story can reach the world just because this is New York. But along with the megaphone comes the microscope. In New York you might have a loyal following, but there are also people ready to pounce on your every foible. There is enormous competition and scrutiny, and these factors present a challenge. But they also raise the bar for excellence, and I have come to crave this dynamic atmosphere.

When a worthy competitor opens next door, of course it initially sends a shiver. But if your neighbor's business is good, it actually brings in new patrons for your restaurant and helps you maintain your edge. So many of our customers have become more sophisticated and demanding, which keeps our outlook fresh and vital. You cannot coast in New York.

Chefs were the trailblazers as professionals. They ratified the field for everyone. Now, along with restaurateurs and wine professionals, they have become entrepreneurs. When I started in this business you did not have the fine dining restaurant groups that exist and thrive today. Hospitality is a field in which anyone who works hard can rise. The profession has constantly welcomed and supported immigrant groups and their success stories are legendary.

Although the competition is fierce, the New York restaurant community is also tightly knit and incredibly collegial, especially when compared with many other industries. We collaborate effectively on cause-related work as well as promotional events. We are there for each other.

The community spirit of the hospitality industry was defined by the events of 9/11. Literally within moments of the horrific attacks, restaurateurs, chefs, and hospitality employees mobilized to provide relief to rescue workers, grieving families, and everyone else who needed help. With their dining rooms nearly empty or out of commission in the days following 9/11, members of the industry chose to extend their services beyond their own four walls and out into the communities, especially downtown, that needed them most. They could do no less.

Throughout the year, quietly and instinctively, restaurant professionals voluntarily do well by doing good. Scores of New York restaurants package leftover food to contribute to City Harvest, the organization that rescues leftover food and redirects it to where it is needed the most. Restaurants have generously provided leadership and talent to raise millions of dollars and to help Share Our Strength feed the needy, to help Citymeals-on-Wheels provide meals for the homebound elderly, and to help C-Cap to train inner-city students to become chefs and cooks. These efforts have helped to bond the members of the community, to bring people together.

I would go as far as to say that the fabric—not just the collective stomach—of New York has been nourished, nurtured, and enriched by this great industry.

But none of this would be possible without the continuing support of the restaurant-going public. By frequenting restaurants and treating them and their staffs with the same respect you expect them to shower on you at dinner, you also sustain the community. It's the best way to ensure that New York will maintain its position as the greatest restaurant city on the planet.

INTRODUCTION

FLORENCE FABRICANT

The kitchen has fascinated me, challenged me, and kept me entertained almost as long as I can remember. And when I say kitchen, I find it hard to separate home from restaurants. New York's restaurant scene has had a profound influence on my life. Do I go out to dinner or light the stove? No contest for some people, but a dilemma for me.

It is not an overstatement to say that I first began tinkering with restaurant recipes when I was about four years old. But please do not imagine some prodigy whipping up Tournedos Rossini for the family instead of playing with blocks. My obsession then, as I still vividly recall, was adding just the right amount of soy sauce to my egg-drop soup until I was satisfied with the flavor and color. It did not matter whether it was in the neighborhood chow mein palace or at Ruby Foo's—the original one—near Times Square.

My parents were avid restaurant-goers and I was a lucky participant. I loved the glitter of fancy places. I remember my father taking me to Chambord on Second Avenue, which had all the different sizes of Champagne bottles in the window. I always insisted that he recite their names—jeroboam, Nebuchadnezzar, and so forth—before we went into the narrow storefront restaurant in the shadow of the "El."

My mother adored the Forum of the Twelve Caesars and The Four Seasons. She did not like Dominick's and Mario's in the Bronx, but my father did; he took me to both, and insisted that my mother prepare steaks for him the way they did, seasoned with garlic and olive oil. Before theater we would go to the Algonquin Hotel, where I liked the creamed chicken served under a glass bell which the waiter removed with great ceremony. After theater, immense, crisply caramelized apple pancakes at Reuben's were a must. We would go to Rumpelmayer's on Central Park South for hot chocolate after skating in the Wollman Rink. Of course, I went to the Automat. And to the Tip-Toe Inn and the C&L when I visited friends on the Upper West Side. I remember these names better than those of some of my old boyfriends.

Although I was born in the Bronx, I grew up in Westchester County, and spent as much time as possible in Manhattan. In my early teens I attended classes at The Art Students League, and before taking the train home from Grand Central Terminal, I would always have a bowl of oyster stew at the Oyster Bar. By myself.

After eating the honey-soaked phyllo dessert called *ekmek kadaif* with *kaymak* at the Balkan-Armenian in the East Twenties, I asked the waiter to find out how it was made, especially the *kaymak*, a kind of dense clotted cream. The next day I spent an hour in the kitchen at home, cooking cream down and ladling it to aerate it as it condensed. My first gâteau Saint-Honoré, an indulgence of cream, caramel, custard, and crisp pastry, beckoned from a tall dessert cart at Voisin on Park Avenue. That one I did not attempt.

Far too few of the restaurant landmarks in the city's history and in my life before I was professionally involved in food linger as more than memories. There is a recipe for Oyster Stew from the Oyster Bar in this book, but I would have loved to include the sweetbreads with peas that I adored at Le Pavillon. I mourn Le Pavillon even as I celebrate Daniel, Jean Georges, and Le Bernardin. The new stars that make New York's restaurant universe shine so brightly fill many of the pages in this cookbook. The restaurants that have been included were selected in consultation with NYC & Company to represent all the boroughs and a cross-section of the city's ethnic fabric. And they are not limited just to high-profile places like Daniel and Jean Georges, or to the newest, hottest venues, but cover quite an array, from standbys like Sardi's and the Carnegie Deli to wd50 on the newly gentrified Lower East Side. Williamsburg, Brooklyn, is represented by the hip, new Relish, and the venerable Peter Luger Steak House.

During the selection process, there were a few brushes with disaster: Lespinasse, Pico, and Pazo were suddenly toast just as the list was being compiled. Others due to open in the coming months, such as the collection taking shape in the new complex at Columbus Circle, did not make the cut. There were also many, many deserving restaurants in the city that, regrettably, were not included. Not only were we limited by the size and scope of the book but we had to be careful to avoid overlapping restaurants that were already on the list. In a few instances we were not able to obtain suitable responses in a timely manner.

I requested two to four recipes from the current menu of each restaurant. The final assortment of recipes had to provide a balance, from appetizers through desserts, including drinks. It was also critical to see which recipes could best be transformed and adapted for the home cook without violating the chef's intention.

Over the years as a food professional, I have spent enough time in restaurant kitchens to learn to deal with chefs' recipes and even to understand the shorthand with which many are written. I have acquired some good habits, like plucking the leaves of herbs off the stems; shocking blanched vegetables in ice water; taking enough time to reduce a sauce before bolstering it with a final dollop of butter; tossing drained pasta in the pan with the sauce and adding some of the pasta water instead of merely dumping the sauce on top; and tweezing out the pin bones from fish fillets. I have incorporated these techniques into the recipes. They are worth adopting and will make you a better cook.

I am not anti-fat, and I use plenty of butter and oil in my own cooking. But I find that most chefs overdo it, or do not really measure when writing their recipes, often calling for six tablespoons when four are enough. Also, the portion sizes in restaurants can be excessive at times. I adjusted the recipes accordingly.

I have also acquired an understanding of how much of a recipe can be done in advance, leaving only the final assembly job before serving. There is more tolerance than one might think. I have incorporated this advice into the recipes, too.

As demanding as it is to be a chef, in some respects they have it easier than home cooks. A chef would walk out the door if asked to prepare Sea Scallops with Caviar and Watercress without the help of underlings to separate the watercress leaves according to size, trim the scallops, and so forth. That recipe, from Alain Ducasse, is in the book, wrestled into submission, step by step. So are The Four Seasons' Crisp Farmhouse Duck, which has to be started four days in advance, and Mario Batali's delicious rabbit from Babbo, which requires disjointing and partly deboning two rabbits, making stock, peeling baby carrots, and shucking peas.

Unlike the home kitchen, restaurants have batches of stock, chopped onions, peeled garlic cloves, rinsed and dried lettuces, properly softened butter, and perfect sorbets ready and waiting, making everything from the prepping to the final assembly of a dish as efficient as possible. Home cooking is not like that. Except for some staples, every recipe requires a shopping list and more than one preparation task. How many cooks know how many pounds of fresh peas in the pod it takes to end up with one cupful, shucked? In a restaurant that cup of peas is on hand, shelled and waiting. I took all these considerations into account when testing, organizing, and writing the recipes.

Because these recipes have come from restaurant kitchens, where the resources are not the same as in a home, some adjustments may be necessary when it comes to ingredients. For example, it is better to use well-flavored homemade stocks instead of the canned variety or bouillon cubes. These days, many fancy food shops and on-line retailers sell high-quality veal, chicken, beef, lamb, and vegetable sauce bases and concentrates, which would be fine to use.

At the same time, though, fresh ingredients should be genuinely fresh and in good condition; the quality of the ingredients is not negotiable. It is better to substitute baby spinach for arugula if the latter looks wilted, or diced sea scallops for bays if the bay scallops have been frozen. Similarly, when you try the recipes in this book, there is no harm in making sensible substitutions like filet mignon for veal or for venison in order to guarantee the best results.

The freshness imperative also applies to spices and herbs. Many of the chefs have specified organic ingredients, but it is not essential that they be used. Some chefs also made a point of insisting on a particular variety of salt. In general, kosher or sea salt would be best. And how much salt to use is a highly personal matter. Oils should be good quality: olive oil should always be extra virgin—those from Greece and Spain often represent the best value. Vinegars should be good quality, too; avoid supermarket balsamic. For most hard-to-find ethnic ingredients, reasonable substitutes have been listed.

Measuring is also important. Chefs usually weigh ingredients instead of measuring them by cups and spoons. Although many of the ingredients for these recipes have been given by volume, in many other books, weighing is essential. A good kitchen scale is a worthwhile investment.

There may still be some imprecision with timing. Not all stoves, ovens, and grills cook the same, and it is important to recognize when the ingredients have reached a certain stage of doneness. I have given guidelines to help, but exactly 25 minutes in my oven might mean 20 or 35 in yours.

Although some of the dishes—such as the rabbit from Babbo—are demanding and involve serious kitchen time, others like City Hall's Delmonico Steak with blue cheese butter and Pearl Oyster Bar's Fried Cod Sandwich, are quite simple to prepare, and none require unobtainable ingredients.

This is New York, after all, and there are very few components for a recipe that are not available somewhere. Butchers sell rabbits, although an advance order might be required. There are Korean supermarkets for sweet potato noodles, and spice merchants who keep smoked paprika on hand. The days when a trip to Chinatown was necessary to buy fresh ginger are past. A list of resources in the back of the book will provide guidance for shopping—whether you live in New York or not, it's easy now to order ingredients by mail through many of the suppliers listed. And the Internet's many grocery sites can also help.

These days chefs devise their dishes with a dozen different components. In adapting the recipes I often simplified them. I omitted the instructions for preparing the carrots and asparagus to go alongside Lutèce's roast chicken, the chestnut puree for the venison at La Côte Basque, and the salad served with the Open-Face Tuna Salad Sandwich at Le Pain Quotidien. Is there a dessert without an ice cream, a sauce or two, a delicate tuile, and a frivolous chocolate garnish? You are likely to find some of these adornments left off the plate, or perhaps merely suggested at the end of the recipe.

Even the presentation of food in a restaurant is different from the way it is served at home. So instead of requiring that four or six portions each be plated separately—usually by a team in a restaurant kitchen, where one cook puts the meat on the plate, another adds the sauce, and yet another drops a cluster of herbs on top—I gave instructions for family-style service in bowls and on platters.

But here is a restaurant tip: Before a plate goes on a waiter's tray and into the dining room, someone with a clean cloth wipes the rim of any extraneous drips of sauce, something that can easily be done at home. And another one: Serve hot food on warm plates.

Wine suggestions made by the chef or the restaurant's wine director have been included with each recipe. Sometimes they are fairly broad—"a Sauternes," for example—but in other instances they are extremely specific, down to the vintage; a more general recommendation is also offered with these. The recommendations are meant only as guidelines.

The recipes provide an excellent cross-section of what dining in New York today has come to represent. Traditionalists will find Chicken Soup from the Second Avenue Deli, Caesar Salad from Tavern on the Green, Onion Soup Gratinée from Capsouto Frères, and a Bittersweet Chocolate Soufflé from Payard Bistro. Nostalgia buffs will not be able to pass on Patsy's Lobster Fra Diavolo, and those with a spirit of adventure may want to try Pampano's Lobster Tacos. For vegetarians, there is Hangawi's Vermicelli Genghis Khan. Cooks who cannot resist a challenge can set off into the wilds of the Ricotta and Spinach Dumplings from Felidia, the Breast of Chicken and Foie Gras Poached in Cabbage from Bayard's, the Goose Fat Potatoes from Strip House, or the Lemongrass-Crusted Swordfish with Thai Peanut Sauce from Roy's New York.

The cuisines range from American, both classic and contemporary, to Chinese, Indian, Thai, Vietnamese, Moroccan, Mexican, Greek, Italian, Italian-American, French, Caribbean, and Spanish. Steakhouse specialties, brunch dishes, and cocktails are all in the book.

Trendy flavors like wasabi, luxury touches like a dollop of caviar or a slice of foie gras, and comfort food like deviled eggs and a version of macaroni and cheese are represented. The secret of Le Cirque's world-famous Crème Brûlée is revealed, as is how to make those omnipresent little molten chocolate cakes.

You might envy my family and many of our friends. We ate spectacularly well while I was testing the recipes. But now, for the big question, my perennial dilemma: Do I go out to dinner or into the kitchen tonight?

APPETIZERS

GOUGÈRES

MARINATED CALAMARI SALAD

CRACKLING CALAMARI SALAD WITH LIME-MISO DRESSING

SEA SCALLOPS WITH CAVIAR AND WATERCRESS

TORO TARTARE

MUSSEL SALAD WITH ARTICHOKES AND HARICOTS VERTS

GREEN ASPARAGUS WITH MORELS AND ASPARAGUS SAUCE

LEEKS BRAISED IN RED WINE

MOULES MARINIÈRES

YACHE PAJUN, VEGETABLE SCALLION PANCAKE

CORNMEAL-CRUSTED OYSTERS

LOBSTER CAKES WITH CUCUMBER-GINGER SALAD

LOBSTER TACOS

FONDUTA

CHICKEN LIVER CROSTINI

SAUTÉED FOIE GRAS WITH APRICOTS

GOUGÈRES

IT's IRONIC THAT ARTISANAL, a brasserie-style restaurant, occupies what once was the New York version of La Coupole, the famous Parisian brasserie. Between incarnations the space had a highly regarded run as An American Place. Now, as Artisanal, it features an enormous Belle Époque painting from a French railway station on one wall and, because the restaurant's emphasis is on cheese, a retail counter along another. Terrance Brennan, the chef and owner, has had a long love affair with cheese. His Lincoln Center–area restaurant, Picholine, is known for its outstanding selection. Brennan has also opened a wholesale cheese center where cheeses are aged and distributed, and where classes and receptions are held.

MAKES 36 PIECES

¾ cup all-purpose flour
¼ teaspoon baking powder
4 tablespoons unsalted butter
¼ cup plus 2 tablespoons milk
1¼ teaspoons sea salt
6 grinds black pepper
3 eggs, at room temperature
1 cup coarsely grated Gruyère
    cheese

Preheat the oven to 375 degrees. Line 2 baking sheets with parchment. Sift the flour and baking powder together and set aside.

Put the butter, ¼ cup of the milk, ¼ teaspoon of the salt, the pepper, and ½ cup of water in a 2-quart saucepan. Set over medium heat, bring to a boil, and cook until the butter melts, then remove from the heat. Dump in the flour mixture all at once, stir well with a wooden spoon, and return to the heat. Cook gently for a minute or two, stirring until the mixture starts to pull away from the sides of the saucepan and forms a ball. Transfer the dough to an electric mixer with a paddle attachment and beat at low speed until the mixture is just warm. You can do this by hand but it's a tough job. A food processor, however is also effective.

Add the eggs one at a time, beating to incorporate after each addition. Add ½ cup of the cheese. Beat until the mixture is smooth and shiny, about 10 minutes.

These gougères are lightened by the long beating and the addition of baking powder.

Though Gruyère is the classic cheese, other varieties, including Parmigiano-Reggiano, Roquefort, or even Cheddar, can be used.

A tablespoon or two of minced herbs can also be added just before the end of beating.

Gougères can be made in advance and frozen, then briefly reheated in a 350-degree oven, 10 to 15 minutes.

Using a pastry bag or 2 teaspoons, form 1-inch mounds on a baking sheet, placing them about an inch apart. You should be able to fit 18 gougères on a baking sheet. Gently brush the tops of the gougères with the remaining milk, and sprinkle each with a generous pinch of the remaining cheese and salt. Bake until puffed and deep gold, about 7 to 10 minutes. Remove from baking sheet and serve while still warm.

Champagne, or a white or red wine from Burgundy

MARINATED CALAMARI SALAD

THIS HISTORIC CHELSEA TAVERN, with its handsome bar anchoring a multi-story restaurant complex, has had several identities. Now with the teaming of executive chef Gerry Hayden, formerly of Aureole, and partner Steve Tzolis, who also owns Il Cantinori and Peryali, the restaurant has become Amuse. The massive bar remains the focus of the tavern area, but the furnishings are contemporary. So is the food served at the low banquettes and little tables, as well as in the adjacent dining room, decorated in a similar warmly modern style. The menu is divided according to price, allowing for informal mixing and matching, with plates both small and large. And for those who need guidance, there is also a set menu drawn from the à la carte choices.

SERVES 6

¾ cup extra virgin olive oil

4 large garlic cloves, minced

2 serrano chiles, seeded and minced

1½ pounds small squid (calamari), cleaned and sliced into thin strips

2 tablespoons sherry vinegar

Salt and freshly ground black pepper

2 tablespoons coarsely chopped celery leaves

2 tablespoons coarsely chopped flat-leaf parsley leaves

12 oil-cured black olives, pitted and halved

Heat half of the olive oil in a large sauté pan and toss in the garlic. Sauté until the garlic is golden. Add the chiles and squid, and cook for no more than a minute, stirring with a wooden spoon. Transfer the contents of the pan to a bowl. Add the remaining oil, the vinegar, and salt and pepper to taste. Cover and leave in the refrigerator for at least 3 hours. Longer, but not longer than another hour, is fine.

Remove the bowl from the refrigerator a half hour before serving. Fold in the celery leaves, parsley, and olives. Check seasoning and spoon the salad onto 6 plates.

This salad is essentially a ceviche of calamari. It can be served in martini glasses garnished with a slender stick of celery. To make hors d'oeuvres to go with cocktails, cut the squid strips into 1-inch-long strips, proceed with the recipe, place them in shot glasses, top each with an olive half, and serve with tiny forks. This version makes about 24 servings.

Fresh celery leaves, with their fragrant pungency, are good to use as an herb.

Domaine Leccia Patrimonio, a Corsican red wine, or another red country wine to serve slightly chilled

CRACKLING CALAMARI SALAD WITH LIME–MISO DRESSING

CHINA GRILL

CHINA GRILL IS THE FLAGSHIP of an ever-expanding restaurant group owned by Jeffrey Chodorow. Represented in Manhattan by the original China Grill, Tuscan, Asia de Cuba, Rocco's (of original reality-TV fame), and the new Mix in partnership with none other than Alain Ducasse, it also has a strong foothold in Miami, San Francisco, Las Vegas, Los Angeles, London, and Mexico City. China Grill, with quotations from Marco Polo's writings embedded in the floor, was one of New York's first Pacific Rim restaurants. This calamari salad, which combines Japanese, Thai, and Italian influences, is a fine example.

SERVES 4

1 tablespoon chopped fresh ginger

1 large garlic clove

2 tablespoons soy sauce

¼ cup mellow white miso paste

¼ cup rice vinegar

¼ cup lime juice

6½ cups soybean oil

1 head radicchio, cored and sliced very thin

1 head frisée, cored and sliced thin

½ cup cornstarch, sifted

10 ounces cleaned squid (calamari), sliced in thin rings, plus the tentacles

Sea salt

To make the dressing: turn on the food processor and drop the ginger and garlic through the feed tube. Process until they are minced. Stop the machine and scrape down the sides. Add the soy sauce, miso, vinegar, and lime juice. Whirl briefly to blend. With the machine running, slowly add ½ cup of the soybean oil, just as though making mayonnaise. Process until the dressing is emulsified, then transfer it to a container with a pouring spout. You should have about 1½ cups of dressing.

Toss the radicchio and frisée together in a bowl, then toss again with half the dressing. Spread it on a rimmed platter.

Heat the remaining 6 cups of oil in a wok or a large, deep saucepan to 360 degrees. Set a large bowl near the stove and line it with paper towels. Place the cornstarch in a bowl, add the calamari rings and tentacles and toss with your fingers until they are well-coated. When the oil reaches 360 degrees, drop in the calamari. Use a wooden fork or a pair of chopsticks to separate the rings as much as you can, and swirl the oil gently as the calamari cooks. When the calamari is golden—and this will take a good 5 to 8 minutes, longer than you might think—scoop it out

Most fried calamari is dusted with flour. This recipe, using cornstarch instead, results in lighter squid rings that stay crisp longer, even when doused with dressing.

with a skimmer or a slotted spoon, place it in the paper-lined bowl and sprinkle it with sea salt. Pull out the paper towel, distributing the salt, then spread the calamari on the salad. Drizzle with the remaining dressing and serve.

Pinot noir or sauvignon blanc

SEA SCALLOPS WITH CAVIAR AND WATERCRESS

ALAIN DUCASSE

I N HIS LUSH, INTIMATE RESTAURANT, which is among New York's most elegantly appointed, Michelin three-star chef Alain Ducasse has brought European fine dining to America. You might begin with a glass of Champagne and gougères served on a Lalique plate in the glowing Art Deco sitting room before being seated in the main room, where your reservation guarantees that the table is yours for the evening. Crisp, slender baguettes or buttery brioche-style breads are offered with two kinds of butter. Most dishes are accompanied by inventive side dishes that use the same ingredients to play raw against cooked or pureed against sliced. For example, in this recipe Ducasse uses what is essentially scallop trimmings to make the scallop butter sauce. And, of course, crowning the dish with a generous dollop of osetra caviar is virtually de rigueur at Alain Ducasse.

SERVES 4

1 bunch watercress, rinsed and
  dried
1 pound sea scallops (8 to 12
  depending on the size)
4 tablespoons extra virgin olive oil
3 tablespoons lemon juice
Salt and freshly ground black
  pepper
4 tablespoons unsalted butter
2 shallots, peeled and minced
1 thyme sprig
1 bay leaf
5 garlic cloves, crushed
½ cup *vin jaune* or dry sherry
1 cup chicken stock
4 ounces osetra caviar or 1½
  teaspoons *fleur de sel*

> It pays to note that when chefs
> use herbs, like the watercress in
> this recipe, they often take the time
> to remove the leaves and discard
> the stems.
> Most of the time the tendons
> from the sea scallops are simply
> discarded. But they do have flavor,
> so in this recipe they're cooked to
> make a base for the scallop sauce.
> Vin jaune, a golden wine from
> the Jura region of France, has
> become extremely popular with
> chefs (see recipes, pages 30 and 51).
> The best vin jaune is Château-
> Chalon. The wine has a sherry-like
> quality.

Pluck the leaves from the stems of the watercress, and separate the large leaves from the small ones. Discard the stems. Painstaking, yes, but that's how it is done when you have three Michelin stars. Trim the hard tendon—that little half-moon ridge attached to the side of the scallop—and reserve. Cut the scallops into ½-inch cubes and toss them with 2 tablespoons of the olive oil, 1½ tablespoons of the lemon juice, and freshly ground black pepper. Refrigerate the scallops to let them marinate.

Place the scallop tendons in a small saucepan. Add 2 tablespoons of the butter and sauté gently for about a minute. Add the shallots, thyme, bay leaf, and garlic. Sauté until the shallots are translucent. Add the *vin jaune* and simmer until the wine has evaporated and just glazes the pan. Add the stock and simmer gently until reduced by half. Strain the contents of the pan, discarding the solids. Pour this sauce base back into the pan and add the remaining butter, bit by bit, until the sauce becomes syrupy. Add ½ teaspoon of the lemon juice and season to taste with salt and pepper. Keep the sauce warm.

Toss the large watercress leaves with the remaining lemon juice and olive oil. Arrange them in a mound on 4 salad plates. Toss the marinated scallops with the small watercress leaves and arrange this mixture in a mound on top of the watercress salad. Top the scallops with caviar or, if not using caviar, sprinkle with *fleur de sel*. Drizzle the warm butter sauce around the outside edge of the salad and serve.

Lieb Family Cellars Pinot Blanc 2001 from Long Island, or another pinot blanc that is fresh-tasting but well-perfumed to complement the sweet scallops and peppery watercress

TORO TARTARE

JEWEL BAKO

J EWEL IS THE OPERATIVE TERM for this tiny Japanese restaurant, which may be the most elegant spot in the still funky East Village. Jack Lamb, a former maître d'hôtel at Bouley Bakery, and his wife, Grace, do not compromise on ingredients or presentation for pricey *kaiseki*, or set dinners. A sushi bar in the rear, beyond the arched wooden ceiling of the main room, has a few seats for those who prefer to pick and choose. The Lambs have also opened Blue Goose around the corner, a blue-and-white striped café serving breads, pastries, and other light fare for breakfast, lunch, and supper.

SERVES 4

2 tablespoons drained capers
2 tablespoons extra virgin olive oil
2 tablespoons grated fresh ginger
Sea salt
12 ounces sushi-quality tuna
½ ripe Hass avocado, peeled
2 teaspoons lime juice
2 teaspoons soy sauce
½ teaspoon prepared wasabi paste
1 ounce osetra caviar

> Salmon or hamachi (yellowtail) can be used instead of tuna.

In a mortar, crush the capers, work in the olive oil, and finally the ginger. Season the mixture with a pinch of sea salt. Finely dice the tuna and fold it into the caper mixture. Do not combine the tuna and the seasoning more than 20 minutes before serving.

Mash the avocado, mixing in the lime juice as you go. Mix in the soy sauce and wasabi, adjusting the amounts to taste.

To serve, pack the tuna so it nearly fills a half-cup metal measuring cup, and turn it out onto a small salad plate. Repeat with the remaining tuna on 3 more plates. Spread the avocado mixture on top of each serving of tuna and top with the caviar.

🍷 Auxey-Duresses, a crisp chardonnay, or a cold, dry sake such as Hakkaisan Jyunmai Ginjyu

MUSSEL SALAD WITH ARTICHOKES AND HARICOTS VERTS

OUEST

Tom Valenti has put to rest the conventional wisdom that there is no room for a fine restaurant on the Upper West Side beyond the Lincoln Center area. After he opened Ouest, a number of other chefs followed suit, so that now the Upper West Side offers more than sushi bars, Tex-Mex joints, and pizza. Valenti's career has taken him to many parts of the city, but he is right at home in his open kitchen on Upper Broadway, producing big flavors for the local regulars and for those who would venture to this part of the city for a meal, not just to shop at Zabar's. His second restaurant, 'Cesca, is nearby.

Do not be daunted by the process of removing all the leaves and the choke from the artichokes and throwing this debris away. The fleshy heart, sometimes called the bottom, is the best part of the vegetable.

Big green-lipped mussels from New Zealand are excellent to use.

See page 65 for directions on making homemade mayonnaise, but omit the anchovies and cheese.

New Zealand sauvignon blanc from the Marlborough region

6 globe artichokes

Juice of 1 lemon

1 cup dry white wine

4 garlic cloves, peeled and smashed

2 pounds mussels, scrubbed and debearded (see tip, page 33)

⅔ cup mayonnaise, preferably homemade (see tip)

1 generous tablespoon Dijon mustard

2 tablespoons minced shallots

Pinch cayenne

Salt and freshly ground black pepper

6 ounces *haricots verts* or fresh green beans, trimmed and cut in thirds

3 tablespoons extra virgin olive oil

6 small bunches mâche or 3 cups fresh watercress leaves

Ouest

Preparing this salad is a multi-step procedure, but once all the components are ready, the assembly becomes a snap. First, trim all the leaves from the artichokes. Use a paring knife to trim away the fuzzy choke, taking care not to cut away the fleshy heart. Neatly trim off the stem and the edges around the heart. Place the hearts in a bowl, add half of the lemon juice plus water to cover, and set aside.

Heat the wine and garlic in a 3-quart saucepan. Add the mussels, cover, and simmer until the mussels open, about 6 minutes. Remove the mussels, leaving any unopened ones in the pan. Steam these for another 2 minutes, then discard any that still have not opened. Remove the mussels from the shells and place the mussels in a bowl. Discard the shells. Strain the mussel cooking liquid and reserve 3 tablespoons.

Beat together the mayonnaise, mustard, reserved mussel broth, shallots, cayenne, and salt and pepper to taste. Fold half this dressing into the mussels. Set aside in the refrigerator.

Bring a 2-quart pot of salted water to a boil. Cook the artichoke hearts until tender, about 10 minutes; remove them with a slotted spoon and set aside. Add the *haricots verts* to the boiling water and blanch for 1 minute. Drain and place in a bowl of ice water. When the beans are cool, dry them on paper towels, then transfer to a large bowl and toss with 1 tablespoon of the olive oil. Add the mâche and the remaining oil and lemon juice to the bowl and toss again.

Slice the artichoke hearts vertically, about ¼-inch thick, and arrange slices in a circle on 6 salad plates. Pile some of the mussels in the center of the artichoke hearts. Make a mound of the mâche and *haricots verts* salad on top of each, drizzle the remaining mayonnaise dressing over and around the salad, and serve.

GREEN ASPARAGUS WITH MORELS AND ASPARAGUS SAUCE

JEAN GEORGES

S OME NEW YORKERS wonder whether Jean-Georges Vongerichten has an identical twin. Although he is the chef and partner in five restaurants in the city and several others around the world with more on the way, he seems almost always to be in the gleaming open kitchen at his flagship restaurant, Jean Georges. He's an inventive cook, one who soaks up new ideas like a sponge and creates food that is original, thought-provoking, and filled with flavor. His tightly wound personality translates into restaurants that inspire passion with every bite.

SERVES 6

1 bunch pencil asparagus, woody ends snapped off

2 tablespoons unsalted butter

3 tablespoons *vin jaune* or oloroso sherry (see tip, page 25)

Salt and freshly ground white pepper

1 shallot, peeled and diced

½ pound fresh morels, rinsed well and dried

2 tablespoons heavy cream

36 jumbo asparagus, ends snapped off and peeled

> Asparagus is always best cooked and served à la minute so the flavor and texture will be more vibrant.
>
> Morels can harbor sand in their deeply pitted surfaces. So be sure to rinse them well and allow them to dry.

Cut the pencil asparagus into 1-inch lengths. Place them in a saucepan with water to cover and boil a couple of minutes until tender. Drain, reserving ½ cup of the cooking water. Puree the asparagus in a blender, adding some of the cooking water to thin the mixture. Strain through a fine sieve into a small saucepan and heat gently over low heat. Whisk in 1 tablespoon of the butter, 2 tablespoons of the *vin jaune* or sherry, and salt and pepper to taste. Remove from the heat and set aside, covered.

Melt the remaining tablespoon of butter in a 10-inch skillet over low heat. Add the shallot and cook until softened. Increase the heat to medium, add the morels, and sauté until the morels are fully cooked, about 10 minutes. Stir in the remaining *vin jaune* and the cream. Simmer a few minutes until thickened. Season with salt and pepper, and set aside.

Cook the jumbo asparagus in a large pot of salted boiling water about 6 minutes, until tender, then drain. Arrange 6 of the spears side by side on each plate. Reheat the asparagus sauce and spoon along one side of the plate. Reheat the morels and spoon along the opposite side of the plate.

A northern Italian white like Ribolla Gialla 2001 from Friuli

LEEKS BRAISED IN RED WINE

BALDORIA

THIS TWO-STORY SPOT IN THE THEATER DISTRICT is the offspring of what is probably New York's most exclusive restaurant—Rao's, an East Harlem bar-restaurant that does not accept reservations from persons unknown to the management. Regulars have their tables, but others who have some insider connection can sometimes secure a spot that's not being used by its "owner." Frank Jr., son of Frank Pellegrino, an owner of Rao's, decided he wanted to strike out on his own, so with his father's blessing he opened Baldoria. Some of the Italian-American specialties for which Rao's is known, such as baked clams, meatballs, and lemon chicken, are on Baldoria's menu, but more ambitious food is also offered in the casual, tiled-floor setting.

SERVES 4 TO 6

12 slender leeks (about 2 pounds), well-trimmed, with about 2 inches of green

1 tablespoon unsalted butter

⅓ cup dry red wine

½ cup veal stock

Salt and freshly ground black pepper

1 tablespoon balsamic vinegar

1 tablespoon minced flat-leaf parsley leaves

Use a sharp knife to quarter the tops of the leeks vertically through the green and to where the white begins. Rinse thoroughly and pat dry.

Melt the butter in a large, heavy sauté pan. Add the leeks, roll in the butter, cover, and cook a few minutes until they begin to sweat. Add the wine, veal stock, and salt and pepper. Cover and braise until tender, about 10 minutes. Baste the leeks with the vinegar, then lift them out of the pan, drain them well, and arrange on a serving platter.

Cook the remaining liquid over high heat until reduced to about ½ cup. Season to taste, then pour over the leeks, scatter the parsley on top and serve hot or at room temperature.

Rutherford Hill Merlot 2000 or another California merlot, or Rosso di Montalcino Collemattoni 2000

Leeks are often sold in uneven 1-pound bunches, with both thick and thin stalks. For this recipe, it's best to buy loose leeks, so you can select uniformly slender ones.

MOULES MARINIÈRES

Few of New York's restaurants evoke Belle Époque France as beautifully as L'Absinthe. The setting, with its globe lights, intricate tile floors, posters, mirrors, and brass trim suggests the ultimate neighborhood bistro or brasserie. But it is not just a pretty face. The chef and owner, Jean-Michel Bergougnoux, has the finest credentials, and offers a menu that covers both traditional dishes, like moules marinières, and more original fare. Perhaps it's the setting, for at L'Absinthe's comfortable banquettes, the classics are what whet the appetite.

Serves 4

6 pounds mussels, preferably Prince Edward Island

2 tablespoons extra virgin olive oil

2 tablespoons unsalted butter

4 shallots, peeled and finely chopped

1 bouquet garni (a few parsley sprigs, thyme sprigs, and a bay leaf tied together)

1½ cups dry white wine

Freshly ground white pepper

Crusty baguette or country bread

Muscadet sur Lie, the most recent vintage, from a producer like Michel Morilleau

In addition to removing the "beard" or byssus, by pulling it off with a knife, a chef will take care to trim off the bit of gray filament along the edge of the mussel.

Scrub mussels and debeard as necessary.

Place a small stockpot over medium heat. Add the oil and butter, stir in the shallots, and cook until the shallots are translucent, about 2 minutes. Add the bouquet garni, mussels, and wine. Turn heat to high. When the wine simmers, reduce heat to medium, cover, and cook until mussels open, about 6 minutes. Discard any that do not open. Transfer mussels to 4 soup plates. Season the broth with pepper to taste, spoon over mussels, being careful not to scoop any sandy residue at the bottom of the pot, and serve, with crusty bread on the side.

YACHE PAJUN, VEGETABLE SCALLION PANCAKE

DO HWA

Growing up in Queens, Jenny Kwak and her sisters were privileged to enjoy their mother's excellent Korean home cooking. To give New Yorkers an idea of just how good Korean food could be, Kwak opened Dok Suni's, in the East Village, using her family's recipes and enlisting her mother to supervise the cooks. A friendly spot that did not seek a Korean clientele like the restaurants in "Little Korea" on West 32nd Street, Dok Suni's was so successful that the mother-daughter team opened Do Hwa, a more sophisiticated venue in Greenwich Village.

2 teaspoons soy sauce

½ teaspoon red pepper flakes

1 teaspoon sesame seeds

⅓ cup rice vinegar

2 medium-size zucchini (about 10 ounces)

1 bunch scallions, trimmed

4 *shiso* leaves, sold in Asian markets (also called beefsteak plant or *perilla)*

1 cup all-purpose flour

¾ teaspoon salt

1 egg

½ teaspoon *dashida* (Korean beef stock base), or beef bouillon powder, optional

¼ cup peanut oil

Unlike most recipes, this one doesn't call for preheating the pan before adding the batter. That's so the vegetables have time to cook before the batter has browned.

This is a last-minute dish: fried, cut in pieces, and served at once. But the various components of the pancake can be readied and the sauce assembled in advance. First, combine the soy sauce, pepper flakes, sesame seeds, and vinegar in a small bowl. This is the dipping sauce. Set aside.

Using a paring knife, slice off wide strips of the zucchini skin, leaving only ⅛ inch of the flesh attached. Julienne the strips lengthwise, then cut them into 1-inch pieces. Discard the rest of the zucchini—it contains too much water for the recipe. Cut the scallions in half lengthwise, then on an angle into 1-inch pieces. Roll the *shiso* leaves and slice them into thin shreds.

When you're ready to cook the pancake, whisk the flour and salt in a large mixing bowl. Beat the egg, ¾ cup cold water, and the beef stock base if using. Whisk the egg mixture into the flour mixture to make a batter. Fold in the zucchini strips, scallions, and *shiso*. Allow to rest 2 minutes so the batter can begin to soften the vegetables.

Pour the oil into a 10- or 12-inch skillet. Nonstick isn't necessary, but it helps. Add the batter to the cold skillet. Turn the heat to medium-high and cook the pancake until it's golden on the bottom. Run a spatula around the edge of the pancake to loosen it, place a large plate over the skillet, flip, then slide the pancake back into the skillet to cook the other side. Remove the pancake to the paper towels to drain it briefly. Cut it into wedges and serve with the dipping sauce.

OB Korean beer, another Asian beer, or the mild Korean sweet potato vodka called soju

CORNMEAL-CRUSTED OYSTERS

VINE

THE HEART OF THE DOWNTOWN FINANCIAL DISTRICT is gradually being transformed as a number of stately office towers, many predating the Depression, have been converted to residential properties. The building that houses Vine is a perfect example. Massive columns and neoclassic detail greet the visitor who rounds the corner to the restaurant's discreet entrance. Inside, soaring ceilings add grandeur to an otherwise modest room which features a bar lining one wall. There's a small food shop and café next door. The real prize, however, is the downstairs bank vault, which is used for private parties and overflowing lunch crowds hungering for Vine's well-focused New American cooking.

SERVES 4 TO 6

1 tablespoon freshly grated
   horseradish
½ cup crème fraîche
½ cup mayonnaise
Salt and freshly ground black pepper
24 oysters on the half shell
½ cup flour
½ cup stone-ground cornmeal,
   preferably a mixture of yellow
   and white
1 teaspoon ground cumin
1 teaspoon cayenne
2 cups peanut oil

Though freshly grated horseradish is best, bottled white horseradish can be substituted. Just be sure to drain it well, and taste the sauce to make sure it has enough zip. A pinch of wasabi powder can be used to enliven it.

To make the sauce, mix the horseradish, crème fraîche, and mayonnaise in a small bowl. Season to taste with salt and pepper, and refrigerate until ready to use.

Remove the oysters from the shells. Rinse the shells, dry, and set aside. Mix the flour, cornmeal, cumin, and cayenne in a shallow dish and season with a teaspoon each of salt and pepper.

Heat the oil to 350 degrees in a wok, deep-fryer, or, if you are not an equipment junkie, a deep saucepan.

Dredge the oysters in the flour mixture, place them in the hot oil, and fry until they're golden brown and crisp, about 2 minutes. Drain them briefly on a paper towel. Arrange the shells on 4 or 6 salad plates, depending on how many servings you want. Place a generous dollop of the horseradish mixture on each shell. Place a fried oyster on top of the horseradish cream in each shell and serve.

A crisp sauvignon blanc or a blanc de blancs Champagne

LOBSTER CAKES WITH CUCUMBER-GINGER SALAD

'21' CLUB

The name of the restaurant refers to the address—21 West 52nd Street—and "club" is a holdover from the days when the premises housed a speakeasy. '21' was founded in 1930, during Prohibition, and in fact, its former wine cellar, now a private dining room, is still reached through a hidden door. The wine collection at '21' even included some so-called "medicinal" wines in an attempt to circumvent the Volstead Act. Today, the double town house, with its wrought iron balustrades and painted jockeys standing at attention, still attracts regulars to its dining room, where the tables are covered with red-checked cloths and the ceiling is hung with toys and souvenirs. And classic old standbys on the menu such as the '21' Burger and the Chicken Hash are still favorites. But chef Erik Blauberg also has a way with modern haute cuisine, like these lobster cakes.

SERVES 4

6 tablespoons extra virgin olive oil

½ jalapeño chile, seeded and minced

½ cup minced, seeded red bell pepper

½ cup minced onion

Salt and freshly ground white pepper

2 egg yolks

1 tablespoon Tabasco

2 tablespoons lime juice

5 tablespoons mayonnaise

2 tablespoons Dijon mustard

1 tablespoon minced chives

½ tablespoon minced flat-leaf parsley

2 teaspoons minced cilantro leaves

Pinch cayenne

Heat 2 tablespoons of the oil in a sauté pan. Add the jalapeño, red bell pepper, and onion. Season with salt and pepper. Sauté over low heat, until the vegetables are soft but not brown. Remove the vegetables to a bowl and set aside to cool about 30 minutes.

In a large mixing bowl, combine egg yolks, Tabasco, and lime juice. Lightly blend in the mayonnaise, mustard, chives, parsley, cilantro, and cayenne. Fold in the lobster, reserved sautéed vegetables, soft bread crumbs, and ¼ cup of the panko. Spread the remaining panko evenly on a pan at least 8 by 8 inches. Pack one-quarter of the lobster mixture into an empty 6-ounce tuna fish can (or a ramekin) and place the can, open side down, onto the panko. Lift off the can. Repeat with the remaining lobster mixture. Sprinkle the extra panko from the pan onto the tops of the cakes, pressing a tablespoon or more of the panko onto each cake. Refrigerate for at least 30 minutes.

½ pound fresh cooked lobster meat cut into ½-inch pieces (see tip)

½ cup soft fresh bread crumbs

1¼ cups *panko* (Japanese white bread crumbs)

1 tablespoon unsalted butter

Cucumber-Ginger Salad (recipe follows)

Preheat the oven to 400 degrees. Heat the remaining 4 tablespoons of oil in a large ovenproof skillet. Place the lobster cakes in the skillet and sauté over medium heat until golden brown on the bottom. Carefully turn the cakes, add the butter to skillet, cook 1 minute, and transfer the pan to the oven. Bake until golden brown, about 4 minutes. Using a spatula, transfer the cakes to individual plates, place some of the Cucumber-Ginger Salad alongside, and serve.

CUCUMBER-GINGER SALAD

Place cucumbers in a bowl. Add the ginger, ginger juice, and vinegar. Mix well. Fold in dill. Season with pepper.

2 medium cucumbers, peeled, halved lengthwise, seeded and sliced thin

⅓ cup Japanese pickled ginger, coarsely chopped

3 tablespoons juice from pickled ginger

3 tablespoons rice vinegar

2 tablespoons minced dill leaves

Freshly ground white pepper

Alsatian gewürztraminer, especially from Domaine Weinbach, Paul Blanck or Zind-Humbrecht

You can buy lobster meat cooked and out of the shell, or you can boil a 1¾-pounder in a large pot of water for about 8 minutes, and you'll have your ½ pound of lobster meat. Two 1-pound lobsters, which cost less, can also be used; boil them for about 6 minutes.

LOBSTER TACOS

PAMPANO

WHAT IS IT ABOUT CELEBRITY RESTAURANTS IN NEW YORK? Sports figures sometimes do well, though most of the time, their places are branches of nationwide franchises. But Marla Maples and Britney Spears could not survive as restaurateurs. Only when the celebrity is discreetly in the background, the way Robert de Niro operates, does it seem to work. Placido Domingo had a hard time fulfilling his restaurant dream with his name on the marquee. First he tried Spanish food, then a blend of Spanish and Mexican. Now, lightened and brightened, and with his presence strictly behind the scenes, the restaurant has become Pampano, specializing in Mexican seafood. Richard Sandoval, who also owns Maya on the Upper East Side, runs the kitchen.

2 live lobsters, each 1½ pounds

1½ tablespoons unsalted butter

1 tablespoon extra virgin olive oil

½ cup finely chopped onion

2 garlic cloves, minced

2 *chiles de arból*, or ½ teaspoon red
    pepper flakes

2 tablespoons tomato paste

1 cup heavy cream

¼ cup chicken stock

Salt

3 tablespoons minced cilantro leaves

½ cup canned black beans, rinsed
    and drained

4 flour tortillas

1 ripe Hass avocado, peeled and
    sliced

If you prefer, you can purchase 1 pound of cooked lobster meat for this recipe.

Caymus Vineyards Conundrum 2001, or another rich California white

There are four separate components to this recipe, each of which needs to be prepared before the tacos can be assembled and served. But all can be done in advance and reheated at the last minute.

Boil the lobsters for about 6 minutes. Drain and set aside. When they're cool enough to handle, crack the shells and extract the meat. Dice the meat into ½-inch pieces and place it in a small pan with the butter, covered.

For the sauce, heat the oil in a medium saucepan, add the onion, garlic and chiles, and gently sauté until the onion is translucent. Stir in the tomato paste, cook for a moment, then stir in the cream. Cook about 5 minutes until thickened; stir in the chicken stock, season with salt and add 1 tablespoon of the cilantro. Set aside.

Puree or finely mash the black beans, adding enough water to make a mixture about the consistency of sour cream.

Just before serving, strain the cream sauce and gently reheat it; keep warm. Reheat the lobster with the butter and keep warm. Heat the beans. Place over high heat a griddle or a cast iron skillet large enough to hold a tortilla. Add one tortilla, heat for 45 seconds, until the tortilla starts to blister, turn and heat another 15 seconds. Remove the tortilla to a flat surface. Spread one-quarter of the black beans in a line down the center, top with one-quarter of the lobster, spoon on about 3 generous tablespoons of the sauce, add about 4 slices of the avocado, and sprinkle with ½ tablespoon of the cilantro. Roll the tortilla around the filling and place it, seam side down, on a warm serving platter. Repeat with the remaining tortillas and serve at once.

FONDUTA

SEBASTIANO MAIOGLIO opened his restaurant, Barbetta, in 1906 in twin brownstone Astor town houses that were built in 1874 and 1881. The restaurant is now owned and run by his daughter, Laura Maioglio. Embellished with crystal chandeliers and fine woodwork, Barbetta also has one of the city's most elegant gardens for outdoor dining on soft summer evenings. It has always specialized in the cooking of the Piedmont region of northern Italy. Fonduta, a simple cheese appetizer that can be ennobled with shavings of white truffle, is a classic of the region. Laura Maioglio serves the fonduta in a nest of crisply cooked Parmigiano-Reggiano and decorates it with whole quail eggs, for a unique dish that has to be prepared one serving at a time. At home, a simple fonduta with a scattering of fresh white truffles in season will do just fine.

SERVES 4

1 (12-inch) baguette, sliced thin

½ cup milk

6 ounces Italian Fontina Val d'Aosta cheese, rind removed, diced

2 egg yolks

1 (1-ounce) fresh white truffle or 2 teaspoons white truffle oil, optional (sold in fancy food shops)

If you use white truffle oil, be sure that it's fresh and of good quality. Always store it in the refrigerator. It can be omitted.

This recipe calls for some fast action. Everything has to be ready to serve as soon as it is finished. So get your crostini ready first. Lightly toast the baguette slices and arrange them on a platter around a shallow 12- ounce ceramic bowl.

Place a heavy 2-quart saucepan over low heat, add the milk, and when it begins to warm, add the cheese. Stir with a whisk. When the cheese and milk are smooth and creamy, add the egg yolks, and beat them vigorously into the cheese mixture. As soon as the yolks are incorporated, remove the pan from the heat. Beat for another minute, then pour the fonduta into the waiting bowl.

If you have a fresh truffle, wait until you present the fonduta at the table before shaving it on top to maximize the aroma. Otherwise, drizzle the white truffle oil on the fonduta right before seving. Guests can dip the crostini into the cheese mixture.

Sparkling white Prosecco from the Piedmont region of Italy

CHICKEN LIVER CROSTINI
TRATTORIA DELL'ARTE

A HUGE ANTIPASTI DISPLAY, copious portions, and decor that is at once rustic Italian and whimsical—with its artistic studies of noses and other body parts that seem to reflect the Art Students League down the street—all set Trattoria dell'Arte apart. Shelly Fireman, who owns this restaurant and several others nearby—including Brooklyn Diner, Red Eye Grill, and Shelly's New York; and Fiorello's, another Italian fantasy, across from Lincoln Center—doesn't mind a touch of whimsy in his places. Consider the noses.

SERVES 4

¾ pound chicken livers,
   well-trimmed and cut into
   1-inch pieces

Salt and freshly ground black pepper

4 (¾-inch thick) slices Tuscan bread
   or other crusty bread

1 garlic clove, cut in half
   lengthwise

3 tablespoons extra virgin olive oil

¼ cup balsamic vinegar, at least 10
   years old

The secret to this dish is to make sure the livers are seared on the outside, pink in the middle, and well-glazed with the balsamic reduction. It is best to accomplish this by cooking one portion at a time, restaurant-style. At home though, cooking them all at once is easier and still gives a good result.

Dry the livers on several sheets of paper towel. Season with salt and pepper.

Toast the bread slices, rub them with the garlic halves, and drizzle them with 1 tablespoon of the olive oil. Cut each slice in thirds. Arrange the bread on a warm serving plate and set aside. Heat the remaining oil in a large nonstick skillet. When the oil is very hot, add the livers, being careful not to crowd them. If all the pieces don't fit in skillet, cook them in two batches. Sear the livers on one side, then turn and sear the other side, reduce heat to medium and continue cooking 3 to 5 minutes for each side. The livers should still be pink inside. Add the vinegar and turn the livers in the pan juices to baste. Spoon the livers and warm sauce over the toast slices, re-season with salt and pepper, and serve.

A robust Chianti

TRATTORIA DELL'ARTE

TRATTORIA DELL'ARTE   57TH & 7TH   TRATTORIA DELL'ARTE

SAUTÉED FOIE GRAS WITH APRICOTS

TERRE

CHRISTIAN DELOUVRIER'S STURDY CAREER as a highly rated chef in New York's best hotel restaurants—Maurice in Le Parker Meridien, Les Célébrités in the Essex House, and Lespinasse in the St. Regis—came to an abrupt end when Lespinasse closed early in 2003. But instead of moving to yet another hotel dining room, Delouvrier finally broke away and followed the dream of many a chef. With no shortage of backers, Delouvrier was able to take a brief respite before opening Terre in the Meatpacking District. The name is French for earth, and shorthand for food that is indeed earthy and honest, and still rooted in Delouvrier's talent for finesse. And if sautéed foie gras seems fancy to Americans, one must remember that Delouvrier comes from Gascony, a part of France where it's everyday fare.

SERVES 8

12 ounces dried apricots

24 whole blanched almonds

¼ cup apricot jam

4 tablespoons Armagnac

1 whole fresh duck foie gras, about 1½ pounds (sold by fancy butchers)

Sea salt and freshly ground black pepper

Fleur de sel

A Sauternes

Place the apricots in a bowl, cover with 2 cups of very hot water and set aside for 1 hour to soften. Lightly toast the almonds and set aside.

When the apricots have softened, reserve 8 of them. Puree the rest with the soaking liquid in a food processor. Transfer the puree to a heavy saucepan and cook over low heat about 10 minutes until smooth and soft. Stir in the jam and half of the Armagnac. Transfer the apricot mixture to a coarse strainer suspended over a bowl and set aside to drain about 1 hour.

Place the apricot liquid that has passed through the strainer in a small saucepan, along with any puree clinging to the outside of the strainer. Do not discard the solids. Bring the liquid to a simmer, add the remaining Armagnac and cook a few minutes, just until syrupy. Add the toasted almonds. Transfer the apricot solids from the strainer to another saucepan. This much of the recipe can be prepared in advance.

French *fleur de sel*, the best coarse sea salt, adds the necessary seasoning plus a bit of crunchy texture to the foie gras.

Gently separate the foie gras into its two natural sections. With a thin, sharp knife dipped in hot water, cut it into 16 slices, each about an inch thick. Use a sharp paring knife to pluck out any little blood clots or pieces of vein from the slices. Season the pieces of foie gras on both sides with sea salt and pepper.

When you're ready to cook the foie gras, bring both of the apricot mixtures to a gentle simmer.

Heat a cast-iron skillet or heavy sauté pan until very hot. Add as much of the foie gras as you can in a single layer without crowding. Cook over medium-high heat less than a minute, then turn and sear the other side. Do not overcook. The foie gras should be cooked no more than medium-rare. Divide the seared foie gras among 8 plates. Sprinkle with a little *fleur de sel*. Drizzle a little of the apricot sauce with the almonds on the plate along one side of the foie gras, and spoon some of the warm puree on the other side. Garnish with reserved apricot halves. Serve at once.

SOUPS

WARM LENTIL SOUP WITH CRISP PANCETTA

CHICKEN SOUP

ONION SOUP GRATINÉE

GARBURE

SUNCHOKE SOUP WITH BLACK TRUMPET MUSHROOMS

OYSTER STEW

CHILLED SPRING PEA SOUP WITH PEA SALAD
AND MINTED CRÈME FRAÎCHE

WARM LENTIL SOUP WITH CRISP PANCETTA

STACKED, NOT SPRAWLING, DEFINES URBAN LIVING. And Town, as its citified name suggests, complies with that concept. The restaurant, designed by David Rockwell, starts with a narrow bar at street level, then descends a couple of steps to an area with small tables for lounge dining, then on to the restaurant proper, resulting in a soaring atrium effect. Chef Geoffrey Zakarian's food is suitably urban-contemporary, calling on some inventive ingredients such as buckwheat and, in this creamy lentil puree, a moderately sweet, but little-known French wine called *vin jaune*.

1 box (17.5 ounces) French Le Puy lentils

1 thick slice smoked bacon, diced

1 medium onion, peeled and chopped

1 carrot, peeled, in chunks

2 celery stalks, in chunks

2 thyme sprigs

1 bay leaf

1 head of garlic, halved horizontally

8 cups well-flavored chicken stock

2 tablespoons heavy cream

¼ cup *vin jaune* or medium-dry sherry (see tip, page 25)

1 tablespoon white wine vinegar

Salt and freshly ground black pepper

3 (¼-inch thick) slices pancetta, cut into julienne

2 bunches scallions, trimmed and thinly sliced

French Le Puy lentils are green instead of brown and are smaller and somewhat nuttier-tasting than American lentils. They're what most chefs prefer.

Chefs also like to place a warm garnish in the center of a bowl, serve it , and then ladle the hot soup over the garnish at the table. It's a lovely way to serve a soup that's worth remembering.

Place the lentils in a bowl, cover with cold water to a depth of 2 inches, and allow them to soak overnight. Drain.

In a large, heavy saucepan, gently sauté the bacon, and when it renders some of its fat, add the onion, carrot, celery, thyme, bay leaf, and garlic. Cook over medium-low heat until the vegetables are very tender, about 10 minutes. Drain the lentils, add them to the pot, cook a few minutes longer, then add the stock. Bring to a simmer, and cook gently until the lentils are very tender, about 40 minutes.

Remove a few tablespoons of the lentils and set aside. Remove garlic, thyme, and bay leaf. Transfer the contents of the pan to a food processor or blender and puree until smooth. You may have to do this in two batches. Pass the puree through a fine strainer. Clean the saucepan and add the puree to the pan. Bring the soup to a simmer, and add the cream, *vin jaune,* vinegar, and salt and pepper to taste. Remove from heat.

Heat a sauté pan, add the pancetta, and sauté until crisp. Add the scallions, allow them to wilt, then fold in the reserved lentils. Divide this mixture among 8 soup plates. Reheat the soup, thinning it with a little water if necessary, and ladle it over the pancetta mixture, then serve.

The wine in the soup, *vin jaune,* is a good accompaniment. The best of the lot is Château- Chalon. In its place, an oloroso sherry will do nicely.

CHICKEN SOUP

T HESE DAYS "DELI" OFTEN MEANS A CORNER GROCERY with a salad bar and flowers for sale. But in New York restaurantese, a delicatessen is also a place to find a mile-high corned beef sandwich on rye with a sour pickle on the side, smoky pastrami with a lush rim of fat, lox and eggs, and chicken soup. New Yorkers who have moved to far-flung places—California, Hong Kong, Phoenix—long for old-fashioned deli food, the contribution made by immigrant Jews from Eastern Europe more than 100 years ago. The Second Avenue Deli is one of the few remaining authentic sources. Its clientele is multi-generational and not dominated by tourists, and its waiters are gruff old-timers. You can find foie gras almost anywhere now, but good chopped liver?

SERVES 8

1 pound chicken wings and
    drumsticks
2 celery stalks, cut into 3-inch
    pieces, including leaves
1 (3½- to 4-pound) chicken, rinsed
Kosher salt
1 large unpeeled onion, roots
    trimmed, and rinsed
1 large carrot, peeled
1 parsnip, peeled
Freshly ground white pepper
4 fresh dill sprigs, tied with string

The onion is left unpeeled because the skin adds a golden color to the soup.
For the clearest possible soup, line your strainer with a clean linen napkin.

Pour 3 quarts of cold water into a large stockpot. Add the chicken wings, drumsticks, and celery. Bring to a boil.

Rub the whole chicken inside and out with salt. Add it to the pot and boil for 5 minutes, skimming any residue that rises to the surface. Lower the heat to a simmer, cover, and cook until the whole chicken is cooked through, about 40 minutes. Transfer the whole chicken to a platter.

Add the onion, carrot, and parsnip to the pot, season with salt and pepper to taste, and simmer 1 hour and 15 minutes. Remove the carrot and set aside. Strain the contents of the pot into a clean saucepan, discarding the solids.

The whole chicken may be added to soup or reserved for chicken salad. If serving it in the soup, cut it up, and remove the skin and bones.

Dice the carrot and add it to the soup along with dill. Reheat, adding salt and pepper if needed. Remove the dill, ladle the soup into plates, and serve.

Wine? Beer? Not at all. The libation of choice in an old-fashioned deli is celery tonic.

ONION SOUP GRATINÉE

CAPSOUTO FRÈRES

FOR MORE THAN 20 YEARS, Jacques Capsouto has welcomed those who seek French comfort food and are willing to venture south of Canal Street to his romantic restaurant in the semi-wilderness of the streets near the Holland Tunnel. Capsouto Frères has become inextricably woven into the fabric of New York, and despite its hip downtown location, it caters to those with a taste for more traditional fare. The Capsoutos' family tree is Sephardic-Jewish, and the Passover seders held annually in the restaurant are filled to capacity. And when it comes to French comfort food, what could be better than a steaming bowl of rich onion soup paved with melted cheese on toast?

SERVES 6 TO 8

2 tablespoons unsalted butter
2 tablespoons vegetable oil
5 large onions, peeled and sliced thin
¼ cup brandy
¼ cup dry white wine
8 cups well-flavored beef stock
Salt and freshly ground black pepper
1 or 2 slices of toasted country bread
    or baguette for each serving
6 to 8 large slices Gruyère cheese

Instead of ladling the soup into individual bowls or crocks, it can be put into an ovenproof tureen or serving bowl, topped with all of the bread and cheese, then broiled until the cheese melts. Bring the tureen to the table and serve. But have a knife or even kitchen shears ready to cut through the stringy melted cheese as you serve each portion.

The soup is child's play. Begin by heating the butter and oil in a heavy 4- to 5-quart saucepan. Add the onions, and allow them to cook over medium-low heat, stirring from time to time, until they are meltingly soft and barely colored, 20 to 30 minutes. Do not rush this part of the preparation. Onions take time.

Add the brandy and wine, and cook them down until they have nearly evaporated. Add the stock and simmer for 30 minutes. Season with salt and pepper. The soup is ready to serve at this point, needing only its cap of bread and cheese, but there's no harm in setting it aside for several hours, or even refrigerating it overnight.

Reheat the soup if necessary and transfer it to individual ovenproof bowls or crocks. Top each with one or two slices of toast and cover the toast with the cheese. Preheat the broiler and run the bowls or crocks under it just until the cheese melts and bubbles. Serve at once.

A Beaujolais cru, a Fleurie for example

GARBURE

ARIANE DAGUIN IS A REVOLUTIONARY. As a native of Gascony in Southwest France, who comes from a family of restaurateurs, it would seem natural that she would go into the business. But first she had other fish to fry, or foie gras to sauté. She was instrumental in putting American duck foie gras in just about every important restaurant kitchen in the country, and she even served it to more than one president of France. This she accomplished as a founding partner of D'Artagnan, a company which specializes in foie gras, game, mushrooms, and pâtés. Its success led to the opening of the restaurant, a two-story affair with French country antiques. There is also a retail shop that sells D'Artagnan products such as the duck fat, duck stock, and duck confit used in this recipe.

1 small head Savoy cabbage, well-trimmed, cored, and cut into 4 wedges

5 tablespoons duck fat

6 garlic cloves, chopped

½ pound pancetta, diced

2 onions, chopped

2 celery stalks, chopped

2 quarts duck or chicken stock

4 carrots, peeled and cut into 1-inch pieces

2 confit duck legs and thighs, cut apart at the joint

Salt and freshly ground black pepper

4 confit duck gizzards , thinly sliced, optional (sold in fancy-food shops)

8 roasted garlic cloves, peeled

Crusty country bread, for serving

To make roasted garlic, brush a head of garlic with olive oil, wrap it in foil, and place it in a 400-degree oven until the cloves are tender, 30 to 40 minutes. Peel and use as many cloves as needed and refrigerate the rest.

Bring a large pot of water to a boil. Add the cabbage and blanch it for 5 minutes. Drain it well. Place it in a colander and set aside.

Heat 3 tablespoons of the duck fat in a 4- or 6-quart pot. Add the cabbage, and sauté it briefly in the fat, turning it with tongs to coat it well. Remove the cabbage and set aside. Add the remaining duck fat to the pot along with the garlic, pancetta, onions, and celery. Sauté over low heat until the vegetables are tender. Add the duck stock and bring it to a simmer. Return the cabbage to the pot, add the carrots and the duck confit, and simmer for 45 minutes. Season with salt and pepper. Just before serving, add the gizzards confit and the roasted garlic.

To serve, ladle the soup into flat soup plates, evenly dividing the vegetables and the pieces of duck.

A Madiran, a rich red wine from the southwest of France. It is a Gascon tradition to pour some of the wine into the plate when there is a little broth left, and then drink directly from the plate.

SUNCHOKE SOUP WITH BLACK TRUMPET MUSHROOMS

AQUAVIT

THIS SCANDINAVIAN RESTAURANT tucked in a town house that was owned by the Rockefellers is unique. Its main dining room, on the lower level, is a soaring, multi-story atrium with a gentle waterfall spilling down the back wall. In addition, there is a bar and café on the ground floor. Heading the kitchen is Marcus Samuelsson, a Swede who was originally from Ethiopia and who is bringing a global outlook to traditional dishes and ingredients such as herring platters and lingonberries—staples of the Scandinavian kitchen. Here you'll find herring sushi and Kobe beef paired with aquavit spirits that are infused with uncommon flavors.

3½ tablespoons unsalted butter

1 pound fresh sunchokes (Jerusalem artichokes), peeled and chopped

2 shallots, finely chopped

2 garlic cloves

½ pound Yukon gold potatoes, peeled and cut into ½-inch cubes

4 cups chicken stock

2 cups mild fish stock

½ cup dry white wine

2 bay leaves

4 Chinese dried black mushrooms

2 fresh thyme sprigs

2 tablespoons crème fraîche

Salt and freshly ground white pepper

2 cups (about 8 ounces) fresh black trumpet mushrooms or fresh chanterelle mushrooms

2 tablespoons minced chives

½ teaspoon black truffle oil, optional

The dried Chinese black mushrooms add a great deal of flavor but are too woody to be pureed. The black trumpet mushrooms, a variety of chanterelle also called *Trompettes de la Mort* (trumpets of death, because of their color), are the chef's choice because of the stunning color contrast they provide. But other mushrooms, including regular chanterelles, can be used instead.

Melt 1 tablespoon of the butter in a large saucepan over medium heat. Add the sunchokes and sauté until they begin to soften, about 5 minutes. Add the shallots and garlic, sauté 2 minutes more, then add the potatoes. Add the chicken stock, fish stock, wine, bay leaves, dried mushrooms, and thyme. Bring to a boil, reduce heat, and simmer gently until the vegetables are very tender, about 25 minutes.

Remove the soup from the heat, and discard the bay leaves, thyme, and dried mushrooms. Add the crème fraîche and 2 tablespoons of the butter, and puree the soup in a food processor, blender, or in the pot using a hand-held blender. You may have to puree the soup in two batches if using a food processor or regular blender. Return the soup to the saucepan and reheat. Season with salt and pepper.

In a sauté pan heat the remaining ½ tablespoon of butter. Add the trumpet mushrooms, and sauté over high heat until they just start to wilt, about 1 minute. Add the chives, stir, and remove from heat. Divide the mushroom mixture among 6 shallow soup plates. Ladle the hot soup over and, if desired, garnish with a few drops of truffle oil. Serve at once.

A white Châteauneuf-du-Pape such as Domaine de la Solitude, 1999

OYSTER STEW

THANKS TO LOVING RESTORATION WORK and sensitive realignment of its commercial space, Grand Central Terminal, the world's largest railway station, has recently become an important New York dining venue. But the Oyster Bar, located off the ramp that connects the upper and lower levels of the station, was there before the other fine restaurants now found in Grand Central. Its landmark interior, arched with Guastavino tilework, was where travelers who were about to step aboard the 20th Century Limited dined. And the restaurant remains most famous for its oysters on the half shell, its oyster stews, and its oyster panroasts, which are prepared in specially designed silver bowls that swivel to allow the cook to pour out the contents.

SERVES 2

2 thin slices white sandwich bread, crusts removed

½ cup clam broth or clam juice

2 tablespoons unsalted butter

1 teaspoon Worcestershire sauce

½ teaspoon celery salt

12 oysters, shucked, with their liquor

1½ cups half-and-half

1 teaspoon sweet Hungarian paprika

Add 2 tablespoons of Heinz chile sauce just after the oysters have been added, replace the half-and-half with ½ cup heavy cream, and you'll have an oyster panroast instead of oyster stew.

Toast the bread. You'll want it on the dark side so it will add a bit of smoky flavor to the stew. Place each slice of the toast in a shallow soup plate. Now it's minutes until the dish is ready to serve.

Combine the clam broth, butter, Worcestershire sauce, and celery salt in the top of a double boiler set over boiling water. When the mixture is hot and the butter has melted, add the oysters and their liquor, and allow to cook for 30 seconds. Add the half-and-half, and cook just until the mixture is hot, then use a slotted spoon to transfer the oysters to the plates, placing 6 on each slice of toast. Ladle the cream mixture over the oysters, sprinkle with the paprika, and serve without delay.

A pinot noir from Oregon, like St. Innocent; or from Sonoma, the Rutz or Castle Rock

CHILLED SPRING PEA SOUP WITH PEA SALAD AND MINTED CRÈME FRAÎCHE

OLIVES

Todd English first came on the scene with a tiny restaurant in Charlestown, Massachusetts, on the edge of Boston. He has since turned Olives, as the restaurant is called, into an industry, with branches in Las Vegas, Washington, and New York. The settings vary but English's boldly flavored Mediterranean-style cooking is the hallmark of them all. The New York edition is in a stately former insurance company building-turned-hotel in the W chain.

Serves 4

4 tablespoons extra virgin olive oil

1 medium onion, peeled and chopped

½ cup chopped celery

3 cups chicken stock or water

3 pounds fresh peas in the pod, shucked, about 3 cups shucked peas

½ cup sugar snap peas, trimmed

½ cup snow peas, trimmed

4 tablespoons crème fraîche

1½ tablespoons chopped fresh mint

Juice of ½ lemon

Sea salt and freshly ground black pepper

Heat 3 tablespoons of the oil in a heavy saucepan. Add the onion and celery and cook over low heat until translucent. Add the stock and simmer about 5 minutes, then remove from the heat. Transfer to a bowl sitting in an ice-water bath to cool.

Bring a pot with 2 quarts of salted water to a boil, add the shucked peas and blanch for 3 minutes, until tender but still bright green. Use a slotted spoon to remove the peas and place them in the chilling bowl of stock. Add the sugar snaps and snow peas to the boiling water, blanch 2 minutes, then drain and allow to cool in a separate small bowl.

Remove ½ cup of the peas from the stock and add them to the mixture of sugar snaps and snow peas. Coat with the remaining tablespoon of olive oil. Set aside.

Place the stock mixture in a blender and puree. Add 1 tablespoon crème fraîche and ½ tablespoon of the mint, blend briefly, then transfer to a container and chill at least 1 hour.

Mix the remaining crème fraîche with the remaining mint and the lemon juice, and set aside.

If you use chicken stock, it should be light-colored and mild-flavored to allow the flavor of the fresh peas to dominate.

Consider serving the cold soup, without the garnish, in tiny coffee cups or in shot glasses as an hors d'oeuvre.

To serve, check the seasonings of the pea soup, adding salt and pepper as needed. Place a mound of the whole pea mixture in the center of each of 4 soup plates, spoon the soup around it, and top with a dollop of the crème fraîche mixture.

Bertani Le Lave Italian Chardonnay 2001, Livon Tocai Ronc de Zorz 1999, or Antinori Tenute Guado al Tasso Vermentino 2001—in other words, a dry white Italian wine

SALADS

CLASSIC CAESAR SALAD

TOMATO SALAD WITH SHAVED FENNEL AND GORGONZOLA

DEVILED EGGS AND FRISÉE WITH WARM BACON VINAIGRETTE

GIGI SALAD

BEET SALAD WITH BEET VINAIGRETTE

GOI TOM, GRILLED SHRIMP SALAD

CLASSIC CAESAR SALAD

TAVERN ON THE GREEN

ON THE EDGE OF CENTRAL PARK, the historic Tavern on the Green combines the beautiful architectural details of the pavilions that dot the 150-year-old park with the exuberance of the late Warner LeRoy, who will always be remembered as the city's Barnum of dining, the most spectacular restaurant showman ever. His restoration of Tavern on the Green gave its interior a Victorian grandeur and populated its gardens with a topiary menagerie that glitters with lights. The food is designed to please young and old, visitors and residents, who flock to the restaurant for special occasions and weekend brunches.

3 egg yolks or ½ cup commercial
   mayonnaise

2 tablespoons Dijon mustard

4 garlic cloves, minced

6 anchovies, or more to taste,
   drained and mashed

⅓ cup lemon juice

Freshly ground black pepper

¾ cup extra virgin olive oil

1¼ cups freshly grated Parmigiano-
   Reggiano

2 heads romaine lettuce, trimmed,
   rinsed, dried, and torn into
   pieces

🍷 A Sancerre, especially the Henri
Bourgeois 2001

At Tavern on the Green the salad
is made with romaine hearts that
are split but have part of the stem
left intact to hold them together.
The dressing is then spooned
around. That's fine when a single
portion is involved, but to assemble
several servings at home, it's easier
to use torn lettuce. It's up to you.

This dressing calls for raw egg yolks. If you feel that using them poses a risk—although you might consider that organic, free-range eggs are less likely to cause problems—you can omit them and substitute ½ cup of commercial mayonnaise, in which case reduce the oil to ½ cup.

Place the egg yolks, mustard, garlic, anchovies, and lemon juice in a food processor and whirl until smooth. Season with pepper. With the machine running, slowly pour in the oil through the feed tube to make a thick, creamy dressing. Add ¼ cup of the cheese and blend briefly. Set aside in the refrigerator.

Next make the Parmesan crisps, which take the place of traditional croutons. You'll need a baking sheet with a nonstick Silpat liner, or a small but reliable nonstick skillet. If you have a liner, place it on a baking sheet and cover it with the remaining cup of grated cheese in a thin layer. Preheat the oven to 350 degrees, and bake the cheese until it has melted and turned golden brown. Remove the baking sheet from the oven, allow it to cool, then break up the cheese into 1-inch pieces and set aside. An alternate method is to place a small nonstick skillet over medium heat, spread about ½ cup of the cheese evenly over the bottom, and cook it until the cheese melts and starts to brown. Remove the skillet from the heat, allow it to cool, and use a spatula to lift off and break up the layer of crisp cheese. Repeat the process with the remaining cheese.

To assemble the salad, put the lettuce in a big bowl. Give the dressing a quick whisk and pour it over the greens and toss. Consider using your hands, which are the most effective utensils of all. Scatter the cheese crisps over the top and serve.

TOMATO SALAD WITH SHAVED FENNEL AND GORGONZOLA

GOTHAM BAR & GRILL

GOTHAM BAR & GRILL WAS MEANT TO BE A TRENDSETTER when it opened. Housed in a handsome, soaring loft space on the edge of Greenwich Village, it was dedicated to cutting-edge American food. It almost did not make it. But then the owners hired Alfred Portale, a Culinary Institute of America graduate who had trained in France. They made a daring move introducing him and their restaurant to an uptown crowd by opening for a charity dinner for 200 people— who wound up loving the food and the restaurant. A loyal following soon developed. For his part, Portale capitalized on the *haute* in haute cuisine with towering presentations. He was devoted to the nearby Greenmarket, and his commitment to the farmers led owners Jerome Kretchmer, Jeff Bliss, and Richard and Robert Rathe to back Bill Telepan, one of Portale's disciples, in another venture, JUdson Grill, where "farm fresh" is also the mantra.

1 small fennel bulb

3 pounds assorted heirloom tomatoes of varying sizes and colors

Salt and freshly ground black pepper

½ cup finely chopped red onion

1 garlic clove, peeled and mashed to
a paste with salt

2 teaspoons fresh thyme leaves

⅓ cup extra virgin olive oil

1 tablespoon aged red wine vinegar

1 tablespoon balsamic vinegar, aged
at least 10 years

½ pound *haricots verts*, trimmed

2 tablespoons minced chives

2 cups loosely packed baby arugula
or regular arugula (leaves only),
rinsed and dried

5 ounces crumbled Gorgonzola

To slice the fennel, use a light-
weight, inexpensive Japanese-
style mandoline or a heavy-duty
French one if you prefer.

Plan on serving this salad when
ripe tomatoes are in season and
sold at farmers' markets.

Ice water is the secret ingredi-
ent in this recipe, used to crisp
and curl the fennel and, as chefs
say, to "shock" the cooked beans so
they keep their color.

Cut the fennel into ⅛-inch-thick slices vertically, and
place in a bowl of ice water. Refrigerate for 1 hour.

Cut the tomatoes into slices, wedges, or halves, depending
on their size and shape; you want pieces that will fit on a
fork and are not much larger than bite-size. Place the
tomatoes in a bowl and season with salt and pepper. Scatter the onion, garlic, and thyme on top. Whisk together
the oil and vinegars, and drizzle on the tomatoes. Set aside
for 15 minutes.

Bring a small saucepan of salted water to a boil, add the
haricots verts, and cook until bright green, about 4 minutes. Drain and plunge the *haricots verts* into a bowl of
ice water to stop the cooking. Drain and set aside.

Add the chives to the tomatoes and toss gently. Place the
arugula in the center of 6 salad plates. Using a slotted
spoon, lift the tomatoes and onions out of the bowl, allowing the dressing to drain off, and place them on the
arugula, mounding them as high as possible. Arrange the
haricots verts around the tomatoes. Drain the fennel and
arrange it around the *haricots verts*. Sprinkle the Gorgonzola on top, spoon the dressing left in the bowl on the
haricots verts and fennel, and serve.

A rich sauvignon blanc, such as Cloudy Bay from New
Zealand, is an excellent complement, although a summery
rosé that's not too sweet would work well, too.

DEVILED EGGS AND FRISÉE WITH WARM BACON VINAIGRETTE

RELISH

HIP NEW NEIGHBORHOODS NEED HIP NEW PLACES TO EAT. Relish, in Williamsburg, Brooklyn, fills the bill. Diner-style with dim, lounge-like lighting, a lovely indoor patio, and food best described as trendy American seem to satisfy the skinny young jeans-and-black-clad patrons. A frisée salad with eggs is typical bistro fare, but here it has been crossed with comfort food, deviled eggs substituting for poached. It can be hors d'oeuvres—pick off the deviled eggs first—a starter or, for some, dinner.

6 hard-cooked eggs, peeled and
halved

1 teaspoon coarse (whole grain)
mustard

3 tablespoons mayonnaise

¼ teaspoon paprika

Salt and freshly ground black
pepper

4 slices bacon

6 tablespoons extra virgin olive oil

2 teaspoons Dijon mustard

2 tablespoons white wine vinegar

1 tablespoon minced red onion

2 tablespoons minced chives

2 teaspoons chopped fresh tarragon
leaves

2 small heads frisée, cored, rinsed
and dried

10 cherry tomatoes, cut in half

Why not triple the recipe for the
eggs and serve them—without
the salad—with drinks?

Unlike the classic bistro salad, *frisée aux lardons,* Relish's version without poached eggs is much easier to prepare. To make the deviled eggs: scoop the yolks into a bowl, mash them with the coarse mustard, mayonnaise, paprika and a touch of salt and pepper. Pile this mixture back into the whites, put the eggs on a plate, cover, and set them aside in the refrigerator. (Try to resist eating a couple of them on the spot. You may, but then you won't get any later.)

Fry the bacon, drain it on paper towels and chop it. To the fat in the pan add the oil, Dijon mustard, vinegar, onion, 1 tablespoon of the chives, and the tarragon. Return the chopped bacon to the pan.

Pile the frisée in a salad bowl and toss it with the rest of the chives and the tomatoes. This is far as you can go in advance. If you're not serving this right away, put the salad in the refrigerator.

Minutes before you're about to serve the salad, warm the dressing in the pan, stirring it, and season to taste with salt and pepper—you will not need much. Pour the warm dressing over the frisée, toss it and divide the salad among six plates. Top each with two deviled egg halves and serve.

Bloody Marys

GIGI SALAD

THE FIRST PALM OPENED IN NEW YORK in 1926. It is still owned by descendants of the founders, John Ganzi and Pio Bozzi, Italian immigrants who turned a spaghetti joint into a magnet for celebrities. The restaurant's name is a bureaucratic misspelling of the owners' intentions. They wanted "Parma." It became Palm, and it stuck. The walls are covered with cartoons of regulars, the oldest ones drawn by King Features Syndicate artists in exchange for dinner. Although the Palm is best known for steaks, the Gigi Salad is the dish that is ordered more than any other. It was named for its creator, the late Louis "Gigi" Delmaestro, who was the general manager of the Palm in West Hollywood for 27 years. There is now a Palm Too across the street from the original, as well as a Palm West in the theater district. Another 24 restaurants are scattered across the country and in Mexico.

SERVES 4 TO 6

¼ pound bacon

2 tablespoons red wine vinegar

½ cup extra virgin olive oil

1 garlic clove, crushed

3 basil leaves, torn into pieces

Salt and freshly ground black pepper

1 pound fresh green beans, ends trimmed

1 pound (about 2) ripe beefsteak tomatoes, cored and cut into ½-inch chunks

1 medium sweet onion such as Vidalia, cut into ½-inch dice

½ pound jumbo or large shrimp, cooked, peeled and cut into ½-inch-thick pieces

 An Australian chardonnay

Fry the bacon until crisp, drain on paper towels, and crumble. Set aside the crumbled bacon and discard the fat. Whisk the vinegar, oil, garlic, and basil in a bowl. Set aside.

Bring a quart of water to a boil, add the beans and cook for 4 minutes. Drain the beans and run them under cold water until they are cool. Drain well, shaking off excess water, and spread them on paper towels to dry. Cut the beans into 1½-inch lengths.

Combine the beans, tomatoes, and onion in a salad bowl. Briefly whisk the vinaigrette, pour ½ cup of it over the vegetables, and toss. Add additional vinaigrette if needed, and season with salt and pepper.

Mound the salad on plates and top each serving with some of the shrimp and crumbled bacon. Serve at once.

To make the West Coast variation of the salad, in addition top each serving with a hard-boiled egg, cut in quarters, and ½ of a peeled and diced Hass avocado,.

BEET SALAD WITH BEET VINAIGRETTE

CRAFT

People love going to salad bars and picking and choosing, so why not give them the chance to design a whole meal that way? That was chef Tom Colicchio's concept: offer each component á la carte, making it possible to order, say, a first course of seafood and decide whether the fennel salad or the lentils would be best alongside it, then go on to a main course of chicken or sea bass with a choice of several kinds of potatoes, grains, vegetables, and sauces. Everything is served family style, and the restaurant has more or less stayed the course, though for the indecisive there is a prix fixe tasting menu. Even the design of the room emphasizes the craftsmanship of the materials—stone, wood, leather, and metal—and the tables are extra large, with plenty of room for the various copper pots and serving dishes that accumulate. The success of Craft has led to two adjacent spin-offs: the informal Craftbar, an Italian-style wine bar, and 'Wichcraft, a sandwich café with plenty of preset combinations, of course, but you can always design your own.

Serves 4

16 baby beets, each about 2 inches
   in diameter
2 tablespoons grapeseed oil
Kosher salt and freshly ground
   black pepper
1 cup extra virgin olive oil
1 large shallot, peeled and sliced
¼ cup red wine vinegar
½ teaspoon Dijon mustard

Preheat the oven to 325 degrees. Trim the roots and green tops from the beets. Scrub them to remove any soil.

Place the beets in a bowl, add the grapeseed oil, and toss the beets to coat. Season with salt and pepper. Wrap the beets in a sheet of heavy-duty foil. If using a variety of beets, wrap each color in a separate sheet of foil so they don't bleed onto each other. Place the foil pouches in a large roasting pan. Roast until tender, about 1 hour—a paring knife should penetrate easily. Remove the beets from the oven and let cool.

When the beets are cool enough to handle, rub off the outer skin with a paper towel. Set aside all but 3 beets. Coarsely chop the 3 beets and set them aside separately.

Heat 1 tablespoon of the olive oil in a skillet. Add the shallot, and cook over low heat until it's soft and translu-

Try to find an assortment of beets —golden, Chioggia (candy cane), and purple—to use in this recipe.

Consider using disposable plastic gloves or even baggies when handling beets so you do not stain your hands.

cent but not colored—the technique chefs call "sweating." Place the shallot in a blender jar with the vinegar, mustard, the chopped beets, and salt and pepper to taste. Puree the mixture, then add the remaining olive oil in a thin, steady stream.

Slice the reserved beets in half and arrange them on 4 plates. Drizzle with the beet vinaigrette and serve.

A rosé wine, preferably Greek, such as Xynomavris rosé, or Kiryannis, or Skakis

GOI TOM, GRILLED SHRIMP SALAD

LE COLONIAL

L E COLONIAL IS THE CATHERINE DENEUVE OF VIETNAMESE RESTAURANTS, presenting a lushly beautiful and decidedly romantic setting with lots of greenery, bamboo, and carved Asian woodwork. The second-floor lounge is even more lush. The menu gives a complete overview of the cooking of Vietnam, and the kitchen interprets that fresh yet complex cuisine with care. The crunch of lettuce, bean sprouts, and herbs contrasts with tender meats or fish charred on the grill. The flavors are at once herbaceous, fiery, and tart—an appetite-whetting combination if there ever was one.

8 jumbo shrimp, shelled and
   deveined

1 teaspoon minced shallot

1 teaspoon minced garlic

2 tablespoons peanut oil

1 tablespoon Chinese oyster sauce

½ seedless English cucumber,
   peeled, halved lengthwise,
   and sliced paper thin

1 carrot, peeled and sliced paper thin

1 cup thinly sliced peeled daikon
   (long, white radish)

¼ cup thinly sliced red onion,
   separated into rings

1 teaspoon kosher salt

2 teaspoons *nuoc mam* (Vietnamese
   fish sauce), available in Asian
   stores

1 tablespoon sugar

1 tablespoon lime juice

2 teaspoons minced seeded fresh red
   chile pepper

2 tablespoons extra virgin olive oil

2 tablespoons roughly chopped
   fresh basil leaves, preferably
   purple opal basil

1 tablespoon roughly chopped fresh
   mint leaves

2 tablespoons roasted unsalted
   peanuts, chopped

1 tablespoon fried shallots,
   optional (see tip)

Place the shrimp in a bowl and toss with the minced shallot, garlic, the peanut oil, and the oyster sauce. Set aside in the refrigerator to marinate for at least an hour.

Meanwhile, mix the cucumber, carrot, daikon, and onion in a bowl. In a separate bowl mix the salt, fish sauce, sugar, and lime juice together until the sugar dissolves. Add the chile pepper and whisk in the olive oil. Pour this dressing over the cucumber salad mixture and toss. Set aside.

Heat a grill or a griddle. Toss the shrimp with 1 tablespoon of the basil. Grill, turning once, until well-seared and cooked through. Mound the salad on a serving dish. Arrange the shrimp over it. Scatter the remaining basil, the mint, peanuts, and fried shallots on top and serve.

Burgess Cellars Napa Valley Chardonnay 2000

Try to find the fried shallots. They are sold jarred in Asian shops and also online, from web sites that specialize in ethnic ingredients. They are also excellent to keep on hand to use as a crunchy garnish for other salads, baked potatoes, and eggs.

Le Colonial

PASTA & RISOTTO

SPAGHETTI WITH FRESH TOMATO AND BASIL SAUCE

NORCINO, SPAGHETTI WITH CHIANTI AND SAUSAGE

LINGUINE WITH SALSA MONACHINA

PENNE GRATIN

TAGLIOLINI WITH SHRIMP AND LOBSTER

RICOTTA AND SPINACH DUMPLINGS WITH BUTTER AND SAGE

VERMICELLI GENGHIS KHAN

SMOKED TOMATO RISOTTO

RISOTTO WITH RADICCHIO AND SHRIMP

ENGLISH PEA RISOTTO

SPAGHETTI WITH FRESH TOMATO AND BASIL SAUCE

L'IMPERO

L'IMPERO IS PROOF THAT NEW YORKERS WILL FLOCK to any neighborhood for good food. Although Tudor City is on the edge of Midtown, it is an out-of-the-way enclave, one that has never been known for its restaurants. But Scott Conant, whose reputation as a first-rate interpreter of Italian food has been building over the years, and his partners, especially a wine expert, Chris Cannon, have changed all that. Sheer curtains and romantic candlelight soften the tailored room. In this setting, Conant's inventive pastas are not to be missed.

SERVES 4 TO 6

2½ pounds ripe plum tomatoes (about 20)

½ cup extra virgin olive oil

Pinch red pepper flakes

Kosher salt and freshly ground black pepper

1 pound spaghetti, preferably *alla chitarra* or another artisanal cut

6 large fresh basil leaves

1 tablespoon unsalted butter

2 tablespoons freshly grated Parmigiano-Reggiano, plus additional for serving, if desired

L'IMPERO

TUDOR·CITY

Rosso di Montalcino Solaria 1998 or another Rosso di Montalcino

Bring a large pot of water to a boil. Have a large bowl of ice water ready near the stove. Cut a small "X" in the bottom of each tomato. Ease 5 of the tomatoes into the boiling water; scoop them out and transfer them to the ice water after 15 seconds. Repeat this with the rest of the tomatoes. Starting at the X, peel the skin off each tomato and cut away the core. Cut each tomato in half lengthwise and use your fingers to flick out the seeds.

Heat 5 tablespoons of the oil in a wide saucepan. Add the tomatoes and red pepper flakes and season with salt and pepper. Once the tomatoes have started to soften, after about 10 minutes, mash them with a potato masher. If you don't have a potato masher, you'd be surprised how well pounding them with the bottom of a sturdy coffee mug works. Cook the tomatoes another 15 to 20 minutes, until they're tender and the sauce has thickened. Set them aside.

Bring 4 to 5 quarts of well-salted water to a boil in a large pot and add the spaghetti. While the spaghetti cooks, stack the basil leaves, roll them up tightly and use a sharp knife to slice the roll into fine shreds, making a chiffonade. Set the basil aside. Gently reheat the sauce and check the seasonings.

Spaghetti *alla chitarra* is often homemade, although it is also sold in packages, dried. Its fairly thick, squared-off strands are made by rolling the dough over a wooden box closely fitted with wires that cut it. The device is called a chitarra, or guitar. Good artisanal dried spaghetti can be substituted.

Cook the spaghetti until al dente, 7 to 8 minutes, then drain, reserving about a half-cup of the cooking water. Add the pasta and the remaining oil to the sauce and toss gently with a couple of wooden spoons so you don't break the pasta, using a generous motion, until the pasta is well-coated. If necessary, moisten the spaghetti with some of the reserved cooking water. Add the butter, grated cheese, and basil chiffonade, toss again, and serve at once.

NORCINO, SPAGHETTI WITH CHIANTI AND SAUSAGE

CESARE CASELLA, whose family has had a restaurant in Lucca, Italy, for several generations, worked in a number of New York restaurants before opening his own place, Beppe, a rustic corner of Tuscany in the Flatiron District. It boasts a wood-burning oven in which casseroles roast. Photographs of his family adorn the brick walls. And Casella can be counted on to tuck his signature bunch of fresh herbs in the pocket of his chef's jacket. To make sure his food reflects the cooking of his native region, he even imports some of his ingredients, including dried beans. This hearty, simple pasta dish is typical of his cooking: Note the rather unusual touches of spice in the sauce.

¼ cup extra virgin olive oil

6 garlic cloves, peeled and chopped

1 medium onion, peeled and minced

¼ cup chopped celery

1 tablespoon chopped fresh
  rosemary

½ pound Italian sweet sausage,
  removed from its casing

½ pound Italian hot sausage,
  removed from its casing

1½ cups Chianti or other dry red
  wine

1½ cups peeled, chopped fresh or
  canned plum tomatoes (about 1
  pound tomatoes)

Salt and freshly ground black
  pepper

Pinch ground cinnamon

Pinch ground cloves

Pinch grated nutmeg

1 pound spaghetti

6 tablespoons freshly grated
  Parmigiano-Reggiano

Pasta dishes in Italy are invariably prepared by draining the pasta, then cooking it in the sauce for several minutes to integrate all the ingredients.

Heat the oil in a large skillet. Add the garlic, onion, celery, and rosemary and sauté over medium heat until the ingredients begin to color. Add the sausage meat, breaking it up with the back of a wooden spoon, and cook, stirring, until the sausage loses its redness. Add the wine. Cook it down until it barely films the pan, then stir in the tomatoes. Cook over low heat for 30 minutes.

Add salt and pepper to taste and the cinnamon, cloves, and nutmeg. Add 2 cups of water, reduce the heat to very low and simmer, partly covered, for 1 hour. Add a little more water if it starts to dry out too much.

Bring 4 quarts of salted water to a boil in a large pot, add the spaghetti, and cook until al dente, about 6 minutes. Drain and add the pasta to the skillet. Cook the pasta in the sauce for 5 minutes. Serve with a dusting of Parmigiano-Reggiano.

Badiola Castella di Fonterutoli 2001 or another earthy Tuscan red wine

LINGUINE WITH SALSA MONACHINA

MARIO'S

Arthur Avenue is the main thoroughfare of the Belmont section, the Bronx's Little Italy. Old-fashioned pasta shops, bakeries, cheese shops, fish markets, and groceries still thrive. Mario's has been in business there since 1919. The fifth generation of the Migliucci family runs the restaurant. The specialties of the house are what have become known as "Italian-American" food—the Neapolitan-style cooking of immigrant families—that remains beloved in America. But it is not just spaghetti and meatballs at Mario's. More sophisticated fare, such as potato gnocchi and osso buco, are also on the menu. The Salsa Monachina in this recipe is the same as the popular puttanesca. Joseph Migliucci, one of the owners, says they use monachina because it is a more polite term than puttanesca, which means streetwalker.

SERVES 4 TO 6

1 (28-ounce) can San Marzano tomatoes

¼ cup salt-packed capers

3 salt-packed anchovies

¼ cup extra virgin olive oil

3 large garlic cloves, sliced thin

8 oil-cured black olives, pitted and sliced

Salt and freshly ground black pepper

1 pound dried linguine

Place the tomatoes in a large bowl and crush them with your hands. Rinse the capers and anchovies and pat dry.

Heat the oil over low heat in a 4-quart saucepan. Add the garlic and sauté until lightly browned. Stir in the capers and olives. Add the anchovies and stir until they dissolve. Add the tomatoes and their juice. Cook, stirring occasionally, about 1½ hours, until the sauce has thickened, darkened, and intensified. Season to taste with salt and pepper. Remove from the heat.

Bring a large pot of salted water to a boil for the linguine. Cook the pasta until it is al dente, about 6 minutes. Drain. Reheat the sauce and add the pasta to the sauce. Stir the pasta in the sauce for a few minutes, then serve.

Capers that are packed in salt instead of vinegar, and anchovies that are packed in salt instead of oil, are plumper and have better flavor.

A pinot grigio if you like white, or Vino Nobile di Montepulciano for a red

PENNE GRATIN

FRESCO BY SCOTTO IS A FAMILY AFFAIR. It opened in 1993 and immediately attracted the power elite from politics and the entertainment world. Four members of the Scotto family are involved in the day-to-day operations, and you are likely to see one or more of them on hand at any time. Marion Scotto, the matriarch of the family, had a political background in Brooklyn; Rosanna Scotto is a television news anchor; Elaina Scotto, a former publicist, was in fashion; and Anthony Scotto Jr. came from the food service industry. Their restaurant is bright and lively, decorated with murals that illustrate the bounty of Italy. This dish, nicknamed Penne from Heaven, is Fresco's interpretation of macaroni and cheese.

SERVES 6

Salt

1 pound penne pasta

3 tablespoons extra virgin olive oil

6 ounces prosciutto, diced

2 tablespoons unsalted butter

1 cup half-and-half

9 ounces freshly grated
   Parmigiano-Reggiano
   (about 3 cups)

Freshly ground black pepper

> The penne can be prepared in advance and baked at the last minute. But it is best to transfer the mixture from the sauté pan to a bowl and refrigerate it, because the pasta may soak up too much sauce while it waits. Before transferring it to the baking dish and running it under the broiler, you may need to moisten it with another ½ cup of half-and-half.

Bring four quarts of salted water to a boil in a large pot. Cook the pasta until al dente, about 8 minutes. Drain and keep warm.

Preheat the broiler.

While pasta is cooking, heat the oil in a large sauté pan. Add prosciutto and sauté over low heat, stirring, until it loses its color. Add the butter. When the butter has melted, add the half-and-half, about 2 cups of the cheese, and freshly ground pepper to taste. Bring to a simmer, add the penne, and toss to mix. Transfer to a shallow baking dish. Sprinkle with the remaining cup of cheese.

Place under the broiler and broil about 5 minutes, until the top is golden. Serve at once.

Vernaccia di San Gimignano, especially Teruzzi & Puthod 2001

TAGLIOLINI WITH SHRIMP AND LOBSTER
FIAMMA OSTERIA

FIAMMA OSTERIA IS ONE OF A LARGE GROUP OF RESTAURANTS that caters to a youngish crowd. But unlike the others in restaurateur Stephen Hanson's portfolio (Dos Caminos, Ruby Foo's, Blue Water Grill, Park Avalon, Ocean Grill, Isabella's, Atlantic Grill, and even Blue Fin), Fiamma has succeeded in aiming high. It has emerged as one of a crop of outstanding new Italian restaurants. It's a comfortable, well-appointed multi-story venue with inventive food that remains true to its Italian roots.

⅓ cup extra virgin olive oil

2 (1-pound) lobsters, cut up

Salt

½ pound medium shrimp, shelled
and deveined

Freshly ground black pepper

6 garlic cloves, sliced

1 medium zucchini, about 8 ounces,
trimmed and sliced ⅛-inch thick

½ cup brandy

½ cup dry white wine

½ pint grape tomatoes, cut in half

½ cup fresh tarragon leaves,
chopped

1 tablespoon unsalted butter

8 ounces fresh *tagliolini* noodles or
fresh linguine

First sautéing the lobsters in the shell, then extracting the meat, allows the shells to contribute flavor to the dish.

Place the oil in a large sauté pan over very high heat. Add the lobster pieces and sauté until the shells turn bright red. Remove from the pan and set aside to cool.

Bring a large pot of salted water to a boil for the pasta.

When the lobsters are cool enough to handle, extract the meat from the shells, cutting it into 1-inch chunks. Discard the shells and return the lobster pieces to the sauté pan. Add the shrimp, season with salt and pepper, and add the garlic and zucchini. Sauté about 1 minute. Add the brandy and wine, cook a few minutes, then add the tomatoes and tarragon. Cover and cook over low heat 4 to 5 minutes. Swirl in the butter. Keep warm.

Cook the noodles until al dente, about 3 minutes, then drain. Transfer the noodles to the sauté pan and toss with contents of the pan, then transfer to a warm serving dish or to individual soup plates and serve immediately.

Blanco della Castellada, 1999, a blend of tocai friuliano, pinot grigio, and sauvignon blanc from Friuli, or another dry white wine from Friuli or the Veneto

FiAMMA
OSTERIA

RICOTTA AND SPINACH DUMPLINGS WITH BUTTER AND SAGE

FELIDIA

A BEAUTIFULLY APPOINTED TWO-STORY TOWN HOUSE RESTAURANT is where Lidia Bastianich established a Manhattan beachhead after developing a following for her cooking in Queens. Her cuisine combines the food of her native Istria, the easternmost region of Italy, with high-end northern Italian specialties and hearty home cooking. A well-stocked cellar emphasizes the wines of Friuli, including some from the family's own vineyards. Bastianich has become an important culinary figure, and is one of too few women chefs who have outstanding restaurants in New York.

SERVES 10

2½ pounds whole milk ricotta cheese

Salt

4 eggs, beaten

1 pound stemmed spinach leaves, cooked, squeezed dry, and finely chopped

¾ cup freshly grated Parmigiano-Reggiano, plus extra for serving

6 tablespoons fine dry bread crumbs

3 to 4 cups all-purpose flour

Freshly ground black pepper

1½ cups chicken broth

5 tablespoons unsalted butter

10 fresh sage leaves

Place the ricotta in a sieve lined with cheesecloth and placed over a bowl. Cover with plastic wrap and allow to drain in the refrigerator for 8 to 24 hours. This removes the excess moisture from the ricotta so the dumplings will hold their shape.

Bring a large pot of salted water to a boil.

In a medium mixing bowl combine the eggs, drained ricotta, spinach, 6 tablespoons of the Parmigiano-Reggiano, bread crumbs, and 4 tablespoons of the flour. Season with salt and pepper.

Dust a baking sheet generously with some of the flour. Line a second baking pan with a lightly-floured kitchen towel. With floured hands, roll about 2 tablespoons of the ricotta mixture into a ball about 1½ inches in diameter. Roll it in the baking sheet of flour until well-coated. Test by dropping it into boiling water. It should hold its shape and rise to the surface within a minute. Cook another minute, then remove with a slotted spoon. If the dumpling does not hold its shape, add some more flour to the mixture and test again. Taste, and adjust seasonings if necessary.

Form remaining mixture into balls, roll in flour, and set on the lightly floured towel.

In a skillet large enough to hold all the dumplings in a single layer, heat the broth, butter, and sage leaves until just simmering. Simmer for 3 minutes, then remove from heat. If you do not have a skillet large enough, divide the sauce ingredients between two skillets or prepare the dish in two batches.

Place half the dumplings in the pot of boiling water and stir gently until they rise to the surface, about 1 minute. Cook until firm, about 1 minute more. Remove with a skimmer, drain, and transfer to the skillet with the sage sauce. Cook the remaining dumplings and add them to the skillet. Place the skillet over medium-low heat and gently shake the pan to coat the dumplings with sauce. Remove the pan from the heat, add the remaining 6 tablespoons of cheese, and swirl the dumplings in the sauce until they are coated. Serve in bowls, spooning any extra sauce over them. Pass additional cheese alongside.

The pound of spinach amounts to about 20 cups, loosely packed. Be sure it is well rinsed to remove all sand and grit.

The dumplings are called gnudi, meaning naked, because they essentially consist of spinach-ricotta filling without any surrounding pasta.

Rudd Napa Valley Sauvignon Blanc 2000 or another full-bodied California sauvignon blanc

VERMICELLI GENGHIS KHAN

HANGAWI

IT ONLY TAKES ONE CITY BLOCK, but from the hustle and bustle of Little Korea (West 32nd Street from Fifth to Sixth Avenues), one can step out of one's shoes—literally—and into the peaceful serenity of Hangawi. It is a vegetarian Korean restaurant, with a Buddhist philosophy and food that explores the seemingly infinite possible uses for burdock, sweet potato, tofu, and other nonmeat ingredients. Korean teas, including rare wild green teas, are another specialty. A spin-off called Franchia, which specializes in teas and light food, including noodle dishes, salads, and dumplings, is another welcoming oasis nearby.

SERVES 4

6 ounces *jap chae* (Korean dried sweet potato vermicelli)

¼ cup soy sauce

1 tablespoon sake

1 tablespoon Asian sesame oil

2 tablespoons dark brown sugar

1 tablespoon grated fresh ginger

3 ounces fresh shiitake mushrooms, stemmed and sliced thin

4 ounces oyster mushrooms, stems trimmed, torn in strips

4 ounces cremini mushrooms, sliced thin

1 small onion, sliced thin vertically

1 small zucchini, trimmed, quartered lengthwise, and cut in thirds

1 cup broccoli florets

12 snow peas, trimmed

2 cups sliced napa cabbage

1 carrot, peeled and slant-cut into ½-inch slices

2 scallions, trimmed and cut into 1-inch lengths

Place the noodles in a large bowl, cover with warm water, and allow to soak at least 2 hours. Drain well.

Combine the soy sauce, sake, sesame oil, brown sugar, and ginger in a wok or large sauté pan. Add 1 cup water. Bring to a simmer and cook over very low heat about 5 minutes, stirring. Stir in the drained noodles and the remaining ingredients. Cook, stirring over low heat, about 10 minutes, until the mushrooms have wilted and the other vegetables are tender but still bright-colored. Transfer to a platter and serve.

🍷 Nonju, a milky Korean rice wine traditionally served in a ceramic pot with a gourd as a ladle. Green tea or saké are also suitable.

🧂 Korean vermicelli is sold in Korean supermarkets and some other Asian stores. Chinese glass or cellophane noodles can be substituted.

SMOKED TOMATO RISOTTO

BRASSERIE

WHEN RESTAURANT ASSOCIATES OPENED THE BRASSERIE IN 1959 in the Mies van der Rohe–designed Seagram Building, it was a revelation. It served breakfast, and dinner, and was open around the clock, providing a classy alternative to the neighborhood diner. It's had its ups and downs since then, and after having been closed for several years, was reinaugurated after a complete redesign. It is still owned by Restaurant Associates, which also runs the restaurants in most of the city's museums and concert halls, as well as Sea Grill and Rock Center Café in Rockefeller Center. It's very modern now, designed by Diller + Scofidio and done mostly in pale, glowing, translucent greens. The food, too, has moved from a mostly French brasserie style to a more international menu. It still offers many brasserie favorites such as handsome seafood platters, *steak-frites*, and mussels; but there are Asian touches in some of the seasonings; and Italian, too, such as this risotto, with its cutting-edge smoked tomatoes to brighten the dish and play their subtle flavor off the piney touch of rosemary.

8 medium ripe plum tomatoes, halved lengthwise and seeded

5 tablespoons extra virgin olive oil

1 tablespoon balsamic vinegar

5 garlic cloves, minced (about 1½ teaspoons)

Salt and freshly ground black pepper

3 fresh rosemary sprigs

2 tablespoons unsalted butter

1 small yellow onion, peeled and minced

2 shallots, peeled and minced

1 cup Italian rice, preferably Carnaroli or Arborio

1 cup dry white wine

2 cups well-seasoned chicken stock

⅓ cup freshly grated Parmigiano-Reggiano

2 tablespoons fresh thyme leaves

The tomatoes are not literally smoked, but acquire their smokiness from the high heat in the pan.

It's a good idea to turn on your kitchen exhaust or open a window while you smoke the tomatoes.

If you have a small stove-top smoker, you can use it for the tomatoes. But do not overdo it; five minutes are enough.

Place the tomatoes in a bowl with 3 tablespoons of the oil, the vinegar, 1 teaspoon of the minced garlic, and salt and pepper to taste. Mix everything thoroughly and set it aside for an hour.

Heat a large cast-iron skillet until it starts to smoke. Put two sprigs of the rosemary in it, and when the herb is fragrant and starts to brown, add the marinated tomatoes, cut side down. Remove from the heat, cover the pan, and set it aside for about 20 minutes or so.

Heat the remaining 2 tablespoons of the oil and the butter in a heavy 3-quart saucepan. Add the rest of the garlic, the onion, and shallots, and sauté everything, stirring over medium heat, until the vegetables are soft. Stir in the rice and cook it about 1 minute, until it starts to whiten. Pour in ½ cup of the wine and cook, stirring, until the wine is absorbed by the rice. Repeat with the rest of the wine. Meanwhile, heat the chicken broth in a small saucepan. After the wine has been absorbed, start adding the chicken broth a ½ cup at a time, stirring and adding more as it is absorbed.

By the time all the broth is used up, the rice should be al dente. Fold in the cheese and season to taste with salt and pepper. Add the smoked tomatoes along with any liquid in the skillet. Strip the leaves from the remaining sprig of rosemary and fold those in, too, along with the thyme leaves. At this point the rice should be al dente but creamy, and ready to serve. You do not need additional grated cheese.

White St. Joseph from the Rhone, preferably Alain Graillot 2000, or a viognier

RISOTTO WITH RADICCHIO AND SHRIMP

REMI

W ITH ITS MURANO GLASS CHANDELIERS, its canal-side mural, nautical stripes and the crossed gondolier's oars, or remi, over the door, Remi is a tribute to Venice. Francesco Antonucci, the chef who owns the restaurant with its designer, Adam Tihany, is a native of Mestre, on the mainland across from Venice. His food is devoted to the specialties of the region.

SERVES 4

Salt

20 large shrimp, shelled and deveined

6 tablespoons unsalted butter

1 medium onion, peeled and minced

1 cup Italian short-grain rice, preferably Vialone Nano or Arborio

5 cups well-seasoned fish stock (approximately)

½ cup dry white wine

10 to 12 leaves radicchio, preferably the long Treviso variety, chopped

1 tablespoon Cognac

Freshly ground black pepper

1 tablespoon finely chopped flat-leaf parsley leaves

In the Venice area, Vialone Nano, which is slightly more slender than arborio and makes the risotto a trifle moister, is preferred. A good Venetian risotto is called alla onda, or wavy.

Bring 2 quarts of well-salted water to a boil. Add the shrimp, cook 30 seconds, then drain them.

In a heavy 3-quart sauce pan, melt 4 tablespoons of the butter. Stir in the onion and sauté over low heat until it's translucent. Add the rice and allow it to cook about 1 minute, stirring, until it begins to whiten. Meanwhile, bring the fish stock to a simmer in a separate saucepan.

Add the wine to the rice, stir and cook until it is nearly absorbed. Stir in the radicchio. Begin adding the fish stock, about ½ cup at a time, stirring fairly steadily, and adding additional stock as it becomes absorbed by the rice. Just keep the saucepan at a steady simmer and the rice will soak up the stock. After about 15 minutes, when all but about ½ cup of the stock is used, the rice will be nearly tender. Fold in all but 4 of the shrimp. Stir, and add the remaining stock. The rice should be al dente and creamy, in an almost-sauce. Fold in the Cognac and the remaining 2 tablespoons of butter and season to taste with salt and pepper.

Divide the risotto among 4 plates, top each with a reserved shrimp, and sprinkle with parsley. Serve hot.

Prosecco, preferably Primo Franco

ENGLISH PEA RISOTTO

PETROSSIAN

ALTHOUGH PETROSSIAN IS BEST KNOWN as the New York branch of the French caviar house, and dining in its opulent headquarters invariably means beginning with caviar or foie gras, the restaurant offers much more. Refined service and elegantly appointed tables provide the setting for finely wrought contemporary French food. Should caviar be the mealtime requirement it will be served in a special presentoir, with silver and vermeil paddles for spooning it up. Petrossian's caviars range from the finest beluga to American farm-raised transmontanus, which today can stand up to sevruga.

SERVES 4

4 cups vegetable stock (approximately)

2 cups shucked garden peas, about 2 pounds peas in the pod

Salt and freshly ground black pepper

4 tablespoons soft unsalted butter

1 medium onion, finely minced

4 garlic cloves, finely minced

1 cup rice for risotto, preferably Vialone Nano or Arborio

2 cups fruity white wine such as riesling

2 teaspoons chopped rosemary leaves

½ cup freshly grated Parmigiano-Reggiano

> The risotto can be garnished with fresh pea shoots.

Heat ¾ cup of the vegetable stock in a small saucepan until just warmed. Place it in a blender jar, add 1 cup of the peas and puree. Season to taste with salt and pepper and set aside.

Bring 2 cups of water to a boil in a small saucepan. Add remaining peas and cook for 2 minutes. Drain and chill in a bowl of ice water. Heat the remaining vegetable stock and keep at a simmer.

In a 3- to 4-quart saucepan, melt 1 tablespoon of the butter over medium heat. Add the onion and garlic and sauté until soft but not brown. Add the rice and stir until it begins to whiten. Add the wine and cook until it just moistens the rice mixture. Add half the vegetable stock. Cook, stirring, over low heat, until most of the stock has been absorbed. Add another cup of the remaining stock and cook, stirring, until it has been absorbed by the rice. By this time the rice should be nearly al dente. Continue to add the stock until the rice is al dente but not hard. Fold in the pea puree and the remaining butter and cook, stirring, until the mixture is creamy. Season to taste with salt and pepper. Fold in the cooked peas, rosemary, and cheese. Serve at once.

An Albarino Rias Baixas, a dry, fruity white wine from Spain

EGGS, SANDWICHES, PIZZA & BRUNCH

SCRAMBLED EGGS WITH MONTRACHET AND SCALLIONS
ON ROASTED PORTOBELLOS

OEUFS COCOTTE

CALIFORNIA OMELET

CHEESE AND CHILE CORNBREAD

TRE POMODORI PIZZA

FOCACCIA ROBIOLA

LOBSTER CLUB SANDWICH

FRIED COD SANDWICH

OPEN-FACE TUNA SALAD SANDWICHES

SCRAMBLED EGGS WITH MONTRACHET AND SCALLIONS ON ROASTED PORTOBELLOS

@ S Q C

IT DID NOT TAKE LONG FOR SCOTT AND LINDA CAMPBELL's copper greenhouse-style restaurant to become a neighborhood institution. One of a new wave of places opening on the Upper West Side, @SQC started by only serving breakfast, before segueing into lunch, then dinner—making it a welcoming spot for local new-economy types who work at home. The Campbells are also activists, supporting sustainable agriculture in the region.

2 garlic cloves, sliced thin

4½ tablespoons extra virgin olive oil

4 portobello mushrooms, stems removed, brushed clean

6 fresh thyme sprigs

Salt and freshly ground black pepper

4 slices firm white bread, crusts removed, halved diagonally

8 eggs

2 scallions, trimmed and chopped

4 ounces Montrachet goat cheese, crumbled

2 tablespoons minced chives

A smoothie made from milk, plain yogurt, and banana, sweetened with maple syrup. But Champagne would be fine, too.

Lightly brushing the mushrooms is the best way to remove any bits of earth that might be clinging to their surface. Washing will make them soggy.

In a baking dish large enough to hold the mushrooms in a single layer, place the garlic and 4 tablespoons of the olive oil and put the dish in the oven to warm while the oven heats to 375 degrees.

Remove the dish, place the mushrooms in it and brush them all over with the seasoned oil. Scatter with the thyme and season with salt and pepper. Return the dish to the oven and roast the mushrooms stem side up for about 25 minutes. Remove the mushrooms from the dish and wrap in foil to keep warm. Place the bread triangles in the dish, turn them once to coat both sides with the oil, and bake until toasted, turning once, about 15 minutes. Remove the toast and set aside.

When you are ready to serve this dish, beat the eggs in a bowl and season with salt and pepper. Mix the scallions and Montrachet together in another bowl and set near the stove. Place a large nonstick skillet over medium heat, add the remaining ½ tablespoon of oil, add the eggs, and stir them with a rubber spatula. When they're barely beginning to set and are still quite moist, fold in the scallions and cheese and continue to cook until the eggs are softly set. Remove from the heat.

Place a mushroom cap, stem side up, on each of 4 warm plates. Spoon the eggs onto each cap, dust with the chives and place a couple of pieces of the toast alongside. Serve.

OEUFS COCOTTE

BALTHAZAR

THERE ARE DOZENS OF NEW YORK RESTAURANTS that call themselves brasseries—even one that has a lock, pure and simple, on the name Brasserie. But none captures the atmosphere of Paris's glorious Belle Époque and Art Deco dining halls like Keith McNally's Balthazar in SoHo. The name itself evokes Balzar, one of the most beloved of the Left Bank places. And truth be told, New York's Balthazar is lovelier by far than that particular Parisian model. It took an Englishman, not a Frenchman, to accomplish it. McNally brought some of the details for his tile, brass, and dark wood dining room—a former leather goods wholesale store—from France, but many of the fittings, like the mirrors showing their age, came from antiques markets in this country. McNally has a similar way with evocative decor at Pravda, his vodka-and-caviar bar. At Balthazar, from the raw bar selections to the steak with terrific frites to the warm apple tart, the food is exactly what one expects, enhanced by fresh bread from the restaurant's own bakery (there's a retail shop adjacent). And for those in the know, breakfast at Balthazar is a true treasure: relaxed, low-key, and delicious. And not just for indulgences like the croissants, but also for specialties like perfectly scrambled eggs and McNally's favorite Oeufs Cocotte, eggs baked in ramekins with cream and fresh thyme.

The recipe specifies organic eggs, and it's a good idea to use only organic eggs for other dishes, too. They are far less likely to cause problems when undercooked with the yolks still runny, as in this recipe.

1 tablespoon soft unsalted butter

4 tablespoons freshly grated
   Parmigiano-Reggiano

1 teaspoon fresh thyme leaves

Salt and freshly ground black pepper

½ cup heavy cream

8 eggs, organic if possible

4 fresh thyme sprigs

Toast or grilled bread, for serving

Good coffee or a mimosa

Preheat the oven to 325 degrees. Butter 4 shallow 1-cup ramekins, the type used for crème brûlée. Sprinkle each with ½ tablespoon of the cheese and ¼ teaspoon of thyme leaves. Lightly dust with salt and pepper. Place ramekins in a baking pan at least 2 inches deep.

Spoon 2 tablespoons of the cream into each ramekin. Break 2 eggs into each ramekin and season with salt and pepper. Sprinkle on the remaining cheese and lay a thyme sprig on top. Pour hot water into the baking pan to come halfway up the sides of the ramekins. Carefully place the baking pan in the oven and bake 8 to 10 minutes, until the whites are just set and the cream and cheese are bubbling and lightly browned. Serve at once, with toast or grilled bread.

CALIFORNIA OMELET

MICHAEL'S

M ICHAEL McCARTY WAS AMONG THE FIRST to bring California cuisine, with its salads, bright vegetables, and free-range chicken to Manhattan, opening a branch of his Santa Monica restaurant in Midtown. It's a comfortable, understated room enlivened with fine modern art, including paintings by McCarty's wife, Kim. A power crowd, mostly in publishing, are the regulars at breakfast, lunch, and dinner. The menu emphasizes fresh ingredients, organic when available.

SERVES 1 TO 2

3 strips thick-cut smoked bacon

1 tablespoon unsalted butter

2 tablespoons minced onion

3 button mushrooms, sliced

1 tablespoon clarified butter or extra virgin olive oil

3 eggs, beaten until frothy

Salt and freshly ground black pepper

¼ Hass avocado, sliced thin

1 sun-dried tomato, chopped

1 tablespoon sour cream

Fresh blood orange juice

It is important to keep the eggs moving in the pan so they do not take on any color.

Fry the bacon until crisp. Drain well, chop, and set aside. Discard the fat from the pan.

In a 9-inch nonstick skillet, melt the butter. Add the onion and sauté over low heat until the onion is translucent. Add the mushrooms and sauté until they have softened and are barely beginning to brown, about 5 minutes. Remove from the heat. Transfer onions and mushrooms to a plate and set aside.

Wipe out the pan. Add the clarified butter or oil and place over medium heat. Season the eggs with salt and pepper and pour them into the pan. Working quickly with a heatproof rubber spatula, move the outer edges to the center, allowing the uncooked egg to run to the outside. The cooked egg will pile up in the middle of the pan. When very little of the still-liquid egg remains in the pan, place the mushrooms and onion on half of the egg mixture, on the far side of the pan. Place the chopped bacon, avocado, tomato, and sour cream on top of the mushrooms and onion. Use your spatula to fold the plain half of the omelet over the filled half. Roll the omelet out of the pan onto a plate and serve at once.

CHEESE AND CHILE CORNBREAD

PEARSON'S TEXAS BBQ

ROBERT PEARSON IS ONE UNLIKELY PITMASTER. An English gent, he started his company as a take-out stand just off the Interstate in Stratford, Connecticut, and immediately acquired a loyal following among Yalies and others. He then moved with his partner, Ellen Goldberg, to Long Island City, Queens, and flourished a few blocks from the Midtown Tunnel. But that building came down, so he moved his establishment to the back room of a bar in Jackson Heights. Now, in partnership with Ken Aretsky, a New York restaurateur who once ran the '21' Club and who owns Patroon in Midtown and 92 on the Upper East Side, he has opened a place in Manhattan in what was Aretsky's Butterfield 81. An Upper East Side barbecue joint? Now that's class!

SERVES 6 TO 8

½ cup plus 1 teaspoon corn oil

4 eggs

1⅓ cups buttermilk

1 teaspoon baking soda

1 teaspoon salt

2½ cups stone-ground yellow
   cornmeal

1 (15-ounce) can creamed corn

1 jalapeño chile, stemmed, seeded,
   and minced

7 ounces Colby cheese, grated,
   approximately 1¾ cups

A good microbrewed beer

Use the teaspoon oil to grease an 8- or 9-inch square baking pan. If your pan is glass or ceramic, preheat the oven to 350 degrees; otherwise preheat the oven to 375 degrees.

In a large bowl lightly beat the eggs. Whisk in the buttermilk, baking soda, salt, and cornmeal. Add the remaining ½ cup of oil, and mix, then the creamed corn, jalapeño, and cheese. Pour the batter into the oiled pan and bake about 40 minutes, until lightly browned.

Cool on a rack, cut in squares, and serve.

Stone-ground cornmeal is coarser than regular milled cornmeal, giving this recipe better texture. You could use yellow polenta instead.

For this recipe, as with most, it is a good idea to line up your ingredients in order, ready to use.

TRE POMODORI PIZZA

SAPORI D'ISCHIA

SAPORI D'ISCHIA started as an Italian import warehouse and wholesale distributor in Woodside, Queens. Then it opened its doors to the public for retail sales. Gradually it began adding a restaurant, first just pizza and some antipasto items at lunchtime. Eventually it became a full-fledged restaurant in the evening, with a menu of salads, ovenbaked specialties, pastas, pizzas, main courses, and desserts. It is still rather out of the way, but the word is out and it has acquired a following of dedicated shoppers and diners.

½ package active dry yeast,
    approximately 1½ teaspoons

3 tablespoons extra virgin olive oil

2 teaspoons sea salt

1 cup cake flour

3 cups bread flour, approximately

1 cup canned San Marzano
    tomatoes, drained

Freshly ground black pepper

2 cups cherry tomatoes, halved

10 Italian sun-dried tomatoes

1 cup (about 3 ounces) shaved
    Parmigiano-Reggiano

2 sprigs fresh basil

A white wine from Ischia or
Campania, in southern Italy

Instead of simmering and sea-soning the San Marzano toma-toes, Sapori D'Ischia recommends simply buying their own brand of tomato sauce made with San Marzano tomatoes, the best Italian canned tomatoes.

Place the yeast, 1½ tablespoons of the oil, and 1 teaspoon of the salt in a large mixing bowl. Stir in 1⅓ cups of warm water. Use a wooden spoon to stir in the cake flour. Add the bread flour, ½ cup at a time, until a soft dough begins to leave the sides of the bowl. You should have added a total of 3 to 3½ cups of flour at this point. Spread the last ½ cup of bread flour on a work surface and knead the dough, adding additional flour as necessary, until a soft, pliable dough has formed that's not sticky. Shape it into a ball, cover it with a towel, and allow to rest 10 minutes.

Divide the dough into 2 equal balls, brush them lightly with a little of the remaining olive oil, cover them with a clean towel, and set aside to rise for about 1 hour, until doubled.

While the dough is rising, crush the San Marzano toma-toes and place in a nonreactive saucepan. Bring to a sim-mer, add the remaining oil, and season with the remaining teaspoon of salt and pepper to taste. Remove from the heat.

Preheat the oven to 500 degrees. Set the oven rack to the lowest position. Punch down one ball of the dough and knead briefly. Stretch and roll it into a very thin, 10-inch round. Place it on a pizza stone or a pizza pan. Spread it with half of the tomato sauce and scatter half of the cherry tomatoes on top. Bake about 10 minutes or longer, if needed, until the crust is golden brown. Strew half of the sun-dried tomatoes, half of the Parmigiano-Reggiano, and half of the basil over the pizza and serve at once. Bake a second pizza with the remaining ingredients.

FOCACCIA ROBIOLA

LE MADRI

Pino Luongo changed Italian restaurants in New York, introducing a rustic Tuscan farmhouse style in a city where Italian food had been served either on red-checked tablecloths in old-fashioned "Little Italy" neighborhoods, or in fancy surroundings that mimicked French restaurants. From Il Cantinori, where he first made his mark as a waiter and later a manager, to Le Madri, his first venture as an owner, in partnership with the Pressmans, formerly of Barney's, he refined his vision. Simple pizzas sizzled in a wood-burning oven, an antipasto was arrayed on a tile counter, many of the pastas were made in-house, and main courses reflected his Florentine tastes. Le Madri was followed by others, including Tuscan Square in Rockefeller Center, and Centolire and Coco Pazzo on the Upper East Side.

Serves 4 to 6

½ package active dry yeast, approximately 1½ teaspoons

4 tablespoons extra virgin olive oil

2 teaspoons sea salt

4 cups all-purpose or bread flour, approximately

6 tablespoons *robiola* cheese or soft goat cheese

6 tablespoons cream cheese

1 shallot, peeled and minced

2 teaspoons white truffle oil, optional (sold in fancy food shops)

Place the yeast, 1½ tablespoons of the oil, and 1 teaspoon of the salt in a large mixing bowl. Stir in 1⅓ cups warm water. Use a wooden spoon to stir in 1 cup of the flour. Continue adding the flour, ½ cup at a time, until a soft dough begins to leave the sides of the bowl. You should have added about 3 to 3½ cups of flour at this point. Spread another ½ cup of the flour on a work surface and knead the dough, adding additional flour as necessary, until a soft, pliable dough has formed that's not sticky. Shape the dough into a ball, cover it with a towel, and allow to rest 10 minutes.

Divide the dough into two equal balls, brush them lightly with a little of the remaining olive oil, cover them with plastic, and refrigerate for 2 hours.

Preheat the oven to 425 degrees. Set the oven rack to the lowest position. Knead the two balls of dough back together, and stretch and roll the dough into a 14-inch round. Prick it all over with a fork and place it on a pizza stone or a pizza pan. Brush it with the remaining olive oil, sprinkle with the remaining teaspoon of salt, and bake un-

 Italian white truffle oil gives this focaccia its unique personality. Truffle oil is highly perishable and should be kept in the refrigerator or freezer, and used sparingly.

Sparkling Prosecco

til it is lightly browned, about 20 minutes. If any part of the dough is puffing up during the first 5 to 10 minutes, prick that area again. Remove the focaccia from the oven and allow it to cool to room temperature.

Slice the focaccia in half horizontally with a sharp bread knife, taking care not to break the surface as you go. Combine the cheeses and the shallot and spread the mixture over the cut side of the bottom half. Sandwich on the top half and return the focaccia to the oven just long enough to reheat it and melt the cheese, about 10 minutes. Sprinkle with truffle oil, if using, and serve in wedges.

LOBSTER CLUB SANDWICH

AN AMERICAN PLACE

A S RESTAURANT NAMES GO, An American Place could not be more fitting. Larry Forgione, who first attracted attention for his determination to use the best American ingredients when he was the chef at the River Café in Brooklyn back in 1979, went on to open An American Place at Lexington Avenue and 70th Street in 1983. He did not hesitate to serve mashed potatoes and fruit cobblers in a fine-dining setting. In those days, before anyone dreamed of American foie gras or goat cheese, even obtaining first-rate local ingredients was a challenge. Since then, An American Place has moved three times, finally landing in the Lord & Taylor department store—a pleasant setting for his summertime lobster club sandwich.

SERVES 4

8 slices thick-cut bacon

2 large ripe tomatoes

8 leaves Bibb lettuce

1 pound cooked lobster meat, cut into ½-inch dice

½ cup plus 2 tablespoons mayonnaise

2 tablespoons chopped tarragon leaves

2 tablespoons chopped flat-leaf parsley leaves

1 tablespoon lemon juice

Pinch cayenne pepper

¼ teaspoon kosher salt

Freshly ground black pepper

8 slices country white or brioche bread

A summer ale or sauvignon blanc

Cook the bacon until it's crisp; drain it on paper towels. Slice the tomatoes. Rinse the lettuce leaves and pat them dry.

Mix the lobster with ½ cup of the mayonnaise, the tarragon, parsley, lemon juice, cayenne, salt, and pepper.

Lightly toast the bread and spread one side of each slice with a little of the remaining mayonnaise. Place a leaf of the lettuce on 4 of the slices. Top with a quarter each of the lobster mixture, the bacon, and the tomatoes, and another leaf of the lettuce. Top with the other slice of the toast. Slice in half. Secure with a toothpick or a bamboo skewer and serve.

For 1 pound of lobster meat you will need to boil two 1½-pound lobsters. It's more work than simply buying the lobster already cooked, but also cheaper.

FRIED COD SANDWICH

PEARL OYSTER BAR

THERE ARE ALL SORTS OF OYSTER BARS in New York, but Pearl Oyster Bar is an uncommon example; a little taste of New England in Greenwich Village. In fact, it's more about beachside fried clams, lobster rolls, and crab cakes than just oysters. Rebecca Charles, the owner, grew up summering in Kennebunkport on the coast of Maine, and began her career at the Whistling Oyster in Ogunquit. Lobster rolls are now on dozens of Manhattan menus, and Charles can claim responsibility. But where else can you order a fried cod sandwich?

SERVES 2

2 (5- to 6-ounce) fillets cod, haddock, flounder, or sole

1 cup milk

Salt and freshly ground black pepper

½ cup all-purpose flour

¼ cup cracker meal

¼ cup canola, peanut, or soy oil

2 ciabatta rolls, Portuguese rolls, or other flat, crusty rolls

½ cup tartar sauce

½ ripe tomato, peeled and thinly sliced

½ small red onion, thinly sliced

4 to 6 Bibb or Boston lettuce leaves

If you use flounder or sole, it will cook faster, about 2 to 3 minutes per side.

Preheat the oven to 450 degrees.

Soak the fish in milk for 5 minutes, drain it, and lay it on a plate. Season the fish with salt and pepper. On a large plate combine the flour and cracker meal. Dredge the fish on both sides with this mixture, dusting off excess.

Heat an ovenproof skillet over high heat, add the oil and when very hot, place the fish in the pan with the whiter side down. When the crust is golden brown, after 3 to 4 minutes, flip the fillets over and place the pan in the oven for 4 to 5 minutes, to finish cooking. At this time place the rolls in the oven, to warm them for a minute or two.

Split the rolls in half horizontally with a sharp, serrated knife. Spread both halves of each roll liberally with tartar sauce. Layer the tomato, onion, and lettuce on the bottom halves and season to taste with salt and pepper. When the fish is done, place it on the bottom halves, close the sandwiches, and serve.

Rebecca Charles admits that beer is best.

OPEN-FACE TUNA SALAD SANDWICHES

LE PAIN QUOTIDIEN

ALAIN COUMONT STARTED HIS CHAIN of farmhouse-style bakery-cafés in Belgium, expanded it to other European countries, and finally brought his concept to New York. There are five restaurant-shops in the city now: the original one on Madison Avenue, and others in the Upper West Side, the Upper East Side, the Flatiron district, and SoHo. What distinguishes these places is Coumont's commitment to using as many organic ingredients as possible. His breads are made with organic flour, his salads rely on organic greens, oils, and vinegars, and even the milk for his organic coffee is organic.

SERVES 2

1 (6½-ounce) can tuna in olive oil, drained

2 tablespoons diced organic celery

2 tablespoons peeled, diced organic onion

2 teaspoons sherry vinegar

1½ tablespoons organic olive oil

2 teaspoons Dijon mustard

2 teaspoons organic mayonnaise

Salt and freshly ground black pepper

2 large slices organic wheat bread

2 tablespoons black olive paste or tapenade

½ roasted red pepper in oil

Mesclun greens and cucumber slices, for serving

Use a fork to break up the tuna in a bowl. Add the celery, onion, vinegar, olive oil, mustard, and mayonnaise, and mix well. Season to taste with salt and pepper. Spread the salad on each of the two slices of bread. Cut each slice into four sections. Spread a little of the olive paste on each section. Cut the roasted red pepper into 8 strips and place one on each section. Transfer the sandwiches to 2 salad plates, garnish with mesclun greens and cucumber slices, and serve.

Organic iced tea

European tuna in olive oil has much better flavor than white albacore tuna in water.

SEAFOOD

GRILLED FILET MIGNON OF TUNA

WILD KING SALMON IN SWISS CHARD WITH QUINOA

LEMONGRASS-CRUSTED SWORDFISH WITH THAI PEANUT SAUCE

HERB-ROASTED SALMON WITH HORSERADISH

KAKAVIA, GREEK FISHERMAN'S STEW

STEAMED BLACK BASS WITH BASMATI RICE

STRIPED BASS WITH RED WINE SAUCE AND SAGE

BLACK COD WITH MISO

SEAFOOD STEW

CODFISH WITH SWEET GARLIC SAUCE AND CHORIZO ESSENCE

OVEN-ROASTED SHRIMP WITH TOASTED GARLIC AND RED CHILE OIL

BUTTER-POACHED LOBSTER WITH CAULIFLOWER PUREE

LOBSTER FRA DIAVOLO

GRILLED FILET MIGNON OF TUNA

UNION SQUARE CAFE

WHEN DANNY MEYER OPENED Union Square Cafe in 1985, the New York restaurant scene was vastly different. The dining public was just starting to be seduced by the allure of new American kitchens and young American chefs; the chefs themselves were beginning to notice the potential that local farmers represented. Union Square Cafe's chef, French-trained Michael Romano, was in the vanguard of those who took advantage of what the burgeoning nearby Greenmarket had to offer. The restaurant's location certainly helped, but the right attitude contributed even more. Union Square Cafe still holds monthly market breakfasts with farmers. But at lunch, it's a downtown version of the Grill Room at The Four Seasons, with publishing moguls, authors, and agents filling the tables. Dinner is for New Yorkers and visitors with the foresight to reserve well in advance, or who do not mind digging into the lusty Italianate food with a glass of wine at the bar. Danny Meyer has added other nearby restaurants to his portfolio: Eleven Madison Park, Tabla, Gramercy Tavern, and Blue Smoke.

2 cups teriyaki sauce

½ cup dry sherry

4 tablespoons minced fresh ginger

½ cup minced scallions

2 garlic cloves, thinly sliced

½ teaspoon cayenne

2 teaspoons freshly ground black
  pepper

Juice of 2 lemons, about ¼ cup

4 yellowfin tuna steaks, each about
  8 ounces and cut 2½ to 3 inches
  thick

2 tablespoons extra virgin olive oil

¼ cup Japanese pickled ginger,
  drained

Most fish markets do not cut their tuna steaks thicker than about 1½ to 2 inches. It will probably be necessary for you to place a special order for the tuna. With thinner steaks, the tuna can be cut in chunks, marinated, strung on skewers, and grilled like kebabs.

Combine the teriyaki sauce, sherry, fresh ginger, scallions, garlic, cayenne, black pepper, and lemon juice in a bowl large enough to hold the tuna. Cut each tuna steak vertically in three equal pieces. Place the tuna in the marinade, cover the bowl, and let it sit in the refrigerator for 3 hours. Turn the tuna every hour.

A half hour before serving, remove the tuna from the refrigerator, drain off the marinade and put the tuna on a platter. Preheat a grill or broiler. You can also use a heavy-duty stove-top grill pan but it will not need to be preheated for more than 10 minutes.

Brush the tuna with olive oil. Grill or broil the tuna a minute or two on each of its 6 sides, so the outside is charred but the center is barely warm and still quite rare. Top each piece of tuna with a little of the pickled ginger and serve at once.

A Cornas from the Rhône, a tokay pinot gris from Alsace, or chilled beer

WILD KING SALMON IN SWISS CHARD WITH QUINOA

RIVER CAFE

T HE BROOKLYN WATERFRONT has perhaps the best views of Lower Manhattan, and that's what makes the River Cafe so magical. It's literally right at the edge of the East River, and were it any closer to the Brooklyn Bridge, it would be under it. But the restaurant, owned by Buzzy O'Keeffe—who has also masterminded places like the Water Club on the Manhattan side of the river in Midtown, and Pershing Square across from Grand Central Terminal—has been an incubator for some of the city's best chefs, including Larry Forgione, Charles Palmer, David Burke, and Rick Laakkonen. When Forgione was at the stove in 1979, the restaurant's mission was to showcase American ingredients at a time when few chefs were paying attention. It still champions that approach.

SERVES 6

1 bunch red Swiss chard, heavy stems removed

6 tablespoons unsalted butter

1 celery stalk, finely diced

2 carrots, peeled and finely diced

2 leeks, white part only, well-rinsed, finely diced

1½ cups quinoa

3 cups hot chicken stock

3 (10- to 12-ounce) king salmon steaks

2 tablespoons finely minced preserved lemon (sold in Middle Eastern food shops)

1 shallot, peeled and minced

½ teaspoon ground star anise or Chinese five-spice powder

1 cup dry red wine

2 cups tawny port

Salt and freshly ground black pepper

½ teaspoon lemon juice

Bring a large pot of water to a boil. Place several layers of paper towels nearby on your countertop. Place a Swiss chard leaf in the water, scoop it out as soon as it wilts, and lay it flat on the towel. Repeat with the remaining Swiss chard leaves. Roll the Swiss chard leaves in the paper towels and set aside.

Heat 1½ tablespoons of the butter in a heavy 3-quart saucepan. Add the celery, carrots, and leeks, and sauté over medium-low heat until translucent. Add the quinoa, stir it for a few minutes, then gradually add the chicken stock. Cover, lower the heat, and cook until the quinoa is tender, about 15 minutes. Remove from the heat and keep covered. The quinoa can be prepared in advance and reheated just before serving.

Remove the skin from the salmon steaks, cut each steak in half, and remove the bones. This will give you six uniform fillets. Spread one side of each piece of salmon with some of the preserved lemon. Then wrap each piece of salmon in a Swiss chard leaf, enclosing it completely like an envelope. You may have to use more than one leaf for each piece of fish. Place two wrapped fish fillets in a Ziploc sandwich bag and seal the bag. Repeat with the remaining fillets. Refrigerate until about 15 to 20 minutes before serving.

Heat ½ tablespoon of the butter in a small saucepan. Add the shallot and star anise and sauté until tender. Add the wine and port, and boil until reduced to about 1 cup. Keeping the wine mixture at a bare simmer, whisk in the remaining 4 tablespoons of butter, bit by bit, until the sauce is thickened. Season to taste with salt and pepper. Add the lemon juice. Keep warm.

Remove the fish from the refrigerator. Bring about 1 inch of water to a boil in a pot or deep covered frying pan large enough to hold the bags of fish in one flat layer. Place a steamer over the boiling water. Place the fish, still sealed in the plastic bags, in the steamer, cover the pot, and cook for about 8 minutes. Remove the fish from steamer and allow to rest 5 minutes. While the fish is resting, reheat the quinoa.

Divide the quinoa among 6 warm dinner plates. Carefully open the plastic bags and place a wrapped fish fillet alongside the quinoa. Drizzle the warm wine sauce over the fish and around the quinoa, and serve.

Zind-Humbrecht Alsatian Riesling 2000, another full-bodied dry riesling, Domaine Drouhin Pinot Noir 1999 from Oregon, or a light red Burgundy

LEMONGRASS-CRUSTED SWORDFISH WITH THAI PEANUT SAUCE

ROY'S NEW YORK

ROY YAMAGUCHI, who brought the luau tastes of Hawaii to New York, was born in Japan, trained at the Culinary Institute of America in Hyde Park, New York, and worked in Los Angeles before settling in Honolulu. From there he created his Roy's empire, with several places in Hawaii, outposts in Tokyo and Guam, and restaurants in California and Manhattan. His cooking is brash and well-spiced, and balances sweet and sour flavors. Seafood is his specialty. This dish is made in Hawaii with a fish called *shutome*, but swordfish is a fine substitute.

Most of the specialized ingredients are sold in Asian stores.

The sauce can be made in advance and reheated when the fish is ready to serve.

1 cup unsweetened coconut milk

⅓ cup packed light brown sugar

⅓ cup soy sauce

1 tablespoon *nam pla* (Thai fish sauce)

2 teaspoons rice vinegar

1 tablespoon lemon juice

2 teaspoons Thai *Masaman* curry paste, or 2 teaspoons curry powder

5 tablespoons creamy peanut butter

¼ cup minced sweet onion such as Maui

2 tablespoons minced cilantro leaves

1 kaffir lime leaf, minced, or 1 teaspoon grated lime zest

2 tablespoons minced fresh basil leaves, preferably Thai opal

1½ tablespoons minced garlic

1½ tablespoons minced fresh ginger

2 tablespoons minced lemongrass bulb

1 tablespoon minced shallots

1 teaspoon *shichimi* (Japanese pepper), or ½ teaspoon each cayenne and black pepper

3 tablespoons canola oil

1½ pounds swordfish steaks, skinned, cut into 4 portions

Salt

Japanese pickled ginger and cilantro sprigs, for garnish

Though this recipe requires what looks like a thousand ingredients, it is actually very simple to prepare.

For the sauce, whisk together in a small saucepan the coconut milk, brown sugar, soy sauce, fish sauce, rice vinegar, lemon juice, curry, peanut butter, onion, cilantro, kaffir lime leaf, basil, and ½ tablespoon each of the garlic and ginger. Bring to a boil, reduce the heat, and simmer about 30 minutes.

Meanwhile, mix the remaining tablespoon each garlic and ginger with the lemongrass, shallots, and *shichimi*. Beat in the oil. You can do this in a food processor. Season the fish with salt. Spread the lemongrass mixture on one side of each piece of the fish.

Heat a large nonstick skillet over medium-high heat. Place the pieces of fish in it, crusted side down, and sauté until golden, about 3 minutes. Use a spatula to carefully turn the fish so as not to lose any of the crust. Continue cooking until the fish is just cooked through, another 5 minutes or so.

While the fish is cooking, reheat the sauce, thinning it with a splash of water if necessary.

Place the fish on a serving dish, garnish with pickled ginger and cilantro, and serve with the sauce alongside.

Passion fruit margaritas made with silver tequila, passion fruit puree, fresh lime juice, and simple syrup. Beer or fruity white wine are good alternatives.

HERB-ROASTED SALMON WITH HORSERADISH

BEACON

A WOOD-BURNING OVEN is a coveted accessory in New York's restaurant kitchens. Often, its use is limited to pizza. But at Beacon the chef, Waldy Malouf, relies on it for cooking everything from the first-course oysters to pears for dessert. The restaurant, which is also owned by David Emil and other partners of the former Windows on the World team, is a spacious room with a mezzanine. But the focus is the hearth, open to view, where the chefs use long-handled peels to move sizzling dishes in and out of the roaring oven.

SERVES 4

2 tablespoons soft white bread crumbs

5 tablespoons prepared horseradish

Freshly ground white pepper

5 tablespoons extra virgin olive oil

2½ tablespoons minced fresh basil

2½ tablespoons minced fresh tarragon

2½ tablespoons minced fresh dill

1½ tablespoons minced fresh mint

Salt

1¼ pounds fresh salmon fillet, skinned and cut into 8 equal pieces

When wild Pacific salmon from Alaska or Washington is in season, it is a better choice for both flavor and the environment than farm-raised Atlantic salmon.

Place the bread crumbs and 3 tablespoons of the horseradish in a mortar and mix well. Season with pepper. Add 3 tablespoons of the oil in a thin stream, beating constantly. Thin the sauce with a tablespoon or two of water so it is slightly thinner than mayonnaise. Set aside.

Preheat the oven to 500 degrees.

Mix 1 tablespoon of the oil with the remaining horseradish. Mix in 2 tablespoons each of the basil, tarragon, and dill, and 1 tablespoon of the mint. Season with salt and pepper. Use a little of the remaining oil to grease a baking dish that will hold the fish in a single layer. Season the fish with salt and pepper and arrange in the pan skinned side down. Spoon the horseradish-herb mixture on top of each piece of the fish, place the pan in the oven, and bake 6 to 8 minutes, until the fish is not quite cooked through.

Remove from the oven and place 2 pieces of fish on each of 4 plates. Spoon some of the horseradish-bread sauce around each portion, sprinkle with some of the remaining herbs and a few drops of the remaining oil, and serve.

Sokol-Blosser Pinot Gris 2000, another Oregon pinot gris, or a light red Burgundy

KAKAVIA, GREEK FISHERMAN'S STEW

ESTIATORIO MILOS

Estiatorio Milos, the New York branch of a popular Montreal restaurant, has generated a trend. The *estiatorio*, or market-style Greek fish restaurant, did not exist in New York before Milos opened. And now it has spawned a handful of imitators which, like the original, specialize in serving fresh fish, by the pound. Milos is a simple, handsome room done in whites and neutrals—more marble quarry than country inn. When diners are seated, the house's own olive oil is poured over crushed herbs as a dip for crusty country bread, then the market choices are described. Greek dishes, both traditional crowd-pleasers and more unexpected items, fill out the menu.

SERVES 6

2 large onions, peeled and cut in chunks

2 pounds Yukon gold potatoes, peeled and cut into chunks

3 pounds assorted fish fillets and steaks, such as striped bass, sea bass, grouper, cod, monkfish

1 cup best-quality extra virgin olive oil

1 tablespoon coarse sea salt

Freshly ground black pepper

18 (2-inch) chunks country bread, toasted

Juice of ½ lemon, about 1 tablespoon

12 sprigs flat-leaf parsley

Ideally, you'll want to use at least three kinds of fish in this stew. In Greece the choices would include a rockfish like rascasse, the fish that is essential to bouillabaisse. But any firm, chunky, lean fish works.

You'll need a deep 6-quart pot to assemble this hearty, amazingly simple fisherman's stew. Put the onions in the bottom of the pot. Cover the onions with the potato chunks. Then add the fish, all of which should be in fairly large pieces. Pour ½ cup of the good olive oil—emphasis on the good, please—over it all.

Measure out 3 cups of water and dissolve the sea salt in it. Add some pepper and pour it into the pot. Cover the pot, and put it on high heat. Once it comes to a boil, lower the heat just a bit and let it cook 12 minutes.

While the kakavia bubbles away, brush the bread cubes with about ¼ cup of the remaining olive oil.

After the 12 minutes are up, remove the pot from the heat and carefully ladle the fish and vegetables out of the pot, into 6 generous soup plates or bowls. Add the lemon juice to the pot. The broth now should be flavorful and slightly thickened from the potatoes and the emulsified olive oil—that's what happens when it boils: it's the bouillabaisse principle. Bring the broth back to the simmer, and ladle it over the fish and vegetables. Drizzle on the rest of the olive oil, top each portion with the bread cubes and parsley, and serve at once.

STEAMED BLACK BASS WITH BASMATI RICE
LA CARAVELLE

O NCE THE "KENNEDY CLUBHOUSE," La Caravelle has evolved over time but has maintained its position among the elite of New York's French restaurants. André and Rita Jammet, the current owners, provide a warm welcome in a setting glittering with mirrors and Dufy-like murals of Paris that could as easily be in the 16th Arrondissement as on West 55th Street. Never mind that a previous executive chef was Japanese and that others have been American. All have maintained the restaurant's classic approach, with dishes such as *quenelles de brochet* and dover sole *meunière*, as well as with more inventive, still French-inspired fare. Black bass steamed as a paupiette, garnished with cucumbers, and served with Indian basmati rice is a fine example.

SERVES 2

½ cup basmati rice

½ English (seedless) cucumber, peeled

1 leek, rinsed, trimmed, and halved lengthwise

2 black sea bass fillets, each about 8 ounces, skinned

Salt and freshly ground black pepper

2 tablespoons minced shallots

2 tablespoons unsalted butter

¼ cup dry white wine

¼ cup fresh orange juice

2 tablespoons extra virgin olive oil

½ tablespoon minced cilantro leaves

La Caravelle

Place rice in a sieve and rinse until water runs clear. Transfer to a bowl, cover with fresh water, and soak 15 minutes.

Use a small melon baller to scoop 10 balls of cucumber flesh. Finely julienne the remaining cucumber and set aside.

Drain the rice and place it in a saucepan with ½ cup water. Bring it to a simmer and cook about 15 minutes, until the rice is tender and water absorbed. Fold in the julienne cucumber and set aside, covered.

Bring a small pot of water to a boil. Peel off two leaves of leek about 6 inches long, place in the boiling water, and cook until just softened, about 5 minutes. Rinse under cold water, pat dry, and cut each leaf in half lengthwise. Cut each fish fillet in half lengthwise, season with salt and pepper, roll each piece up, and tie with a piece of the leek. Place the rolls of fish standing on end in a heat-proof soup plate that will fit into your steamer (or plan to steam the fish in two batches), sprinkle each with shallots, and dot with butter. Place cucumber balls around the fish. Alternatively, the fish and cucumber can be placed in a microwave dish and microwaved instead of steamed.

If you can obtain green papaya, add a little of it, julienned, to the rice to give it a slightly tart flavor.

Instead of serving the fish hot with the rice, it can also be served cold, with a mayonnaise sauce. Thin some mayonnaise with orange juice to dress the rice.

Riesling from Alsace, preferably Trimbach, either Clos Ste.-Hune or Cuvée Frédéric Émile

Combine wine, orange juice, and olive oil in a small saucepan and set aside.

Steam the fish and cucumbers about 10 minutes or microwave for 3 minutes at full power, until just done. Cover loosely to keep warm. Drain the cooking juices into the pan with the wine and orange juice, and bring to a simmer. Season to taste with salt and pepper. Fold the cilantro into the rice, season to taste with salt and pepper, and reheat briefly.

Mound the rice in the center of each of 2 soup plates. Place the fish on top of the rice and scatter cucumber balls around. Spoon the sauce into plates around the fish. Serve immediately.

STRIPED BASS WITH RED WINE SAUCE AND SAGE

CHANTERELLE

CHANTERELLE IS A PIONEER, one of the first fine restaurants to open in SoHo. It has moved since then, conquering new territory in TriBeCa. The dining room is airy and understated, deriving its elegance from stunning sprays of flowers, a few carefully chosen antique pieces, and magnificent chandeliers. David Waltuck, the chef who owns Chanterelle with his wife, Karen, is celebrated for his finely crafted imaginative French-accented American food. The couple have also opened a bistro nearby, Le Zinc.

3 tablespoons fresh sage leaves

½ teaspoon chopped garlic

Juice of ½ lemon, about 1 tablespoon

4 tablespoons soft unsalted butter

Salt and freshly ground black pepper

1½ pounds wild striped bass fillets
    with skin, in 4 equal portions

3 tablespoons red wine vinegar

3 tablespoons minced shallots

1 cup dry red wine

2 tablespoons *glace de viande* (veal
    glaze)

8 tablespoons cold unsalted butter,
    diced

⅓ cup Wondra or all-purpose flour

3 tablespoons extra virgin olive oil

Farm-raised striped bass is more easily obtained than Atlantic wild striped bass, but there is no comparison. The wild fish is meatier and more muscular. Black sea bass and even Pacific king salmon can be substituted.

In this recipe the sage butter actually melts away when the fish is seared but the flavor of sage and butter permeate the fish and the skin becomes extremely crisp.

Place the sage, garlic, lemon juice, and soft butter in a small food processor or in a mortar. Process or pound until smooth. Season with salt and pepper.

Use a sharp knife to lift the skin off the fish, leaving it attached at one edge. Spread the sage butter on the fish, and replace the flap of skin to enclose the butter. Refrigerate until just before cooking.

Place the vinegar and shallots in a small saucepan. Cook until shallots are translucent and vinegar just films the bottom of the pan. Add the wine, cook until reduced to about ¼ cup. Stir in veal glaze, then lower heat. Whisk in the cold butter bit by bit, whisking constantly, until the sauce has thickened. Season to taste with salt and pepper. Cover, set aside, and keep warm.

Fifteen to 20 minutes before serving, dust the fish fillets with the flour and shake off any excess. In a large sauté pan, heat the olive oil until it's nearly smoking. Add the fish, skin side down, and sear until lightly browned. Turn and sear on the second side until cooked through. Count on close to 10 minutes total cooking time. Transfer the fish portions to individual dinner plates, skin side up. Gently reheat the red wine sauce, spoon around the fish, and serve.

Vosne-Romanée Les Malconsorts Jouis Jadot 1997 or another full-bodied red Burgundy

BLACK COD WITH MISO

NOBU

It was inevitable that Nobu Matsuhisa, who opened Matsuhisa in Los Angeles in 1987 to rave reviews, would wind up in New York. Even without having Robert De Niro as a regular at the sushi bar in his Los Angeles spot, a chef whose food is as original as Nobu's would be attracted to New York. Here the design by David Rockwell is stunning, with bare wood and a wall of sea pebbles. Nobu's classic Japanese training fused with a seven-year stint in Lima, Peru, to shape his cuisine. Sashimi meets ceviche. Nobu regulars let the chef decide the menu. But inevitably, they'll want a taste of his famous, often-imitated Black Cod with Miso. Although seats are hard to secure, reservations are not necessary at the sushi bar. And at the equally innovative spin-off, Next Door Nobu, it's first-come, first-served.

SERVES 4

¼ cup sake

¾ cup mirin

2 cups white miso paste

1¼ cups sugar

4 black cod (sablefish) fillets with skin, each about 8 ounces

Japanese pickled ginger, for garnish

Robert De Niro's favorite drink with this dish is chilled sake.

The glaze is also delicious with salmon, tuna, and even beef. But then you may want to reduce the baking time, so the center of the fish or meat is medium rare.

Bring the sake and mirin to a boil in a medium saucepan over high heat. Boil 20 seconds. Reduce heat to low and stir in miso paste with a wooden spoon. When miso has dissolved, increase the heat to medium and stir in the sugar. Cook, stirring constantly, until the sugar dissolves. Remove from heat and cool to room temperature. This mixture is the key to the recipe.

Pat the fish dry with paper towel. Place in a nonreactive dish, pour on the cooled miso mixture, and turn the fish to coat it completely. Cover tightly with plastic wrap and refrigerate 2 to 3 days. The marinating is another key.

Preheat the oven to 400 degrees. Preheat a grill, grill pan, or broiler.

Remove the fish from the marinade, lightly wiping off any excess. Place the fish on the grill or under the broiler with the skin toward the heat, and sear until the skin is just browned. Transfer to a baking dish, skin side up, and bake about 10 minutes, until just cooked through.

Arrange on dinner plates and garnish with ginger.

SEAFOOD STEW

GUASTAVINO

IT IS PROBABLY SAFE TO SAY that no restaurant in New York took longer to create than Guastavino, in the vast, cathedral-like space under the arches of the Queensboro Bridge. The restaurant is named for the designer of the tiles used in the vaulting, Rafael Guastavino, whose work can also be seen in the Oyster Bar in Grand Central Terminal. Back in the 1970s a developer had the idea to turn the vaults under the bridge approach at Fifty-Ninth Street and First Avenue, which had once been used as a market, into a food hall and restaurant. Almost 25 years later, Guastavino finally opened. The bar and the second floor banquet rooms take advantage of the dramatic setting. The restaurant is a modern affair, tucked behind the bar. The chef, Daniel Orr, is French-trained but very American in his culinary outlook.

6 tablespoons extra virgin olive oil

2 cups chopped onions

3 large garlic cloves, minced

2½ pounds ripe plum tomatoes, peeled and coarsely chopped

1½ cups dry white wine

1½ cups seafood stock or clam juice

6 tablespoons tomato paste

2 bay leaves

3 fresh thyme sprigs

½ teaspoon saffron threads

1½ teaspoons grated orange zest

1 teaspoon ground coriander

½ teaspoon ground mustard seed

½ teaspoon ground fennel seeds

¼ teaspoon ground ginger

¼ teaspoon ground cardamom

½ teaspoon freshly ground black pepper

½ teaspoon herbes de Provence

Salt and Tabasco

8 ounces orzo

12 littleneck clams, scrubbed

12 mussels, scrubbed and debearded

¾ pound large shrimp, peeled and deveined

½ pound fresh bay scallops or quartered sea scallops

1 pound cod, in 2-inch chunks

¼ pound squid, cut in rings

2 tablespoons pastis, Pernod or Ricard

12 fresh basil leaves, rolled up and thinly sliced

Heat 2 tablespoons of the oil in a 4- to 6-quart casserole. Add the onions and garlic and sauté until they are soft but not brown. Add the tomatoes, increase the heat to high, and cook until they start to give up their juices, about 5 minutes. Stir in the wine, stock, tomato paste, bay leaves, thyme, saffron, orange zest, ground spices, and herbes de Provence. Bring to a boil. Reduce the heat to a simmer and cook for 45 minutes. Season to taste with salt and Tabasco. Set aside until 15 minutes before serving

Bring 2 quarts of salted water to a boil for the orzo. Add the orzo and cook just until done, about 6 minutes. Drain, season with salt, and toss with the remaining 4 tablespoons of olive oil. Set aside and keep warm.

Reheat the tomato mixture. Add the clams and simmer about 10 minutes, until they open. Add the mussels, shrimp, and scallops. Simmer 5 minutes. Add the cod and squid, simmer about 2 minutes longer, and stir in the pastis. Place some of the orzo in soup plates and spoon the seafood stew on top. Garnish with the basil and serve.

A red Rhone wine or even an Australian shiraz like the McWilliams Hanwood Vineyard

Daniel Orr has his own line of spices called Kitchen Dorr that is sold at the Terence Conran shop next to the restaurant and online. A teaspoon each of the pepper blend, regime blend, Mediterranean blend, and sweet blend can be used instead of the ground spices in the recipe.

CODFISH WITH SWEET GARLIC SAUCE AND CHORIZO ESSENCE

LE BERNARDIN

One month after Le Bernardin opened in 1986, it was acknowledged to be the best seafood restaurant in the city, if not the country. Its reputation has never tarnished. The original chef and owner, Gilbert Le Coze, and his sister and partner, Maguy Le Coze, who transplanted their Paris restaurant to grand quarters in Midtown, did not set about to change the way America eats fish, but their approach, undercooking some varieties ever so slightly and preparing others, like salmon, closer to rare, accomplished just that. Because pristine freshness was so paramount, Gilbert Le Coze became a denizen of the Fulton Fish Market. He led the way so that the freshness he demanded has become much easier to obtain. After his sudden death from a heart attack, he was succeeded as chef and partner by Eric Ripert, who maintains Le Bernardin's high standards, and who has broadened the scope of the menu, with some Asian and Spanish flavors.

SERVES 6

3 heads garlic

½ cup extra virgin olive oil

3 medium ripe tomatoes

4 fresh thyme sprigs

1 link chorizo sausage, preferably Spanish

1 cup chicken stock

½ cup heavy cream

Sea salt and freshly ground white pepper

2 tablespoons canola or grapeseed oil

6 (6-ounce) fillets fresh cod, skinned

Espelette pepper or Spanish hot paprika to taste

12 thin slices baguette, toasted

Chervil sprigs, for garnish

Preheat oven to 200 degrees.

Slice off the top ½ inch of the garlic heads. Place the garlic on a sheet of heavy-duty aluminum foil, drizzle with ¼ cup of the olive oil, wrap tightly, and place on a baking sheet lined with parchment. Core the tomatoes and cut each in 6 wedges. Place on the parchment-lined baking sheet, and drizzle with remaining ¼ cup olive oil. Place the thyme sprigs on top of the tomatoes and place baking sheet in the oven for 2½ hours.

Meanwhile, peel the chorizo and slice it thin. Place in a small saucepan and cook over medium heat until sausage is browned and fat is rendered. Off heat add 1 cup water—it may spatter—and cook until the liquid is reduced by half. Strain through a fine sieve, pressing the chorizo to extract as much liquid as possible. Return the liquid to the saucepan and discard the chorizo slices.

Mas de Daumas Gassac white 2001 or a viognier from the Rhône valley

When the garlic is tender and the tomatoes are cooked, remove them from the oven. Set the tomatoes aside. Using the back of a knife, press out the cloves from the heads of garlic. Reserve 6 cloves. Place the remaining cloves in a blender with ½ cup of the chicken stock. Puree, then pass through a fine sieve into a clean saucepan. Stir in the remaining chicken stock and the cream. Bring to a simmer and cook about 5 minutes, until slightly thickened. Season to taste with salt and pepper. Set aside. (All this preparation can be done hours in advance.)

If necessary, preheat the oven to 200 degrees. Place the tomato pieces and the 6 reserved garlic cloves in the 200-degree oven to warm.

Heat the canola oil in one large or two medium skillets until very hot. Dry the cod, season with salt and pepper, and place in the skillet presentation side down (that is, the whiter side that did not have the skin). Cook about 5 minutes, until golden. Flip and cook the other side until just done, another 3 to 5 minutes. Remove from the heat and transfer to 6 soup plates. Reheat the garlic sauce and spoon around fish. Place the tomato pieces around fish. Slice each reserved garlic clove into 3 slivers, and scatter over the tomatoes. Reheat chorizo essence and drizzle about a teaspoon on each portion. Dust with espelette pepper, place the baguette slices alongside the fish, garnish with chervil, and serve.

OVEN-ROASTED SHRIMP WITH TOASTED GARLIC AND RED CHILE OIL

BOLO

Bobby Flay, the chef and co-owner of Bolo, is a quick study. Having opened Mesa Grill, his interpretation of Southwestern food, he then took off for Spain, and after merely a week or two came back to New York brimming with ideas. In partnership with Laurence Kretchmer and others, he opened the brightly exuberant Bolo. Is it authentically Spanish? Not really, but the essence is there, especially in his *tapas* menu, the wine list, and the sherries. What he has done for Spanish cooking in New York is to remove the cliché-ridden expectations of little else beyond gazpacho and paella, and give it new tastes.

Serves 4

6 dried *chiles de arból*

6 garlic cloves, peeled and chopped

½ cup plus 2 tablespoons extra virgin olive oil

3 fresh thyme sprigs

8 garlic cloves, peeled and thinly sliced

32 large shrimp (about 1½ pounds), shelled and deveined

Salt and freshly ground black pepper

2 tablespoons finely minced flat-leaf parsley

1 tablespoon fresh thyme leaves

Crusty bread for serving

> Depending on the size of the shrimp you use and how many you serve in a portion, this recipe can be an hors d'oeuvre tidbit for 8 or more—a *tapa*, if you will—an appetizer for 6, or a main dish for 4.

Place the chiles in a skillet and toast over high heat for a few minutes, until they're lightly browned and their fragrance is released. Remove them from the heat, crush them, and place them in a small saucepan with the chopped garlic, the ½ cup of oil, and the thyme sprigs. Simmer over low heat about 10 minutes, until the garlic just begins to color. Remove from the heat and allow to steep for 30 minutes. Strain the oil into a small bowl and discard the solids.

Heat the remaining 2 tablespoons of oil in a small skillet, add the sliced garlic, and sauté until the garlic is browned. Remove the garlic and set on paper towels to drain.

Preheat the oven to 475 degrees. Season the shrimp with salt and pepper and place them in a baking dish. Pour the infused oil over the shrimp, turn them to coat evenly, then place in the oven and roast, turning if necessary, until the shrimp are just cooked through, 4 to 5 minutes. Transfer to a serving platter or individual plates. Dust with the chopped parsley and the thyme leaves, scatter the fried garlic on top. Serve with crusty bread for mopping up the juices.

Albariño from Spain

BUTTER-POACHED LOBSTER WITH CAULIFLOWER PUREE

R M

ICK MOONEN, THE CHEF AND CO-OWNER OF RM, is one of New York's most accomplished seafood practitioners. He's also a chef with a conscience, refusing to serve endangered varieties and spearheading consumer awareness campaigns about seafood choices. His cooking at rm is imaginative and luxurious. And as a measure of his honesty, he admits that his butter-poached lobster is not an original recipe, but an adaptation of a recipe by Thomas Keller, the owner of the French Laundry in the Napa Valley, and one of the country's most eminent chefs.

SERVES 4

1 head cauliflower, trimmed of
    leaves, cored, and quartered
1 cup heavy cream
Salt and freshly ground white
    pepper
4 lemons, halved
½ cup white vinegar
½ cup salt
4 live lobsters, each 1½ pounds
6 medium shallots, peeled and sliced
1 pound cold unsalted butter, diced
    into ½-inch cubes
1 Granny Smith apple, quartered
    and cored
1 tablespoon lemon juice
1 cup microgreens or baby arugula

A rich white Burgundy—
Meursault or Puligny-Montrachet

If you have any of the cauliflower cooking liquid left over,
freeze it to use in soups.
The lobster bodies and shells
can be simmered in a mix of
white wine and water to cover for
30 minutes. Strain the broth and
use it as lobster stock.

Place the cauliflower in a saucepan with the cream, 1 cup water, and salt and pepper. Bring to a simmer and cook until the cauliflower is tender, about 15 minutes. Drain the cauliflower, reserving the liquid. Puree in a blender or processor, adding enough liquid to make a smooth puree. Return it to the saucepan and set it aside, covered.

Bring 4 quarts water to a simmer in a large pot with the lemons, vinegar, and ½ cup of salt. Have a large bowl of ice water ready. Remove the claws, knuckles, and tails from the lobsters. Discard the bodies (see tips, following). Add the claws and knuckles to the pot and cook for 2 minutes. Remove and place in the ice water. Add the tails to the pot and cook for 5 minutes. Drain and place in the ice water. Remove the lobster meat from the shells. Reserve the meat and discard the shells. This much is advance work.

Place the shallots in a large saucepan, add 2 cups water and simmer until the shallots are translucent, about 5 minutes. Begin adding the butter bit by bit, using a whisk or a handheld blender to incorporate it. Do not allow the mixture to boil. When all the butter has been added, season to taste with salt and pepper. Hold this mixture at 130 degrees (use a candy thermometer to be sure).

Gently reheat the cauliflower puree. Cut the apple into matchsticks; place in water to cover with the tablespoon of lemon juice.

Place the lobster meat in the butter mixture and cook about 10 minutes. The flesh will remain quite soft.

To serve, place a mound of the cauliflower puree on each of 4 warm plates. Use a skimmer to remove the lobster from the butter bath and place it on the cauliflower. Top with some of the microgreens and a few well-drained apple slivers.

LOBSTER FRA DIAVOLO

THERE IS NO QUESTION that Lobster Fra Diavolo may be a century old, and has long been a favorite in Italian neighborhoods in Manhattan and Boston. Some food historians contend that this combination of lobster, spicy tomato sauce, and pasta is about as Italian as spaghetti and meatballs or veal parmesan—in other words, not. Other say it is authentically Italian, and was brought here by immigrants from Naples. Whichever is true, this dish is popular at Patsy's near Carnegie Hall, once one of Frank Sinatra's favorite hangouts, and in business for nearly 60 years.

4 pounds ripe plum tomatoes

¼ cup extra virgin olive oil

1 medium onion, peeled and minced

4 garlic cloves, peeled and minced

2 teaspoons red pepper flakes,
    or to taste

Salt and freshly ground black
    pepper

2 tablespoons tomato paste

¼ cup finely chopped fresh basil
    leaves

1 tablespoon chopped flat-leaf
    parsley leaves

2 (1½- to 2-pound) lobsters, split
    lengthwise

½ pound dried linguine

Patsy's

The restaurant bottles and sells
its fra diavolo sauce. There's a
shortcut for you.

Use a sharp paring knife to cut a small "X" in the end of each tomato. Bring a large pot of water to a boil and drop in about 12 of the tomatoes, cook about a minute, then use a slotted spoon to transfer them to a bowl of ice water. Repeat with the remaining tomatoes. Core and peel the tomatoes. Chop them by hand or pulse them briefly in a food processor.

In a large saucepan, heat 2 tablespoons of the oil. Add the onion and garlic and cook until softened. Add the tomatoes with their juices and bring to a simmer. Cover and cook about 30 minutes, stirring from time to time. Add the pepper flakes and cook 20 minutes more. Season with salt and pepper, and add the tomato paste, basil, and parsley. Simmer a few minutes longer, check the seasoning, and remove from the heat.

Place the lobsters in a steamer and steam 5 minutes to partially cook them. Cut the lobsters into serving pieces and place in a large sauté pan. Cover with the sauce, adding a little water if the sauce is too thick. Bring to a simmer and cook 15 minutes, covered, basting with the sauce from time to time. When the cooking is finished, set aside, covered.

While the lobsters are cooking, bring a large pot of salted water to a boil for the pasta. Boil the linguine until it is al dente, about 7 minutes, drain and toss with the remaining oil.

To serve, transfer the lobsters to a platter, leaving about 2 cups of the sauce in the pan. Add the linguine to the pan, toss with the sauce, and serve on the side.

Poggione Brunello di Montalcino, Pio Cesare Barolo, or Maestroberardino Fiano di Avellino

POULTRY

ROAST CHICKEN WITH VERBENA

THREE-GLASS CHICKEN

POLLO BORRACHO, DRUNKEN CHICKEN

BREAST OF CHICKEN AND FOIE GRAS POACHED IN CABBAGE

CORNISH HENS WITH LEMON AND OLIVES

GAI PAO PRIK HAENG, CHICKEN WITH CHILES AND CASHEWS

POACHED DUCK WITH FARRO

CRISP FARMHOUSE DUCK

ROAST CHICKEN WITH VERBENA

LUTÈCE

LUTÈCE HAS ENJOYED A LONG RUN among the most famous restaurants in New York, and a reservation there is still coveted. In years past, with André Soltner as the chef and owner, the lovely townhouse restaurant with its authentic zinc bar and wicker chairs was known for classic French food. And its signature dish was as simple a bistro specialty as you could find: roast chicken. Chef Soltner, his tall toque on his head, would be in the dining room to carve it at tableside. Soltner has retired and now Lutèce is the jewel in the crown of Ark Restaurants. Its cachet endures, although today it is no longer the only game in town. But with chef David Féau in the kitchen, the food is still thoroughly French, if more inventive than in the past. The roast chicken, as prepared by Féau, is enhanced by the light citric and herbal notes of lemon verbena.

SERVES 4

2 cups dried verbena

1 (4-pound) free-range organic
   chicken

Salt and freshly ground white
   pepper

½ cup clarified butter

¼ cup sliced shallots

3 fresh thyme sprigs

1 cup chicken stock

1½ cups veal stock

Place the verbena in a bowl, add 2 cups of boiling water, and set aside to steep for 30 minutes.

Preheat the oven to 425 degrees.

Rinse and dry the chicken. Season it inside and out with salt and pepper. When the verbena has finished soaking, remove it from the water, and reserve 1 cup of the water. Stuff the verbena inside the chicken. Place the chicken in a 4-quart flameproof casserole. Pour the clarified butter over it, place it in the oven, and roast about 50 minutes, or until just cooked through, basting every 10 minutes with the butter in the pan.

Set the chicken aside to rest for 10 minutes. Transfer it from the casserole to a dish. Remove and discard the verbena.

Pour off all but 3 tablespoons of the fat from the casserole. Add the shallots and thyme and sauté over medium heat until the shallots have softened. Add the reserved verbena water and chicken stock and cook, scraping the

A rich red Burgundy

pan, until reduced to about ½ cup. Add the veal stock and reduce again, until there is a scant cup of liquid in the pan. Strain the sauce and transfer it to a saucepan.

Return the chicken to the casserole and place it in the oven for about 10 minutes, to reheat. Reheat the sauce. Carve the chicken and serve with the sauce.

Baby asparagus and baby carrots, glazed with a little of the sauce, are an excellent accompaniment.

When fresh morels are available, the chicken can be stuffed with them instead of the verbena, and the morels can then be added to the sauce.

THREE-GLASS CHICKEN

THE ALMOST MINIMALIST DINING ROOM only hints at its Chinese connection. But the menu leaves no doubt. Jimmy Chin's Midtown restaurant combines regional Chinese cooking with some inventive specialties such as Grand Marnier Shrimp. Three-Glass Chicken is a homestyle dish, so named because traditionally the chicken pieces are smothered with a glass of soy sauce, a glass of rice wine, and a glass of water, and slowly baked. That does not quite describe the proportions or the quicker, stove-top method, but Chin Chin's is a lusty, well-seasoned version.

SERVES 2

4 Chinese dried black mushrooms

2 whole chicken legs and thighs

3 tablespoons peanut oil

2 tablespoons Asian sesame oil

10 garlic cloves, peeled

12 thin slices fresh ginger

1 small green chile, sliced

2 scallions, trimmed and minced

1 tablespoon minced cilantro leaves

½ cup rice wine or dry sherry

4 tablespoons soy sauce

1 tablespoon sugar

¼ teaspoon freshly ground white pepper

¼ teaspoon freshly ground black pepper

Steamed long-grain rice, for serving

An Alsatian gewürztraminer, especially Trimbach

Place the mushrooms in a bowl and cover with hot water. Set aside to soak.

Separate the chicken legs and thighs at the joint. Use a heavy cleaver to whack them into 1½-inch pieces, right through the bone. You should have 14 to 16 bite-size pieces. Pat them dry with paper towels.

Heat the peanut oil to very hot in a wok or skillet, add the chicken pieces, and cook, turning, to brown on all sides, about 10 minutes. Remove the chicken, draining it well, and discard the oil. Drain the mushrooms and pat them dry. Add the sesame oil to the wok, then the mushrooms, garlic, ginger, chile, scallions, and cilantro. Stir-fry over high heat for 2 minutes. Add the rice wine, soy sauce, and sugar, and stir. Return the chicken to the wok. Bring to a boil, season with the white and black pepper, reduce the heat to a simmer, cover, and cook for 8 minutes. Steamed rice is a must alongside.

> The Chinese do not simply cut up a chicken at the joints, but go on to chop it into small, almost bite-size pieces irrespective of the bird's skeleton. That way everyone gets the same size pieces.

POLLO BORRACHO, DRUNKEN CHICKEN

ZARELA

W OMEN HAVE LONG BEEN RESPONSIBLE for the strength of the Mexican kitchen, keeping the flame of traditional cooking alive and passing it down through generations. So it comes as no surprise that in New York, where women chefs are in a decided minority, the Mexican women also shine. Zarela Martinez, who was discovered by Craig Claiborne of the *New York Times*, is in the forefront. At her restaurant, Zarela, she produces crowd-pleasing margaritas, guacamole, chilaquiles, enchiladas, and other staples of the cuisine, along with less well-known regional specialties and some inventive dishes, such as this chicken cooked with tequila.

½ cup dry sherry

½ cup golden raisins

½ cup all-purpose flour

Salt and freshly ground white pepper

1 frying chicken (about 3½ pounds), cut in 8 pieces

½ cup corn oil

1 medium onion, peeled and thinly sliced

3 garlic cloves, peeled and sliced

½ cup whole blanched almonds

½ cup small pimento-stuffed olives

2 or more pickled serrano chiles, sliced, optional

1 tablespoon cornstarch

1½ cups chicken stock

1 cup silver or reposado tequila

⅓ to ½ cup sherry vinegar

1 tablespoon sugar

In Mexico this dish would have a more pronounced tartness from as much as a cup of white vinegar. Using sherry vinegar tones it down a bit, but feel free to increase the amount.

Warm the sherry in a small saucepan, add the raisins, and set aside to soak at least 20 minutes. Meanwhile, whisk together the flour and salt and pepper to taste in a shallow dish. Add the chicken pieces and turn to coat them evenly.

Heat the oil in a large skillet to very hot, but not smoking. Add the chicken and sauté until it is golden brown on all sides, about 10 minutes. Transfer it to a 4-quart casserole.

Preheat oven to 350 degrees.

Discard all but 2 tablespoons of fat from the skillet. Add the onion and garlic and sauté over medium heat, scraping up any browned bits from the pan, until the onion is golden, about 4 minutes. Add the almonds and cook for 2 minutes. Add the olives, the pickled serranos if using, and the raisins with remaining sherry, and cook for 2 minutes more.

In a separate dish, dissolve the cornstarch in about ¼ cup of the chicken stock. Add remaining 1¼ cups of the chicken stock and the tequila to the skillet, and bring to a simmer. Add ⅓ cup of the vinegar and the sugar, and give it a taste. Add additional vinegar as desired to make the sauce pleasingly tart with a touch of sweetness. Stir in the cornstarch mixture, bring to a boil, reduce the heat, and simmer the sauce until it thickens somewhat, about 10 minutes. Pour it over the chicken in the casserole, cover and bake about 20 minutes, until the chicken is done. Adjust the seasonings, adding more salt, pepper, or vinegar, as desired, and serve.

A full-bodied viognier

BREAST OF CHICKEN AND FOIE GRAS POACHED IN CABBAGE

INDIA HOUSE, the grand brownstone palazzo that anchors Hanover Square, was built as the Hanover Bank between 1851 and 1854. It housed the Cotton Exchange from 1870 to 1886. Its three floors are filled with period decorations that reflect New York's maritime traditions, including the majestic masthead from the 1854 clipper ship Glory of the Seas. Bayard's is in the spacious second-floor dining room overlooking the square. The restaurant, owned by Harry and Peter Poulakakos, shares the premises with Harry's at Hanover Square, a steakhouse. Both rely on the deep resources of the Poulakakos wine collection. At Bayard's, Eberhard Müller, the chef and a partner, uses a light hand to showcase modern French cooking.

SERVES 4

2 whole chicken breasts, with bone (4 breast halves)

6 to 7 cups chicken stock

1 head savoy cabbage

8 ounces fresh raw duck foie gras

Salt and freshly ground black pepper

1 cup thinly sliced halved leeks, white and light green only

1 celery stalk, sliced thin crosswise

4 ounces baby pearl onions, peeled

12 baby carrots, cut lengthwise into julienne

½ pound medium-small Yukon gold potatoes, peeled and quartered

1 tablespoon chervil sprigs

1 tablespoon flat-leaf parsley leaves

1 tablespoon chopped fresh chives

1 tablespoon tarragon sprigs

Split the chicken breasts in half, place them in a saucepan and cover with the chicken stock. Bring to a simmer and cook gently until cooked through, about 15 minutes. Remove the chicken breasts and set aside to cool. Cook the stock down until it's reduced by one-third. Strain it, transfer it to a container, and refrigerate it. Any fat that congeals on the surface may be removed.

Bring a large pot of water to a boil. Remove the outer leaves of the cabbage and discard them. Gently separate as many inner leaves as you can, at least 10 of them. Add the leaves to the boiling water, a couple at a time, and blanch to wilt them. Remove the leaves and dry them on several layers of paper towel; repeat until all the leaves have been wilted. Cut away any heavy ribs.

Use a thin-bladed knife dipped in hot water to cut the foie gras into 4 slices, each about 2 ounces. Season them with salt and pepper and refrigerate, covered.

Bone and skin the chicken breasts. Remove the narrow strip of fillet from each and reserve for another use, such

There are two ways to purchase the foie gras for this recipe. You can buy a whole lobe, which will weigh from 1¼ to 1½ pounds, giving you extra foie gras to sauté or use in other recipes (see the recipe for Sautéed Foie Gras with Apricots, page 46). You can also buy fresh raw duck foie gras by the slice, in convenient packages of two, with each slice just about enough for each portion in this recipe.

A red Burgundy with good acidity, such as Pernand-Vergelesses

as chicken salad. Slice each of the breast pieces in half horizontally, not quite cutting through at one side, to butterfly them. Place a piece of foie gras on one side of each and cover with the second side to make a sandwich. Wrap each completely in cabbage leaves, pressing the leaves on the chicken with a kitchen towel. Wrap each in plastic wrap and refrigerate.

Bring 4 cups of salted water to a boil in a saucepan. Add the leeks, celery, and onions and cook about 5 minutes. Scoop out with a slotted spoon and transfer to a bowl of ice water. Add the carrots to the boiling water, cook 7 minutes, scoop out, and add to the ice water. Add the potatoes to the pot and simmer until just tender, about 15 minutes. Drain and set aside.

In a saucepan large enough to hold the chicken breasts in a single layer, bring the reserved chicken stock to a simmer. Remove the plastic wrap from the chicken breasts. Add the chicken to the saucepan and cook at a slow simmer for about 7 minutes. Add the leeks, celery, onions, carrots, and potatoes. Simmer 2 minutes more.

Transfer the chicken breasts to 4 shallow soup plates, spoon the vegetables and broth around them, sprinkle with the herbs, and serve.

CORNISH HENS WITH LEMON AND OLIVES
ZITOUNE

THE FRAGRANT SPICES, exotic pottery, draped tents, and generous hospitality of North Africa are starting to enrich the New York restaurant scene. Some Manhattan nightspots are done in Berber style, and, especially in Astoria, carved Moorish doorways open into restaurants that serve couscous, tagines, and bisteeya. Zitoune is one of Manhattan's newer Moroccan-style restaurants, one that does not need belly dancers to attract aficionados. The menu features small plates of typical carrot, tomato, beet, and other vegetable salads to share as appetizers, followed by platters of steaming couscous and typical specialties such as lemon chicken. And for those who want to make these dishes at home, there are new shops which sell the requirements, such as preserved lemons, ras el hanout and other spice blends, and authentic terra cotta tagines.

1½ teaspoons saffron threads

2 large Cornish hens, each about
   1½ pounds, split

Juice of ½ lemon

Salt and freshly ground black pepper

2 tablespoons extra virgin olive oil

1 medium onion, peeled and
   chopped

4 garlic cloves, peeled and crushed

1 teaspoon ground cumin

½ teaspoon ground ginger

1 cup chicken stock

4 small preserved lemons, halved

8 cracked green olives

1 tablespoon chopped flat-leaf
   parsley

2 tablespoons chopped cilantro

Steamed couscous, optional, for
   serving

Preserved lemons, once only
available to those who made
them at home, are now sold in
fancy food shops.

Bring 1½ cups of water to a simmer in a small saucepan. Add 1 teaspoon of the saffron threads and set aside to steep for 30 minutes. Strain and reserve the water.

Rub the Cornish hens all over with the lemon juice and place them in a bowl. Pour in the saffron water, cover, and refrigerate overnight. Turn the hens once or twice in the liquid while they marinate.

Remove the hens from the marinade, discard the liquid, and season the hens with salt and pepper.

In a stove-top casserole or a terra cotta *tagine* large enough to hold the hens in a single layer, heat the oil. Add the onion and garlic and cook over low heat until translucent. Stir in the cumin, ginger, and the remaining ½ teaspoon saffron and cook for about a minute, then add the stock, preserved lemons, olives, parsley, and half the cilantro. Bring to a simmer and add the hens skin side down. Cook, covered, for 10 minutes. Turn the hens and cook for 20 minutes or until cooked through, basting them from time to time. Remove the hens to a deep platter. Simmer the sauce briefly and check seasonings. Pour the sauce over the hens, scatter with the remaining tablespoon of cilantro, and serve. Steamed couscous is a perfect accompaniment.

A Moroccan rosé wine called *vin gris* would be an excellent choice, but of such limited availability that a rosé from Provence or a pinot gris would be a more practical selection.

GAI PAO PRIK HAENG, CHICKEN WITH CHILES AND CASHEWS

KIN KHAO

FOR MORE THAN TEN YEARS, Kin Khao has been a popular spot in SoHo, not just for Thai food, but also as a draw for the social and celebrated. The setting is informal, with just enough artful Asian touches; the food prepared by Thai cooks maintains an authentic identity, perhaps toned down a bit to appeal to American tastes, but otherwise hardly compromised. The prices are reasonable. The owner, Brad Kelley, has traveled all over Asia, and after the success of Kin Khao was inspired to open an Asian market-café, Kelley & Ping, nearby. He also owns Daily Chow, an Asian café in the East Village. Kin Khao means "eat rice."

SERVES 4

1 tablespoon soy sauce

1 tablespoon *nam pla* (Thai fish sauce)

1 tablespoon Chinese oyster sauce

½ teaspoon sugar

2 tablespoons peanut oil

1 medium onion, peeled and sliced thin

4 garlic cloves, peeled and sliced

4 long dried red Thai chiles, chopped, or to taste, or 2 to 4 teaspoons red pepper flakes

3 boneless, skinless chicken breasts, cut into 1-inch pieces

2 celery stalks, slant-cut ½-inch thick

1 cup well-drained canned straw mushrooms

½ cup chicken stock

1 teaspoon cornstarch

¼ cup roasted cashew nuts

½ cup chopped scallions

Mix the soy sauce, fish sauce, oyster sauce, and sugar in a small bowl and set aside.

In a wok or skillet, heat the oil. Add the onion and garlic and stir-fry over high heat until softened. Stir in the chiles and after a minute or so, add the chicken. Stir-fry until the outside has whitened but it's not cooked through. Add the celery and mushrooms, stir-fry another minute, then add the chicken stock and reserved sauce mixture. Stir-fry a few minutes until the chicken is cooked through.

Dissolve the cornstarch in 1 tablespoon of water and mix it in. Add the cashews and scallions. Bring to a simmer and cook until the sauce has thickened slightly. Serve.

A ginger kamikaze, made with ginger vodka (vodka infused overnight with slices of fresh ginger), a splash of lime, one of orange juice, and one of triple sec

Straw mushrooms, which are not available fresh here, are what Thai cooks use. But small fresh mushrooms like chanterelles, hedgehogs, and even morels can be substituted.

POACHED DUCK WITH FARRO

A SMALL AND UNASSUMING RESTAURANT a few steps below street level does not sound like a recipe for success, especially in Greenwich Village, where a certain bohemian flamboyance is often the norm. But Blue Hill, a half-block from Washington Square, has made its mark precisely because it offers elegant food in a subdued, informal setting. Dan Barber, who started as a caterer, has developed a loyal clientele. Like many young and passionate chefs, he relies on first-rate, often artisanal, ingredients that he treats with respect. For this gently-cooked duck breast he discards the fat and skin. But do not be fooled. He substitutes butter to insulate the tender meat. And then he discards the butter, too.

SERVES 6 TO 8

Salt

2 cups farro (Italian spelt grain, similar to bulgur wheat)

2 cups tiny pearl onions

½ pound plus 1 tablespoon unsalted butter

½ cup chicken stock

1 teaspoon sugar

Freshly ground black pepper

4 *magret* (moulard duck breasts)

1 cup dry white wine

1 thyme sprig

1 shallot, peeled and thinly sliced

1¼ cups heavy cream

2 cups veal stock

2 cups dry red wine

1 tablespoon Dijon mustard

Fleur de sel, for garnish

Bring 2 quarts of salted water to a boil. Add the farro and cook until just tender, about 25 minutes. Drain thoroughly and place in a large skillet.

While the farro is cooking, place the onions in a bowl, cover with hot water, and set aside for 10 minutes. Peel the onions, trim, and place in a sauté pan with 1 tablespoon butter, the chicken stock, sugar, and salt and pepper to taste. Place a piece of parchment paper directly on the onions, and simmer until the onions are tender and the liquid is syrupy, about 10 minutes. Add the onions to the farro and set aside covered, ready to reheat just before serving.

Use a small knife to separate the skin and fat from the duck breasts. The skin and fat should come off quite easily; you will not be using them for this recipe but for more on them, see the tip, following. Season the duck breasts with salt and pepper.

Combine the white wine, thyme, and shallot in a 3-quart saucepan large enough to hold 2 of the duck breasts in one layer. Cook the wine mixture over medium-high heat

You can place the slabs of skin and fat in a single layer in a baking dish. Place in a 200-degree oven for about an hour, until the fat has been rendered out and the skin has started to brown. Now you can toss out the skin. Strain the fat into a jar and reserve it in the refrigerator. You'll have about 2 cups of fresh duck fat to use for sautéing. Use it for the Goose Fat Potatoes, page 194, or for the Garbure, page 54.

A medium- to full-bodied pinot noir from Oregon or coastal or central California, or a Burgundy

until it barely films the bottom of the pan. Add the cream and reduce the mixture to ⅔ cup. Strain and return the cream to the saucepan; place over very low heat. Add the remaining ½ pound of butter, ½ tablespoon at a time, whisking it in after each addition. Do not allow the sauce to boil. When all the butter has been incorporated, place 2 of the duck breasts in the saucepan. The sauce should just about cover them. Cook at a bare simmer, swirling the pan to keep the sauce moving, for 4 minutes. Turn the duck breasts in the sauce and cook for 4 more minutes. Remove the duck breasts, scraping as much sauce as possible from them back into the saucepan. Place the cooked duck breasts on a platter and cover with foil. Repeat with the remaining 2 duck breasts. When they have cooked for their 8 minutes, transfer them to the platter and cover with foil. Set aside at least 20 minutes. Discard the butter sauce.

While the duck is resting, in a small saucepan boil down the veal stock until it is reduced to ¾ cup. Boil down the red wine in a separate saucepan until you have just ¾ cup. Combine the veal stock and red wine reductions, whisk in the mustard, and season to taste with salt and pepper.

Reheat the farro mixture and place portions on your dinner plates. Slice the duck breasts on an angle and arrange slices on top of the farro. Garnish with a little *fleur de sel*. Reheat the red wine sauce and spoon it around the plates. Serve immediately.

CRISP FARMHOUSE DUCK

THE FOUR SEASONS

T HE INCOMPARABLE FOUR SEASONS, designed by Philip Johnson for the Mies van der Rohe Seagrams Building, is a landmark that attracts powerful bold-face names to lunch in the Grill Room, and those who wish to dine well on innovative American cuisine to the Pool Room. The seasonal theme that set the restaurant apart when it first opened in 1959 continues. Staff uniforms and flowers change. The food is seasonal, too, relying on timely ingredients, a concept that was devised by the late Joseph Baum, the driving force behind a number of the city's most stunning restaurants. Today it's the way all fine restaurants operate. But one dish ignores the seasons. The gorgeously lacquered roast duck, brought to the dining room and carved tableside, is as much a signature of The Four Seasons as the perennial chocolate velvet cake.

SERVES 2 TO 4

1 (5- to 6-pound) fresh duck
1 (1-inch) piece fresh ginger, peeled and sliced thin
Grated zest of ½ orange
2 garlic cloves, peeled and crushed
2 tablespoons honey
½ cup soy sauce
1½ teaspoons black peppercorns, crushed
1½ tablespoons bitter orange marmalade
⅓ cup fresh orange juice
1 tablespoon Grand Marnier
1 tablespoon red wine vinegar
1 tablespoon tomato paste
⅓ cup dry red wine
½ cup duck or chicken stock
Salt and freshly ground black pepper
Segments from 1 orange

Rinse the duck, pull out all the excess fat, remove the giblets, and cut off the wingtips and the excess skin at the neck. Save the wingtips and giblets for stock, if you wish. Using a sharp paring knife, make lots of ¼-inch incisions along the back of the duck. They'll allow the fat to drain out during cooking.

Place the duck on a wire rack set on a rimmed baking sheet and refrigerate it uncovered for 48 hours. The idea is to dry out the duck so the skin will crisp up better.

Combine the ginger, orange zest, garlic, honey, soy sauce, and peppercorns in a bowl. Cover and leave it at room temperature overnight. Strain this marinade and discard the solids.

Remove the duck from the refrigerator and brush it all over with half the marinade. Leave it for 20 minutes, then brush it with all but 2 tablespoons of the marinade. Refrigerate the unused marinade.

Refrigerate the duck again, for 24 hours more.

The other option, of course, is not to bother with the sauce, and just serve the duck au naturel.

Accomplishing this extra-crisp duck is a four-day project, so plan accordingly. At the Four Seasons the duck is actually dried in the Chinese manner, by hanging it to allow the air to circulate. But putting it on a rack in the refrigerator, uncovered, is an acceptable compromise.

Raphael First Label Merlot 1999 or another American merlot

Remove the duck from the refrigerator 5 hours before serving time. Make sure one oven rack is completely clean, because the duck is going to sit directly on it.

About 2½ hours before serving, preheat the oven to 375 degrees. Place a roasting pan with ¼ inch of water in it on the lowest rack in the oven. Position the clean rack in the middle of the oven. Place the duck, breast side up, on the middle rack, directly over the pan of water. The roasting time is 1½ to 2 hours, depending on the size of the duck, at the end of which your duck should be a gorgeous, shiny mahogany color, and slightly puffed. When it's done, transfer it to a cutting board and allow it to rest for 20 minutes.

To make the sauce, mix the marmalade, orange juice, Grand Marnier, vinegar, tomato paste, wine, and stock in a saucepan Add the reserved marinade and simmer it for about 10 minutes. Strain it, add salt and pepper to taste and the orange segments, and keep it warm until you carve the duck. Spoon the sauce over the duck portions.

MEAT

LAMB TAGINE WITH ISRAELI COUSCOUS

LAMB SHANKS WITH CHILES IN PARCHMENT

RACK OF LAMB WITH WHITE BEANS

SAUTÉED VEAL MEDALLIONS WITH THYME

WIENER SCHNITZEL

VEAL PICCATA

DELMONICO STEAK

BEEF BRAISED IN BAROLO

SHORT RIBS BRAISED IN RED WINE

ROAST BEEF HASH

ROCK CANDY—GINGER SHORT RIBS

ROASTED PORK BUTT AND CLASSIC CUBAN SANDWICH

CALF'S LIVER ALLA VENEZIANA

RABBIT ALLA CACCIATORE

MEDALLIONS OF VENISON WITH SAUCE POIVRADE

LAMB TAGINE WITH ISRAELI COUSCOUS
MARSEILLE

MARSEILLE, THE CITY, IS THE MELTING POT OF FRANCE, and also a gateway to North Africa. Thus it should come as no surprise that the chef at Marseille, Alex Urena, offers a *tagine* here to represent the restaurant. A *tagine* is both a type of braised dish and also the vessel in which it is cooked: a rimmed, shallow, glazed terra cotta platter with a distinctive conical lid. Typically, the inside of the lid is left unglazed so that the steam that rises as the food is cooked can actually be absorbed into the clay and not condense back on the food. The result is a more concentrated sauce. At Marseille, Urena serves a cuisine that represents many areas of the Mediterranean, all in a vaguely Art Deco brasserie setting. The owner, Simon Oren, has a love affair with France, as represented by some of his other restaurants, including Nice Matin and Pigalle.

2 pounds boneless leg of lamb, in 2-inch cubes

Salt and freshly ground black pepper

1 tablespoon ground cardamom

1 tablespoon ground cumin

6 tablespoons extra virgin olive oil

1 medium parsnip, peeled and diced

2 carrots, peeled and diced

2 medium onions, peeled and finely diced

¼ cup tomato paste

1 cup dry red wine

¼ cup Madeira

1 cup veal stock

1 tablespoon lemon juice

1 bay leaf

1 rosemary sprig

5 fresh thyme sprigs

1 cup Israeli couscous (very large grain couscous)

2 cups hot chicken stock

1 tablespoon minced mint leaves

Like most stewed or braised dishes, this *tagine* benefits from resting, then reheating.

Although the couscous can simply be reheated in its saucepan, if it is made well in advance, it can be spread out on a shallow baking pan, coated lightly with olive oil, and set aside. It should then be reheated with some additional stock.

Season the meat with salt, pepper, and ½ tablespoon each of the cardamom and cumin. Use your hands to massage the seasonings into the meat.

In a large, heavy sauté pan heat 2 tablespoons of the oil. Add the lamb and, without crowding it, sear it over high heat until browned on all sides. You may have to sear it in batches. Remove the meat from the pan and add the parsnip, carrots, and half of the onions. Sauté them over low heat— the term the chefs use for this is to "sweat" them—until they're tender but not browned. Add the remaining ½ tablespoon each of the cardamom and cumin, stir, and then stir in the tomato paste. Add the red wine and Madeira and increase the heat so the wine can reduce by half.

If you own a bona fide terra cotta *tagine,* transfer the cooked vegetables and wine to it, add the seared meat and any juices, and the veal stock, lemon juice, bay leaf, rosemary, and 4 sprigs of the thyme. You'll need a *tagine* at least 12 inches in diameter to fit all the ingredients. Cover your *tagine* and either place it on very low heat on the top of your stove, where you will let the contents barely simmer for 2 hours, or put it in a 300-degree oven. Without a *tagine,* use a nice casserole in a 300-degree oven.

After 2 hours, remove the *tagine* from the heat and set the dish aside for at least an hour. Reheat it a few minutes when you're ready to serve.

For the couscous heat the remaining 4 tablespoons of the oil in a heavy saucepan. Add the remaining onions and sauté them until they're tender. Stir in the couscous, then add the chicken stock, salt and pepper to taste, and the last sprig of thyme. Cover and cook until the couscous is tender and all the stock is absorbed, about 20 minutes. Fold in the mint. Serve with the *tagine.*

Las Gravas 2000, Jumilla, Spain. A red Rioja would also complement the dish.

LAMB SHANKS WITH CHILES IN PARCHMENT

ROSA MEXICANO

JOSEFINA HOWARD, THE NOW-LEGENDARY FORCE behind Rosa Mexicano, was among the first in New York to create a Mexican destination for fine dining. Her restaurant near Sutton Place always honored authentic Mexican ingredients, and is filled with Mexcian crafts. She is also the originator of the much-copied concept of making guacamole fresh at tableside. Recently she opened a branch of Rosa Mexicano near Lincoln Center. The food at both restaurants is much the same. Now the day-to-day operation of the restaurants is out of her hands, but she has found a worthy successor in Roberto Santabañez.

SERVES 4

8 dried *pasilla* chiles, cut open, seeds and veins removed

8 dried *guajillo* chiles, cut open, seeds and veins removed

4 lamb shanks, about 14 ounces each

¼ cup white vinegar

¼ cup dark Mexican beer

1 tablespoon silver tequila

¼ teaspoon cumin seeds

5 whole cloves

½ teaspoon dried oregano, preferably Mexican

4 garlic cloves

Salt

8 fresh or dried avocado leaves, optional

Lime wedges and warm yellow corn tortillas for serving

Toast the *pasilla* and *guajillo* chiles in a toaster oven or in a dry skillet about 3 minutes until the insides turn light brown. Place in a bowl, cover with warm water, and soak 15 minutes.

Scrape away enough meat from the bottom of the lamb shanks to expose about 1½ inches of bone.

Preheat oven to 300 degrees.

Drain the chiles and place in a blender with the vinegar, beer, tequila, cumin, cloves, oregano, and garlic. Add enough water to make a thick, textured puree. Season to taste with salt.

Place each lamb shank on a large piece of parchment paper. Spoon some of the sauce onto each lamb shank and rub into the meat, taking care not to spread it on the bone. Top each lamb shank with 2 avocado leaves, if using.

Wrap the shanks in the parchment and tie around the bone with butcher's string. Place shanks on a foil-lined baking pan, place in the oven, and bake about 2½ hours, until tender when pierced with the point of a knife (open the parchment to test).

Place each lamb shank, still wrapped, on a plate. Serve and open the parchment at the dinner table. Pass the lime and tortillas at the table.

1999 Monte Xanic Cabernet Sauvignon-Merlot from Mexico. A cabernet sauvignon from Chile would be another good option.

RACK OF LAMB WITH WHITE BEANS

LE PÉRIGORD

IN SOME RESPECTS, Le Périgord is a neighborhood restaurant. It serves the residents of Sutton Place high-rises as well as diplomats from the United Nations nearby. Georges Briguet, the owner, has continental grace, pampering his elite clientele and seeing to it that their appetites are tempted by French food that is never out of bounds. The room is comfortable and has a pretty glow about it. Fresh flowers, fine tableware, and waiters with great poise round out the picture. A very basic rack of lamb comes on a bed of white beans brought into focus with the peppery sharpness of celery root and the addition of seasonal fresh peas.

6 ounces dried French coco beans (large white beans) or cannellini beans

1 small celery root, about ¾ pound, peeled and quartered

2 carrots, peeled and quartered

1 bouquet garni (see tips)

Salt and freshly ground black pepper

2 racks of lamb, Frenched (see tips)

1 pound fresh peas, shelled

2 tablespoons unsalted butter

Coco beans are dried large white beans, but cannellini beans are a good substitute.

A bouquet garni is a couple of bay leaves, a sprig of thyme, and a few sprigs of flat-leaf parsley tied together or wrapped in a piece of cheesecloth so they can be removed easily.

A Frenched rack of lamb is one that has the meat scraped off the ends of the bones to make for a neater presentation. Little ruffled paper caps are sometimes put on the bones for serving.

Place the beans in a bowl, cover with water to a depth of 2 inches, and soak overnight. Drain the beans, transfer them to a large saucepan, and add the celery root, carrots, and bouquet garni. Add water to cover all the ingredients to a depth of 2 inches. Bring to a boil and simmer until the beans are tender, about 40 minutes. Drain them.

Remove and discard the carrot pieces and the bouquet garni. Cut the celery root in ½-inch dice, fold them into the beans, and place in a clean saucepan. Season to taste with salt and pepper.

Preheat the oven to 425 degrees. Season the lamb with salt and pepper and place in a roasting pan, fat side up. Roast 20 to 25 minutes, until an instant-read thermometer registers 125 degrees when inserted into the meat. Remove the lamb from the oven and set aside 10 minutes.

Bring a small pot of salted water to a boil, add the peas, cook 3 minutes, drain, and place briefly in a bowl of ice water to set the color. Drain the cooled peas well and fold into the bean mixture. Add the butter and reheat the beans, celery root, and peas.

To serve, carve the racks into chops. Spoon a large mound of the beans onto each of 4 warmed plates, arrange the lamb on the beans, and serve immediately.

Chateau Figeac 1995 or another St. Émilion

SAUTÉED VEAL MEDALLIONS WITH THYME
AUREOLE

CHARLES PALMER, THE CHEF AND OWNER OF AUREOLE, describes himself as "a big American guy," and knows that his food reflects his personality. It's robust, abundant. But at the same time, it has the kind of elegance that befits its setting in a lovely Upper East Side brownstone. The restaurant is a special-occasion magnet for New Yorkers and visitors whose main objective is fine food in a gracious setting. Palmer's interpretation of American food comes richly accented with French, Italian, Middle Eastern, and Asian influences. His generosity of spirit goes beyond the walls of the restaurant. He encourages chefs who work with him, and spends time as a mentor to high school students in the city. He is also busy opening moderately-priced neighborhood spots on the Upper West Side, in the Flatiron District, and elsewhere.

SERVES 6

3 tablespoons extra virgin olive oil

4 shallots, peeled and diced

3 tablespoons minced garlic

4 fresh thyme sprigs

2 cups dry white wine

6 cups veal stock (see tip)

Coarse salt and freshly ground
    black pepper

12 baby carrots, peeled, 1 inch of
    green top left on

2 teaspoons unsalted butter

12 (3-ounce) veal medallions,
    ½-inch thick

2 tablespoons minced flat-leaf
    parsley leaves

Heat 1 tablespoon of the oil in a large saucepan over medium heat. Add the shallots, garlic, and thyme and sauté about 4 minutes, until the shallots have softened. Add the wine and simmer 30 minutes or longer, until the liquid just films the bottom of the pan. Add the stock and simmer, stirring from time to time, about 45 minutes, until reduced to 2 cups. Strain through a fine-mesh sieve into a small saucepan. Season to taste with salt and pepper. Set aside.

Bring a small pot of salted water to a boil. Add the carrots and blanch 3 minutes, until crisp-tender. Drain, refresh under cold water, and pat dry. Melt the butter in a small sauté pan, add the carrots, and sauté a few minutes until heated through. Season to taste with salt and pepper and set aside.

Heat the remaining 2 tablespoons of olive oil in a large sauté pan over medium-high heat. When hot, add half the medallions. Sauté 2 minutes on each side, until lightly browned but still pink in the middle. Remove the meat from the pan, and repeat with the remaining veal.

Preparing the sauce is time-consuming but it can be done well in advance, even frozen, making the final cooking quick and convenient.

Though restaurants have veal stock on hand, home cooks may not. Fortunately there are excellent ones sold in fine food shops. Look for one that has no starches, gums, or other additives.

Place 2 medallions on each of 6 warm dinner plates. Reheat carrots, adding parsley. Place 2 carrots on each plate. Reheat the wine sauce and spoon over the veal. Serve immediately.

Veal is a red wine meat. This dish is especially suited to a pinot noir from Oregon.

WIENER SCHNITZEL

I N A CITY SHORT ON AUSTRIAN AND GERMAN RESTAURANTS, Kurt Gutenbrunner's Wallsé on the edge of Greenwich Village stands out. Its two rooms are almost stark, done in a black and white Josef Hoffmann esthetic. And the cooking decidedly puts to rest any notion that Germanic food is heavy. While remaining loyal to the cuisine of his native Austria, Gutenbrunner takes liberties that give everything an uncommon freshness. Of course, when it comes to dessert, there's richness to spare. The food of Wallsé is also served for breakfast, lunch, mid-afternoon tea, and dinner uptown, at Café Sabarsky in the Neue Galerie on Fifth Avenue.

SERVES 4

1 pound veal top round cut into 4-ounce scaloppine but not pounded

Salt and freshly ground white pepper

1 cup flour

2 eggs

2 tablespoons heavy cream

2 cups unseasoned bread crumbs, preferably from a bakery

2 cups vegetable oil

½ cup packed flat-leaf parsley leaves, rinsed, well-dried, and coarsely chopped

3 tablespoons unsalted butter

4 lemon wedges

Cucumber or Bibb lettuce salad with vinaigrette dressing, for serving

An Austrian white wine from the Wachau Valley, especially grüner veltliner or riesling

Place one of the scaloppine in a heavy 1-quart plastic bag and pound it thin with a meat pounder. Repeat with the remaining scaloppine. Place your thin scaloppine on a large platter and season them lightly with salt and pepper.

Place the flour in a shallow bowl large enough to hold one of the scaloppine flat. Place the eggs and cream in a similar bowl, and beat them lightly to blend. Place the bread crumbs in a third similar bowl. Line up the bowls near your stove. Preheat oven to 175 degrees. Line a baking sheet with parchment. Place a platter covered with several thicknesses of paper towel near the stove. Place a small plate, also covered with paper towel, near the stove.

Heat the oil in an 11- to 12-inch skillet or sauté pan, the deeper the better. If you have a chicken fryer, use it. When the oil is quite hot, place the parsley leaves in a metal mesh strainer, place in the oil, and fry 10 seconds. Remove the parsley, draining it well, and put it on the small plate. Add the butter to the skillet and reduce the heat to medium.

Place a slice of the veal in the flour, coat it well on both sides, and shake off the excess. Place it in the egg, turning to coat both sides, then place it in the bread crumbs, coating it well. Shake off any excess. Place it in the skillet and fry it about one minute, gently moving the pan in a circular motion so the oil is frothy. When the breading looks bubbly and starts to brown, turn the veal with a fork or tongs. Cook about another minute, then transfer to the paper-lined platter to drain. Repeat with the remaining veal, adjusting your heat so the crumb coating cooks gradually and evenly.

Transfer each of the finished, drained schnitzels to the baking sheet and hold them in the oven until serving time, no more than 15 minutes. Arrange the veal on a platter or on individual plates and garnish with lemon wedges and the fried parsley. Serve with salad.

VEAL PICCATA

ARESTAURANT WITH ITS SOUL STILL BONDED TO ITALY, Angelina's combines warmth of family with the modern sophistication that fine dining requires today. It has a lovely garden look, and, when the weather permits, outdoor tables under Italian market umbrellas. The kitchen's focus is on upscale Italian food, the kind of menu that everyone has understood as Northern Italian for many years. To its credit, the simple classic Veal Piccata is called just that, and not given the popular but meaningless name of "Veal Francese." The wine cellar offers a well-rounded list of bottles from many regions of Italy as well as selections from France and California.

SERVES 4

1¼ pounds veal for scaloppine, pounded thin, in 8 pieces

Salt and freshly ground black pepper

½ cup flour

3 tablespoons extra virgin olive oil

3 tablespoons soft unsalted butter

1 cup dry white wine

½ cup chicken broth

Juice of ½ lemon

1 tablespoon coarsely chopped flat-leaf parsley leaves

Drying the veal scaloppine will permit it to brown better and faster.

Dry the veal well, season it with salt and pepper, and dip in flour, shaking off excess.

Heat the oil in a large sauté pan. Sauté the veal about 1 minute on each side, until lightly browned. Transfer to a warm platter. You may have to cook the veal in batches. Add 1 tablespoon of the butter and the wine to the pan. Cook down until the wine films the pan. Lower the heat and add chicken broth, salt and pepper to taste, and the lemon juice. Cook briefly over high heat, then lower the heat and add remaining butter, bit by bit, whisking to combine and emulsify. Return the veal to the pan, and briefly baste with sauce. Transfer the veal to a platter, spoon the sauce over it, sprinkle with parsley, and serve.

California chardonnay from Napa Valley, such as Beaulieu Vineyards Reserve

DELMONICO STEAK

THE NAME THAT HENRY MEER SELECTED for his restaurant, City Hall, could not be more appropriate. It's a few blocks from the actual City Hall and from the nearby complex of courthouses and municipal buildings. And it has become a clubhouse of sorts for city officials, lawyers, and judges. The restaurant, a comfortable banquette-filled room in an old cast-iron building, plays on the theme of old New York with historic photographs and a menu that reflects some of the city's venerable dining traditions. The Delmonico Steak, a rib-eye named after a famous nineteenth-century restaurant, is a good example. Meer's version is topped with blue cheese butter. In keeping with his approach to cooking—very contemporary with an emphasis on market-fresh American ingredients—he uses Maytag blue cheese. He is so committed to seasonal freshness in this restaurant that in summer he runs a small farmer's market outside City Hall, where he sells produce from his cousin's farm in Bridgehampton, New York.

SERVES 2

4 ounces (about 1 cup) crumbled domestic blue cheese, preferably Maytag blue

4 tablespoons softened unsalted butter

A few dashes Tabasco

2 rib-eye steaks, preferably dry-aged prime, each about 14 ounces, with bone

Sea salt and freshly ground white pepper

Allowing the steak to rest after it comes off the fire will guarantee its juiciness. It's also a necessary step to make sure that returning it to the broiler to melt the cheese will not overcook it.

The blue cheese butter that tops the steak can be made well in advance, wrapped in plastic wrap, and kept in the refrigerator or frozen. Use a fork to blend the blue cheese and butter, then season the mixture with a dash or two of Tabasco. Mold the mixture into a little log, wrap it in plastic, and refrigerate it. Double or triple this recipe, and you'll have plenty for another meal.

Season the steaks with salt and pepper. Grill, broil, or pan-sear the steaks to the desired degree of doneness. Set the steaks on a platter to rest for 7 minutes. Preheat a broiler. Slice the blue cheese butter into individual medallions of about ½-inch thickness. Place a medallion on each of the steaks and run the steaks under the broiler for about 30 seconds, to melt and lightly brown the topping. Serve immediately.

Bodegas Viñedos Maurodos Viña San Roman 1998, from Spain, or a red Rioja

BEEF BRAISED IN BAROLO

SAN DOMENICO NY

Tony May, for decades one of New York's most outspoken ambassadors of fine Italian cooking, opened the elegant leather-upholstered San Domenico NY with a team of chefs who had worked at the Michelin three-star restaurant of the same name in Imola, Italy. The New York version has since evolved and is no longer associated with the one in Italy, but it remains an essential member of the city's Italian restaurant community. Who else sponsors truffle hunts in Central Park and auctions off supersize white truffles for charity? His daughter, Marisa May, helps run the restaurant. The current chef, Odette Fada, interprets Italian food with great flair and finesse.

SERVES 4

2¼ pounds beef rump or top round in one piece, well-trimmed of fat

Salt and freshly ground black pepper

2 medium onions, peeled and quartered

2 carrots, peeled and quartered

3 celery stalks, quartered

2 thyme sprigs

6 rosemary sprigs

2 bay leaves

2 garlic cloves, crushed

½ teaspoon coriander seeds

1 bottle Barolo wine, plus additional if needed

2 tablespoons extra virgin olive oil

½ cup all-purpose flour

2 ounces pancetta, diced

Soft polenta or mashed potatoes, for serving

Place the meat in a large bowl, season with salt and pepper, and add the onions, carrots, celery, thyme, 2 sprigs of the rosemary, the bay leaves, garlic, and coriander. Add the wine, cover, and allow to marinate at room temperature for 2 hours, then refrigerate for at least 8 hours. Remove from the refrigerator 2 hours before cooking time.

Preheat the oven to 325 degrees. Remove the meat from the marinade, reserving the marinade. Dust meat with flour. Heat the oil in a 4- to 5-quart flameproof casserole over medium heat. Brown the meat on all sides. Take your time, turning the meat as each side browns. Remove the meat from pan, add the pancetta, and cook over medium-low heat until it starts to brown. Return the meat to the casserole along with any juices it has given off while resting, and the reserved marinade with all the vegetables and seasonings. Bring to a simmer, cover, and cook in the oven until fork-tender, about 3½ hours. It will shrink alarmingly, but it's so rich that you will still have enough.

Remove meat from the casserole and cover to keep warm. Remove and discard thyme and bay leaves from the casserole. Puree the cooking liquid and vegetables in a food processor or blender and return the sauce to the casserole.

This traditional Tuscan recipe needs the fresh rosemary—in the marinade, the casserole, and also on the plate—to come alive.

The meat can be larded with herbs and pancetta before marinating.

Season to taste and reheat to sauce. If your sauce is too thick, add a little water or some more red wine. It should be the consistency of heavy cream. Reduce it if it's too thin. Slice the meat across the grain and arrange on a warm platter. Spoon sauce over meat and serve with polenta or mashed potatoes, with any extra sauce on the side. Garnish each portion with a remaining sprig of rosemary.

Barolo, of course. Consider using the same wine for the marinade and at the table.

SHORT RIBS BRAISED IN RED WINE

DANIEL

DANIEL BOULUD'S RESTAURANT EMPIRE in New York covers all bases. Café Boulud is a comfortable Upper East Side restaurant that draws from well beyond the neighborhood for food inspired by France and beyond. DB Bistro Moderne in Midtown has a chic informality and food, including an elaborate burger with fries, that combines down-market inspiration with up-market execution. But the jewel in the crown is Daniel, a room with a slightly Orientalist sensibility, where a team of chefs turns food into art. Nonetheless, the chef-owner has not forgotten his background in a simple family restaurant kitchen in Lyon. And he does not hesitate to include lusty braised meats like short ribs on his exacting, exquisite menus.

3 bottles dry red wine

2 tablespoons canola or grapeseed oil

8 short ribs, about 8 pounds,
   cut in 24 pieces and trimmed
   of excess fat

Salt

1 teaspoon black peppercorns,
   crushed

All-purpose flour, for dredging

10 garlic cloves, peeled

8 large shallots, peeled, trimmed,
   split, rinsed, and dried

2 medium carrots, peeled and cut in
   1-inch pieces

2 celery stalks, peeled and cut in
   1-inch pieces

1 medium leek, white and light
   green parts, trimmed, rinsed,
   and coarsely chopped

6 flat-leaf parsley sprigs

2 thyme sprigs

2 bay leaves

2 tablespoons tomato paste

3 quarts unsalted beef stock

Freshly ground white pepper

Like many stewed meat dishes, this one benefits from being made a day in advance and reheated. The best plan is to cook the ribs, then refrigerate the whole affair overnight right in the pot so the fat on the surface will congeal and you can simply lift it off.

Pour the wine into a large saucepan set over medium heat. When the wine is hot, carefully set it aflame; stand back when you do this. When the flames die down, increase the heat and boil the wine until it is reduced by half to 4½ cups. Remove it from the heat.

Position a rack in the middle of the oven, and preheat the oven to 350 degrees.

Place a large, heavy casserole or Dutch oven on the stove, add the oil, and turn the heat to medium-high. Season the ribs all over with salt and crushed pepper. Lightly dust half the ribs with flour, then slip them into the pan and sear them on all sides, until well-browned. Transfer them to a plate and repeat this process with the rest of the ribs.

When all the ribs are brown, pour off all but a tablespoon of the fat in the pan and toss in the garlic, shallots, carrots, celery, leek, parsley, thyme, and bay leaves. Cook them over medium heat about 5 minutes, until they begin to color, then stir in the tomato paste. Cook another minute. Pour in the cooked wine and the stock, return the ribs to the pot, and bring everything to a boil. Cover the pot and place it in the oven to braise for about 2½ hours, until the ribs are fork-tender. While the meat is braising, lift the lid every 30 minutes or so to skim off excess fat.

Carefully transfer the meat to a warm serving platter that has a rim to catch the sauce. Tent the platter with foil to keep the meat warm.

On top of the stove, boil down the sauce until it has thickened and is reduced to about 4 cups. Pass it through a strainer (discard the solids), season it with salt and white pepper, spoon it over the meat, and serve.

A young, brawny Bordeaux from the Médoc, especially a Pauillac or a St. Julien

ROAST BEEF HASH

SMITH & WOLLENSKY

THERE IS NO SMITH AND NO WOLLENSKY. But Alan Stillman, the restaurateur who created TGI Friday's, is never short on cleverness. Another of his restaurants, Maloney & Porcelli, is named for his lawyers. He also owns the Manhattan Ocean Club, filled with Picasso ceramics; Park Avenue Café and the Post House, which showcase American folk art; One CPS, a brasserie in the Plaza Hotel; and Cité and Cité Grill, also done in brasserie style. Smith & Wollensky is the steakhouse that drives the company, with branches in 9 cities. It is also a place for a great red wine to go with that steak.

SERVES 4

2 baking potatoes, each about 8 ounces, peeled and cut in ½-inch dice

Salt

2 tablespoons unsalted butter

2 tablespoons vegetable oil

1 cup diced onion

½ cup diced green pepper

4 cups finely diced cooked roast beef, preferably the deckle meat, not the eye

Freshly ground black pepper

2 tablespoons bottled steak sauce

4 poached eggs, optional

Place the potatoes in a pot of well-salted water to cover, bring to a boil, and cook 5 minutes. Drain well.

Heat the butter and oil in a large skillet. Add the onion and green pepper and sauté over medium heat. When they have softened, fold in the potatoes and cook the mixture, stirring occasionally, until the vegetables are lightly browned, at least 20 minutes. Fold in the roast beef, season with salt and pepper, and add the steak sauce. Continue to sauté about 15 minutes, until the mixture starts to crisp. Serve with a poached egg on each portion, if desired.

Ravenswood Sonoma Valley Lodi Zinfandel 1999

If you do not have leftover roast beef, you can prepare the hash by first roasting to medium a pound of meat from the rib section, preferably the top, or deckle, meat, the strip of meat that surrounds the eye of the rib.

ROCK CANDY—GINGER SHORT RIBS

SHUN LEE PALACE

THERE IS AN ENORMOUS DIVIDE IN NEW YORK between Chinatown Chinese restaurants and uptown Chinese palaces. Connoisseurs insist the food is best in Chinatown, assuming that unless the napkins are paper and the lighting is fluorescent, the food cannot be good. Michael Tong's restaurants—Shun Lee West and its café near Lincoln Center, and Shun Lee Palace on the East Side—expose this fallacy. Although his menus are filled with crowd-pleasers, it pays to explore the menu for less obvious, often seasonal, treasures, like a stir-fry of dried eels with Chinese chives, gray sole with ginger on a bed of crackling, deep-fried edible bones, and Rock Candy—Ginger Short Ribs. Dishes like these are served with elegance in plush surroundings.

SERVES 6

3 pounds beef short ribs, cut in 10 to 12 pieces, with bone

Salt and freshly ground black pepper

⅓ cup all-purpose flour

2 tablespoons peanut oil

⅓ cup dark soy sauce

⅓ cup light or thin soy sauce

2 cups *Shao Hsing* Chinese wine or dry sherry

1¼ cups sugar crystals or granulated sugar

1 piece star anise

1 cinnamon stick, broken in half

1 teaspoon black peppercorns

4 slices fresh ginger, each about ⅛ inch thick

2 whole scallions, trimmed

Dry the meat, season it with salt and ground pepper, and dredge it in the flour. Dust off any excess. Heat the oil in a heavy 4-quart casserole. Add the meat and sear it on all sides. You may have to do this in more than one batch.

Add the soy sauces, wine, sugar, star anise, cinnamon, peppercorns, ginger, and scallions. Bring to a simmer and stir in 8 cups of water. Bring to a fast boil, lower the heat to medium, cover the pan, and allow everything to cook for 2½ hours. Check from time to time to make sure that there is still enough liquid in the pot.

Carefully transfer the meat from the pan to a serving platter with a rim, and try to keep the bones attached. Pour the sauce into a bowl through a strainer (discard the solids), then return it to the casserole. Cook it until it has reduced to about 1½ cups and is syrupy. Pour the sauce over the meat and serve with steamed rice and Chinese broccoli.

A cabernet sauvignon, especially Robert Mondavi

• Dark Chinese soy sauce is thicker and less salty than thin or light (but not "lite") Chinese soy sauce.

ROASTED PORK BUTT AND CLASSIC CUBAN SANDWICH

NOCHE

N OCHE IS A LATIN FANTASY just steps from Times Square. David Emil, his partners, who owned Windows on the World, and Michael Lomonaco, who was the chef there, have opened this lively, multi-story Cuban–South American–Caribbean restaurant and nightclub. From Argentine empanadas—you're served not one but an assortment—to Cuban sandwiches, daiquiris, and mojitos, it offers lusty food and music with a beat. The place has a disappearing stage, revolving banquettes, and several bars.

10 garlic cloves, peeled

2 large Spanish onions, peeled and quartered

2 large bunches cilantro, heavy stems trimmed, thoroughly rinsed

2 bay leaves

¼ cup ground cumin

2 cups white vinegar

¼ cup salt

¼ cup ground black pepper

1 (4- to 5-pound) Boston pork butt or picnic, boned but not tied

1 bunch fresh thyme, rinsed

1 bunch fresh oregano, rinsed

2 soft hero rolls, split; unsalted butter, mustard, 4 to 6 slices ham, 4 to 6 slices Swiss cheese, dill pickle slices, all optional

For 2 Cuban sandwiches, spread the hero rolls with butter, then mustard, and layer with slices of roast pork, ham, and cheese, and top with pickles. Press down on sandwiches with a spatula. Heat a cast-iron skillet or a sandwich press and cook until the cheese has melted, turning once, pressing on the sandwiches or using a weight on them as they cook.

Pork butt is actually a boneless rolled pork shoulder, also called a picnic or Boston butt.

Place the garlic, onions, cilantro, bay leaves, and cumin in a food processor and process to make a rough puree. Place in a nonreactive stock pot or large, deep bowl and add 8 quarts water, the vinegar, salt, and pepper.

Lay the pork butt flat on a work surface and pile the thyme and oregano in the center. Fold over the outer edge of the pork and roll to enclose the herbs. Tie at 2-inch intervals to make a rolled roast. Place pork in the brine marinade, cover, and refrigerate 2 days.

Preheat the oven to 275 degrees. Remove pork from pot and place on a rack in a roasting pan. Roast about 3 hours, turning occasionally, until tender when pierced with a skewer or a fork. Remove and allow to cool. Slice to serve warm or cold, with your choice of sauce, or use in Cuban sandwiches.

Pesqueria Tinto 1999 from Spain or another robust Spanish red with the roast; a mojito (page 244) with the sandwiches

CALF'S LIVER ALLA VENEZIANA

AL DI LA

AN UNPRETENTIOUS, ALMOST BARE-BONES ROOM and exceptional Italian food that focuses on the cooking of the North around Venice have made Al Di La a magnet for lovers of Italian food, notwithstanding the wait for tables. The restaurant does not accept reservations. Among the first attention-getting spots to open on the now restaurant-heavy Fifth Avenue strip in Park Slope, Brooklyn, it attracts an audience far beyond its neighborhood precinct. But success has not gone to its head. It has maintained its local popularity as a family-friendly place for groups with children in tow.

SERVES 4

4 pieces calf's liver, each 4 to 5 ounces, cut ¾ inch thick

6 tablespoons unsalted butter

4 medium onions, peeled, halved, and sliced ⅛ inch thick

4 bay leaves, preferably fresh

Salt and freshly ground black pepper

4 tablespoons extra virgin olive oil

Leaves from 1 bunch fresh sage

1 cup chicken stock

1 teaspoon aged balsamic vinegar, at least 10 years old

A muscato giallo, a sweet white wine with high acidity. A red wine from the Veneto, such as a merlot, would pair nicely with the dish, too.

Trim the liver of any veins and outer membrane. Line a platter with paper towel and place the slices on it. Cover with another sheet of paper towel.

Melt 3 tablespoons of the butter in a large skillet, preferably nonstick, that can accommodate the liver in a single layer. Add the onions and bay leaves and cook over low heat, stirring frequently, until the onions become meltingly soft and golden, at least 15 minutes. Stir up any browned bits from the pan as you go. Transfer the onions to a smaller pan and remove the bay leaves. Wipe out the skillet.

Season the liver with salt and pepper. Heat the oil in the skillet and when it's hot, add the sage leaves. Stir-fry them briefly until they begin to crisp, and remove them to a plate. Add the liver and sear it over medium heat until it's browned but still rare in the middle, about 3 minutes per side. Remove the liver from the pan and pour off any excess oil. Add the remaining 3 tablespoons of butter to the pan and return the liver to the pan. Cook over medium heat about 5 minutes, basting the liver, until it becomes nicely glazed and is cooked medium-rare to medium. Transfer the liver to a plate and cover loosely with a piece

This recipe, perhaps the ultimate liver and onions, is a classic on the Venetian table. The first step in the preparation, sautéing the onions, must be done slowly, over moderate heat. But the liver needs a quick sauté in a hot pan, so it will be seared but not overcooked.

of foil. Add the chicken stock to the pan and cook, stirring with a wooden spoon to scrape up any browned bits, until the sauce has reduced by half. Season to taste with salt and pepper and stir in the vinegar. Reheat the onions in the small pan, then divide them among 4 dinner plates. Slice the liver on the bias about 1 inch thick and arrange the slices on the onions. Spoon the sauce over the liver, scatter on the sage leaves, and serve.

RABBIT ALLA CACCIATORE

Babbo is the capital of the Batali-Bastianich restaurant empire. Occupying the premises that once housed the legendary Coach House in Greenwich Village, it offers a robust personality in a straightforward, bustling trattoria setting. Tables are always in demand for those whose appetites are ready for hearty, inventive Italian food, so Chef Mario Batali and his partner in wine, Joseph Bastianich, offer alternatives nearby: Lupa, a minimally furnished country-style spot that accepts no reservations; and Otto, a vast pizzeria where the side dishes and the desserts demand as much attention as the thin-crusted pizzas. But Babbo, which means "daddy" in Italian, a name that was attached to the place because both partners had just become parents, is where Batali's skill and invention shine. "I love the idea of garden peas and carrots in a rabbit dish," he said.

2 whole rabbits, each about 3 pounds

⅔ cup extra virgin olive oil

2 carrots, peeled and coarsely chopped

1 large onion, peeled and coarsely chopped

2 celery stalks, coarsely chopped

1 cup dry white wine

2 cups chicken stock or water, approximately

1 tablespoon fresh rosemary leaves, chopped

1 tablespoon fresh thyme leaves, chopped

Salt and freshly ground black pepper

1 cup Thumbelina or baby carrots, peeled

½ cup sugar snap peas, trimmed

1 small onion, peeled and minced

1 cup dry red wine

1 tablespoon capers, rinsed and drained

2 tablespoons anchovy paste

2 tablespoons tomato paste

1 (12-inch) baguette, sliced thin on the bias and lightly toasted

1 cup pea shoots

Remove the livers, kidneys, and hearts from the rabbits. Remove the thighs and rear legs from the rabbits and separate the legs from the thighs. Refrigerate the thighs and the innards. Remove the front legs from the rabbits. Cut the remaining rabbit carcasses in half just where the rib cages end, separating the front part of the rabbits from the loins. Carefully cut the tenderloins from the backbones, keeping the flap that extends from the tenderloins intact. This sounds complicated but with the rabbits on your cutting board, it is easy to understand the business about the flaps. Refrigerate the tenderloins. Chop the rest of the carcasses in 3 pieces.

Heat 2 tablespoons of the oil in a large casserole. Add the rabbit carcass pieces and all the rabbit legs, and cook until well-browned on all sides. You may have to do this in more than one batch. Remove the rabbit pieces, add the chopped carrots, onion, and celery, and cook until browned. Add the white wine. Return the carcass pieces and legs to the casserole and add enough water or chicken stock to barely cover the bones. Cover and cook over low heat for 2 hours. Strain through a fine sieve. Discard the vegetables and bones.

While the stock is cooking, place the 4 tenderloins on a work surface, spreading out the flaps. Season the flaps with the rosemary, thyme, salt, and pepper. Roll the flap around the tenderloin and tie with a piece of butcher's string. Refrigerate.

In a 3- to 4-quart flameproof casserole, heat 4 tablespoons of the olive oil over medium-high heat. Add the thigh pieces in a single layer and cook until brown on all sides, about 6 minutes. Add 2 cups of the strained rabbit stock, reduce the heat to low, cover the pan, and braise for 15 minutes. Remove the thighs from the casserole and reduce the sauce until it's the consistency of heavy cream. Check the seasonings. Return the thighs to the casserole and set aside.

Heat a grill or a grill pan until hot. Add the tenderloin pieces and cook, turning, until browned on the outside and cooked to about medium in the center, 6 to 8 minutes. An instant-read thermometer will register about 135 degrees. Transfer the tenderloins to the casserole.

In a small sauté pan heat 2½ tablespoons of the oil. Briefly sauté the whole carrots and sugar snap peas. Set aside.

In a small sauté pan, heat the remaining 2 tablespoons oil until very hot. Add the minced onion, sauté briefly, then add the livers, kidneys, and hearts and sauté until browned. Add the red wine, capers, anchovy paste, and tomato paste. Cook until the wine has reduced and the mixture has thickened. Transfer to a food processor and pulse to get a coarse puree. Season with salt and pepper and spread on the baguette slices to make crostini.

Briefly reheat the rabbit thighs and tenderloins in the sauce. Remove the tenderloin pieces, remove the strings, and cut each piece in half at an angle. Arrange the rabbit thighs and tenderloins on a serving platter. Stir the carrots and sugar snaps into the sauce, fold in the pea shoots, heat gently, and when they wilt, spoon the sauce onto the platter over and around the rabbit. Serve garnished with the crostini.

A light Tuscan red like Morrelino di Scansano

MEDALLIONS OF VENISON WITH SAUCE POIVRADE

LA CÔTE BASQUE

L A CÔTE BASQUE REMAINS NEW YORK'S LINK to an era when only French restaurants with French chefs in the kitchen qualified as fine dining. After the 1939 World's Fair in Flushing Meadow, a number of the chefs who cooked at the highly regarded French government pavilion remained in New York, mostly because war had broken out in Europe and they could not get home. Henri Soulé who, at 35, was in charge of the French pavilion, then opened Le Pavillon on East 55th Street. He was not much taller than Napoleon and just as imperious. Le Pavillon moved to 57th Street and Park Avenue, and the 55th Street location was turned into a social watering hole, La Côte Basque. Jean-Jacques Rachou eventually became the owner, and he subsequently moved the restaurant to West 55th Street, where it is now one of the city's last bastions of French classicism.

SERVES 4

4 tablespoons unsalted butter

½ cup minced shallots

2 teaspoons whole black peppercorns

8 juniper berries

1 thyme sprig

1 cup dry red wine

2 cups veal stock

5 rosemary sprigs

Coarse salt and freshly ground black pepper

1½ pounds boneless loin of venison, cut in 4 thick medallions

Braised red cabbage, a fruit garnish, and chestnut puree are some classic accompaniments to this venison dish.

Melt 1 tablespoon of the butter in a 2-quart saucepan. Add the shallots and cook over medium heat until they start to brown. Stir in the peppercorns, juniper berries, and thyme, cook 2 minutes longer, then add the wine. Reduce to ½ cup over high heat. Add the veal stock and 1 sprig of rosemary and simmer about 30 minutes, until you have about 1 cup of liquid remaining in the pan. Remove from the heat and strain the sauce (discard the solids). Return it to a clean saucepan and over very low heat, whisk in 2 tablespoons of the butter, bit by bit. Season the sauce to taste with salt and pepper and keep warm.

Season the venison with salt and pepper. Melt the remaining tablespoon of butter in a heavy skillet over high heat. Sear the venison about 5 minutes on each side, to medium rare. Set it aside to rest for 5 minutes, then transfer the steaks to warm dinner plates, spoon the sauce around the venison, and garnish each portion with a rosemary sprig.

A St. Joseph or other sturdy Rhône red

SIDE DISHES

FINGERLING POTATO PUREE

GERMAN FRIED POTATOES

GOOSE FAT POTATOES

FRIED RED TOMATOES

MUSHROOM KASHA

ROASTED MUSHROOMS

SAUTÉED ZUCCHINI WITH TOASTED ALMONDS AND PECORINO

SPINACH GRATIN

BHINDI DO PIAZA, SAUTÉED OKRA

GRILLED EGGPLANT WITH GINGER-LIME SAUCE

The best potato to use for this puree is the ratte, a French variety that some farmers now grow and sell in the Greenmarkets. Other fingerling potatoes or even Yukon golds are also suitable.

FINGERLING POTATO PUREE

BOULEY

ART MEETS FOOD IN THE KITCHEN OF DAVID BOULEY. His restaurant, Bouley, in TriBeCa, is now in its third incarnation, having started a block away, then relocated as Bouley Bakery in its present location, and finally been transformed back into Bouley with the antique carved door in front and shelves of apples perfuming the vestibule. Inventive French-accented American cooking, grounded in the best local ingredients, are Bouley's hallmarks. Around the corner, his interpretation of Austrian food at Danube sets another standard in an opulent room that suggests Klimt and his school of gilded artists of early twentieth-century Vienna. As for Bouley's satiny potato puree, it was inspired by none other than the great French master, Joël Robuchon, one of Bouley's mentors.

SERVES 2

1 pound fingerling potatoes, preferably *ratte* (see tip, opposite), peeled

Salt

⅓ cup heavy cream

2 cups milk

½ tablespoon pistachio oil or another nut oil such as hazelnut

½ tablespoon extra virgin olive oil

4 tablespoons soft unsalted butter

1 roasted garlic clove, mashed (see tip, page 55)

Freshly ground white pepper

🍷 Two people could polish off the potatoes, especially if some fresh black truffles are shaved on the top, making Champagne or a rich white Burgundy the wine of choice. Otherwise, what to drink alongside depends on what accompanies the potatoes.

Cut the potatoes into ½-inch pieces, place in a pot of well-salted cold water, bring to a boil, and cook until just tender, 15 to 20 minutes. Drain and pass through a ricer. Return to the cooking pot and stir them slowly over low heat with a wooden spoon for about 5 minutes to evaporate the excess moisture and concentrate the potato flavor.

Mix the cream, milk, pistachio oil, and olive oil together in a small saucepan and heat until just under a simmer. Add this mixture slowly to the potatoes, stirring lightly, until the puree is smooth and very creamy.

Now pass the puree through a fine sieve—a tamis or a chinois is best—into the top of a double boiler or a bain-marie. Do this a little at a time, but quickly so you do not overwork the potatoes, which is likely to happen if you try to sieve them all at once. Fold in the butter and the roasted garlic and place over boiling water to keep warm. Place the wrapper from a stick of butter directly on top of the potatoes.

Just before serving, whip the potatoes with a whisk to smooth them, and check seasoning. Serve hot.

GERMAN FRIED POTATOES

PETER LUGER STEAK HOUSE

NEW YORK BOASTS A NUMBER OF FAMOUS STEAK HOUSES. Peter Luger Steak House, in Williamsburg, Brooklyn, is in a class by itself. A holdover from another era, it does not accept credit cards, offers an extremely limited menu, does not pride itself on its wines, and is still family-owned and -run. As for the prime beef that is butchered into its steaks, it is hand-selected daily from a number of purveyors. Peter Luger broils only the loin cuts—the short loin or porterhouse—no rib-eye, and the steaks are glossed with butter as they come to the table. It would be next to impossible to reproduce one of the steaks at home, but the potatoes can be done, to serve with the best steak you can find. Try them with City Hall's Delmonico Steak with Maytag blue cheese, page 171.

SERVES 4 TO 6

5 medium-large Idaho potatoes

3 cups vegetable oil

1 large Spanish onion, peeled and diced

Salt

Pinch paprika

6 tablespoons unsalted butter

Freshly ground white pepper

The preliminary frying is the first step in making classic french fries. The second step is to refry the potatoes until they are brown.

The potatoes and onions can be served as soon as they are browned, without reheating.

This recipe is accomplished in three stages and all but the final 10 minutes can be prepared in advance.

Peel the potatoes and cut them in ½-inch thick sticks as for french fries. As they're cut, put them in a bowl of cold water so they do not discolor. In a deep-fryer, a deep sauté pan, or a wok, heat the 3 cups of oil until very hot. While the oil is heating, take the potatoes out of the water and spread them on several layers of paper towel to dry thoroughly. When the oil is hot, about 375 degrees, fry the potatoes until they're barely colored, 4 to 5 minutes. It's best to do this in batches; three should work well. Use a skimmer to drain the potatoes as they are done and transfer them to paper towels.

When all the potatoes are fried, spoon 3 tablespoons of the oil into a large skillet and sauté the onion over medium heat, stirring frequently. Dust them with a little salt and paprika as they fry. When they're soft and golden, remove them.

When the potatoes have cooled, place them on a cutting board, all facing in one direction, and cut them into dice.

At Peter Luger it is likely to be Scotch on the rocks.

Melt the butter in a large skillet. Fry the potatoes, stirring from time to time, for 5 minutes or so, until they are nicely browned. Fold in the onion, 1 teaspoon of salt, and some pepper, and fry another few minutes until everything is browned. Transfer the mixture to a 10-inch pie pan or baking dish. Set it aside until just before serving.

Preheat the oven to 400 degrees. Place the potatoes in the oven for 10 minutes, then serve.

GOOSE FAT POTATOES

$\mathcal{S}$TRIP HOUSE, A PLAY ON WORDS, is a steak house designed to have a rather "louche" and playful bordello look; lots of red, and walls lined with vintage French photos of strippers set the tone. The success of Strip House has led the Glazier Group, which also owns Michael Jordan's The Steakhouse NYC in Grand Central Terminal, to turn its other restaurant, the Monkey Bar, into a steak house. Strip House has also branched out to other cities. There are several cuts of steak on the menu, along with veal, chicken, and seafood. And as well as creamed spinach and french fries, the star of the side dishes is chef David Walzog's Goose Fat Potatoes. Dessert at any table is bound to include the famous 12-layer chocolate cake.

SERVES 4

3 cups goose or duck fat
  (sold in fancy food shops,
  see tip, page 155)

5 fresh rosemary sprigs

5 fresh thyme sprigs

½ tablespoon whole black
  peppercorns

8 garlic cloves

Kosher salt

3 large Idaho potatoes, peeled and
  cut in ½-inch dice

½ tablespoon chopped thyme

½ tablespoon chopped rosemary

Freshly ground black pepper

1 tablespoon minced flat-leaf
  parsley

Preheat oven to 400 degrees.

Bring fat to a simmer in a 3-quart saucepan. Place rosemary and thyme sprigs, peppercorns, and 6 of the garlic cloves, split, in a 12-inch length of cheesecloth. Tie securely and place in the fat. Season the fat with salt. Add the potatoes and cook at a steady simmer until potatoes are tender but still hold their shape, about 10 minutes.

Use a slotted spoon to transfer the potatoes to a bowl, draining them well. Discard the cheese cloth package. Strain the fat and refrigerate it. Fold the chopped thyme and rosemary into the potatoes and season them to taste with salt and pepper. Pack the potatoes into 4 (4-ounce) cupcake molds or in a muffin tin. Bake 20 minutes, until they start to brown. Remove pan from oven, allow to cool 30 minutes, then refrigerate at least 4 hours or overnight.

Preheat oven to 450 degrees.

Line a baking sheet with parchment and brush with a little of the reserved fat. Run a knife around the inside of the molds, invert molds onto the parchment, and tap so

The recipe can also be prepared with olive oil or half olive oil and half clarified butter. Another way to reheat the potatoes and crisp them is by deep-frying. Remove the chilled potato cakes from the molds and set in a deep saucepan that will hold them in a single layer. Heat goose or duck fat—you can use the fat reserved from the first cooking, it might be just enough—and carefully pour it over the potatoes. Bring to a simmer and cook until the potato cakes are crisp and golden. Remove the cakes with a slotted spoon or a spatula, drain them briefly, then serve.

What to drink with goose fat potatoes depends on what main course they accompany. With a steak, a good California cabernet sauvignon is always on target, or a sturdy pinot noir like the Artesa Pinot Noir 2000 from Santa Barbara, California.

the potatoes are released onto the parchment. Brush with a little of the fat. Mince the remaining 2 garlic cloves and place on top of the potato mounds. Place potatoes in the oven and bake about 20 minutes, until lightly browned. Garnish with parsley and serve.

FRIED RED TOMATOES

JIMMY'S UPTOWN

Beginning in the Bronx, at Jimmy's Bronx Café, Jimmy Rodriguez has put his name all over town. His first expansion was to Jimmy's Uptown in Harlem, then Jimmy's Downtown near Sutton Place and Jimmy's City Island on City Island in the Bronx. He is also running a lounge that serves light food in the 30-30 Hotel on Madison Avenue and 29th Street. Although each of his restaurants has a distinctive menu, they share the influences of the South and of Hispanic food, often updated, like these tomatoes, tweaked with Parmigiano-Reggiano.

Serves 6

6 medium ripe tomatoes, about 2 pounds

2 eggs

1 cup flour

⅔ cup yellow grits or polenta

⅔ cup fine yellow cornmeal

⅓ cup freshly grated Parmigiano-Reggiano

½ teaspoon cayenne

2 teaspoons salt

Vegetable oil for frying

The tomatoes can be served on their own as a first course with an arugula salad dressed with lemon and olive oil, or they can accompany grilled meat or fish.

A German riesling that's not bone-dry, like the Riesling Kabinett Graacher Himmelreich, Friedrich-Wilhelm-Gymnasium, Mosel-Saar-Ruwer

Cut a thin slice from the top and the bottom of each tomato, removing the core as you go. Cut each tomato horizontally in thirds.

Beat the eggs with 2 tablespoons water in a shallow bowl. Place the flour in another bowl and the grits, cornmeal, and cheese in another. Whisk the cayenne and salt into the grits mixture. Set the bowls in a row on your counter: first flour, then eggs, then grits. Have a large platter ready at the end of this assembly line.

Dip each slice of tomato first in flour, coating it well, then in the egg, and finally in the grits mixture. Each time be sure to shake off any excess. Arrange the slices in a single layer on the platter or, if necessary, two platters.

Heat the oil to a depth of ¼ inch in a large skillet. Have several thickness of paper towel ready. Fry the tomato slices, turning once, over medium-high heat a few minutes until golden brown on each side. If necessary, fry the tomatoes in two or three batches, but use fresh oil each time. Drain the fried slices on paper towel, then arrange on a serving platter. The fried slices can be kept warm on a parchment-lined baking sheet in a 200-degree oven for up to 30 minutes.

MUSHROOM KASHA

NEW YORK HAS SEVERAL RUSSIAN COMMUNITIES, the most famous of which is Brighton Beach, Brooklyn, where the avenues are lined with boisterous Russian night club–restaurants. But in Manhattan's Theater District, an elaborate double town house furnished with Imperial Russian accessories is the setting for New York's most elegant Russian restaurant. From the cozy ground floor bar, to the dining room with its golden pear tree centerpiece, to the second floor decorated with ballet costumes, stepping into Firebird is like entering a Fabergé egg. The food is Russian, with vodka and caviar, hors d'oeuvre plates called *zakuski*, and classics like beef stroganoff, borscht, chicken Kiev, and *shashlik*. But the menu also offers an array of contemporary dishes as well, such as lobster bisque, filet mignon, and hot-smoked salmon, for those who want a Russian atmosphere but may not want St. Petersburg on the plate.

SERVES 4

1¼ cups chicken stock

Salt and freshly ground black pepper

1 cup whole buckwheat groats (kasha)

2 tablespoons soft unsalted butter

1 tablespoon extra virgin olive oil

6 ounces button mushrooms, trimmed and coarsely chopped

2 tablespoons sour cream

1 teaspoon minced chives

If desired, wild mushrooms such as chanterelles or morels can be used instead of white button mushrooms.

Bring the chicken stock to a boil in a 2-quart saucepan. Season it well with salt and pepper, stir in the kasha, cover the pan, and set it aside off the heat for 15 to 20 minutes, until the stock has been absorbed and the kasha is tender.

While the kasha is steeping, heat 1 tablespoon of the butter with the olive oil in a skillet. Add the mushrooms and cook, stirring, over medium heat, until they are tender, have given up their liquid, and the liquid has evaporated. Season to taste with salt and pepper and fold in the sour cream and chives.

When the kasha is ready, toss it with a fork, then fold in the remaining tablespoon of the butter. Fold in the mushroom mixture and serve.

A rich red wine

ROASTED MUSHROOMS

FAIRWAY STEAKHOUSE

A MARKET-RESTAURANT IS A NATURAL FIT. In Sheepshead Bay, Brooklyn, clam bars share the space with fish markets; the Old Homestead and Frank's sell their steaks retail; and many bakeries have café tables for those seeking instant gratification. For about 3 years the second floor at the original Fairway market on the Upper West Side has housed a café for breakfast and lunch. Now, at dinner, it becomes a steakhouse with a straightforward menu offering slabs of prime meat, plus a few chicken, fish, and pasta selections, and a roster of appealing appetizers, side dishes, and desserts. Mitchel London, an uncompromising culinary wizard who once cooked for Mayor Ed Koch at Gracie Mansion, is at the stove. His roasted mushrooms are a good partner for the rib-eye.

2 garlic cloves

½ bunch flat-leaf parsley

¼ cup plus 1 tablespoon extra virgin olive oil

½ pound oyster mushrooms

½ pound chanterelle mushrooms

½ pound shiitake mushrooms

2 tablespoons clarified butter

Sea salt and freshly ground black pepper

The selection of mushrooms is pretty basic, and if there are other, more exotic varieties like morels, hedgehogs, or bluefoots in the market, they can be added to or used instead of the list in the recipe.

Turn on the food processor and toss the garlic in through the feed tube. When it's finely chopped, scrape down the sides of the work bowl, add the parsley, and process until finely chopped. With the machine running, pour in ¼ cup of the oil in a thin stream. Scrape down the sides of the bowl, then pulse to make a fairly fine mixture but one that's got some texture. You do not want a smooth puree. Set the mixture aside.

Preheat the oven to 475 degrees.

Trim the mushrooms; separate the oyster mushrooms and leave only about ½ inch of stem; scrape and trim the stems of the chanterelles; and discard the stems of the shiitakes. Halve or quarter the shiitake caps to make fairly uniform pieces.

Heat the clarified butter and remaining tablespoon of olive oil in a large skillet (about 14 inches) that can hold all the mushrooms. Alternatively, you can divide every-thing between two pans. Add the mushrooms and toss over high heat 3 to 4 minutes, until they wilt. Transfer the mushrooms to a shallow roasting pan and roast in the oven for 15 minutes.

Remove the mushrooms from the oven and toss with the parsley mixture. Season with salt and pepper and serve.

A robust red wine with a nice amount of bottle age that will also complement your steak

SAUTÉED ZUCCHINI WITH TOASTED ALMONDS AND PECORINO

RED CAT

JUST ABOUT EVERY NEIGHBORHOOD IN NEW YORK TODAY boasts at least one restaurant that counts on a loyal local clientele but, because the food is a good notch above everyday, also attracts visitors from far and wide. The Red Cat in Chelsea is just such place, serving forthright Mediterranean-style cooking in a simple whitewashed room. Its success has led the owners, chef Jimmy Bradley, and his partner, Danny Abrams, to open The Harrison in TriBeCa and The Mermaid Inn, a seafood restaurant, in the East Village.

SERVES 4

4 tablespoons extra virgin olive oil

½ cup sliced almonds

1½ pounds zucchini, trimmed and cut in julienne

Salt and freshly ground black pepper

3 ounces Pecorino Romano cheese, shaved in thin slices

Heat the oil in a large skillet. Add the almonds and fry until golden. Use a slotted spoon to scoop out the almonds, leaving the oil in the pan. Add the zucchini and stir-fry about 30 seconds, long enough to warm it and coat it with the oil without really cooking it. Remove the pan from the heat. Season the zucchini with salt and pepper. Return the pan to the heat to rewarm, transfer the zucchini to a warm serving dish, top with the cheese and almonds and serve.

A dry Italian white such as Gavi di Gavi

Be careful not to overcook the zucchini. It should still be slightly crisp so it does not give off much liquid as it cools.

Use a vegetable peeler to shave the cheese.

SPINACH GRATIN

PETER HOFFMAN, THE CHEF AND OWNER OF SAVOY, a two-story spot on a back street in SoHo, is a farmer's chef. He consults the calendar and features produce only when it is in season. "At one time a fine restaurant was one that served asparagus and raspberries in December," he once said. "Today it is one that doesn't." And he refuses to compromise. The main floor of his sleek yet cozy wood-paneled restaurant is a bar and lounge. Upstairs, the dining room features a wood-burning fireplace, which he uses frequently to roast fish, meats, poultry, and vegetables.

SERVES 4

2½ tablespoons extra virgin olive oil

1 garlic clove, sliced

¾ cup *panko* (Japanese white bread crumbs)

½ teaspoon fennel seeds

4 tablespoons unsalted butter

2 pounds fresh spinach, stemmed and rinsed thoroughly

2 tablespoons flour

1¼ cups milk, scalded

2 eggs, beaten

Salt and freshly ground black pepper

🍷 With the gratin alone, the Standing Stone Gewürztraminer or another fruity California gewürztraminer

🧂 Try to find good, locally grown spinach. Other greens, such as kale or Swiss chard, can be used in place of spinach.

Heat 2 tablespoons of the oil in a small skillet. Add the garlic and cook a few minutes, until it starts to brown. Remove and discard the garlic and stir in the panko. Sauté until they're lightly toasted. Stir in the fennel seeds and set the crumbs aside.

Preheat the oven to 375 degrees. Use the remaining half tablespoon oil to grease a 4-cup baking dish.

Heat 2 tablespoons of the butter in a large skillet. Add the spinach and cook, stirring, over high heat about a minute just until it starts to wilt. Remove from the heat and set aside.

Melt the remaining butter in a 2-quart saucepan. Whisk in the flour, cook a few minutes, then whisk in the milk. Simmer a few minutes until this white sauce has thickened. Remove from the heat. Beat a little of this mixture into the eggs, then whisk the eggs back into the sauce. Season with salt and pepper.

Remove the spinach from the skillet, draining it thoroughly, and place on a cutting board. Chop roughly. Fold the spinach into the sauce. Taste and correct seasoning. Transfer to the baking dish, top with the crumbs, and bake 20 to 25 minutes, until lightly browned on top.

BHINDI DO PIAZA, SAUTÉED OKRA
TAMARIND

Sixth Street in the East Village, Lexington Avenue in the 20s, and Jackson Heights, Queens, are New York's major low-price Indian restaurant quarters. There are Indian restaurants in Midtown too, but they tend to be maharajah-style palaces. Tamarind, in the Flatiron district, with its clean, monochromatic, modern decor and fine Indian art, is in a class by itself. Although the food is clearly rooted in the Indian idiom, it ventures beyond the typical dishes such as chicken tikka masala and tandoori chicken. Giant filled *dosa* pancakes, spiced lamb sandwiches on Indian bread, tandoori lobster tails, and beans with coconut and curry leaves define what the restaurant calls modern Indian cooking. There is a little tea-and-snacks café next door.

SERVES 4 TO 6

6 tablespoons vegetable oil

1 tablespoon cumin seeds

1 pound okra, trimmed and sliced
    ½ inch thick

2 large onions, peeled and chopped

4 garlic cloves, chopped

1 tablespoon minced fresh ginger

1 jalapeño chile, stemmed, seeded,
    and minced

½ tablespoon ground coriander

½ tablespoon chile powder

½ tablespoon turmeric

Salt

1 pound ripe tomatoes, chopped

½ tablespoon *amchoor* (mango powder), optional

2 tablespoons cilantro leaves

A chardonnay or a pinot noir

Heat 3 tablespoons of the oil in a large skillet. Add the cumin seeds, and when they crackle, toss in the okra and cook over high heat, stirring, until the okra starts to brown, about 5 minutes. Remove the okra from the skillet and set it aside.

Add the remaining 3 tablespoons of oil, half the onions, and the garlic to the skillet. Cook until lightly browned, then stir in the ginger, jalapeño, ground coriander, chile powder, and turmeric. Add 1 teaspoon salt, or to taste. Add the tomato and *amchoor* and cook, stirring, until the ingredients are softened and cling together. Return the okra to the pan, along with the remaining onions. Cook briefly, then fold in half of the cilantro. Check seasoning and serve with the remaining cilantro sprinkled on top.

Purchase okra with bright green pods, the smaller the better. Baby okra does not have to be sliced for this recipe.

Mango powder is available in Indian grocery stores.

GRILLED EGGPLANT WITH GINGER-LIME SAUCE

FOR MANY YEARS THERE WERE NO VIETNAMESE RESTAURANTS in Manhattan. They first began seeping into corners of Chinatown, then into other neighborhoods. Now there are many, and fine ones, too, from little spots that specialize in the restorative and ubiquitous soup, pho, to more elaborate fare. Stephen Duong's Vietnamese restaurants are a stylish group: Cyclo in the East Village, Nam in TriBeCa, and O Mai in Chelsea. Of the three, Nam, in a TriBeCa building with stately columns out front, is the most alluring. The almost bare white interior glows with warm light, softened with gauzy curtains and punctuated with discreet black-and-white photos of old Hanoi. Vietnamese women do the cooking, often producing family recipes and homestyle dishes. Their cuisine blends the richness of China with the perfumed freshness of Southeast Asia.

SERVES 4

⅓ cup extra virgin olive oil

1 scallion, minced

1 tablespoon Vietnamese or Thai fish sauce

1 tablespoon sugar

1 tablespoon lime juice

1 garlic clove, finely minced

1 small fresh red chile, stemmed, seeded, and minced, or to taste

1 (1-inch) piece fresh ginger, peeled and thinly sliced

3 teaspoons minced cilantro leaves

4 slender Japanese eggplants, each about 8 ounces

> Regular eggplant can be used instead of the slender Asian variety, but the skin will not be as tender.

Heat the oil until very hot in small saucepan. Remove from the heat, add the scallion, stir, and set aside.

Combine the fish sauce, sugar, lime juice, garlic, chile, ginger, and 2 teaspoons of the cilantro in a blender. Blend until well combined but only until the ginger is minced, not pureed. Set aside.

Trim the stems from the eggplants and slice each in half lengthwise. Pare off a wide strip of the skin lengthwise, with a vegetable peeler. Place the eggplants in a bowl and massage with the reserved scallion oil.

Preheat a grill to medium-hot. Grill the eggplant halves about 2 minutes on each side, until nicely seared and tender. Remove the eggplant from the grill and cut into 1-inch chunks. Arrange in a shallow serving dish, pour the sauce over it, toss lightly, sprinkle with the remaining cilantro, and serve.

🍷 A dry Alsatian riesling

DESSERTS

CRÈME BRÛLÉE

YOGURT PANNA COTTA WITH MIXED BERRY SOUP

MANGO AND PAPAYA CARPACCIO WITH CILANTRO CANDY

WHITE SESAME MOUSSE

CHEESECAKE

BITTERSWEET CHOCOLATE SOUFFLÉ

CHOCOLATE FONDANT

WARM WALNUT TART

STONE FRUIT CRISP

CHERRY CLAFOUTI

RASPBERRY CROSTADA

VANILLA CAKE

WARM ORANGE CAKE WITH GRAND MARNIER ICE CREAM

PINEAPPLE UPSIDE-DOWN CAKE

ILONA TORTE

RAVANI, ALMOND CAKE WITH CITRUS SYRUP

CRÈME BRÛLÉE

LE CIRQUE 2000

SIRIO MACCIONI, THE QUINTESSENTIAL RESTAURATEUR, has made Le Cirque the ultimate of New York restaurants, and perhaps the world's most famous restaurant. It is on the "must list" for celebrities in society, politics, fashion, and entertainment. It survived a move from East 65th Street to the landmark Villard Houses at the New York Palace where, as Le Cirque 2000, it boasts a vast, gleaming kitchen and brilliantly dazzling decor by Adam Tihany. The menu is French-Italian but the chefs also dote on the clientele, and offer everything from pristine grilled fish to elaborate pot-au-feu and bouillabaisse. Maccioni's three sons participate in running Le Cirque, the Osteria del Circo across town, and branches of Le Cirque and Circo in Las Vegas and Mexico. Travel to France or Italy, and chances are some of the best restaurants will feature Crème Brûlée Le Cirque on their menus, just as Paul Bocuse does.

1 quart heavy cream
1 Tahitian vanilla bean, halved
   lengthwise and seeds scraped out
½ cup granulated sugar
8 egg yolks
8 tablespoons light brown sugar

🍷 Chateau Rieussec Sauternes or
   another Sauternes

🧂 Shallow fluted oval white porce-
   lain ramekins are the classic
dishes for serving crème brûlée.
But Le Cirque also serves minis,
in small 2-ounce glass cups.

🧂 Because the custards can be
   prepared in advance and refrig-
erated until just before serving,
they are excellent to consider when
entertaining.

Preheat oven to 250 degrees.

Place the cream, vanilla seeds, and granulated sugar in a saucepan. Place over low heat and cook until just warm to the touch, stirring occasionally until the sugar dissolves.

Place egg yolks in a large mixing bowl. Whisk in a tablespoon or two of the warm cream, then lightly whisk in the remaining cream. Pour the mixture through a fine sieve or a chinois into a clean bowl, pressing as much vanilla as possible through the sieve.

Place 8 shallow 4-ounce ramekins in one or two rimmed baking sheets or roasting pans, whichever will accommodate them. Ladle the cream mixture into the ramekins, stirring it well so the vanilla is evenly distributed. Bake 1 hour and 15 minutes, rotating the pans once so the custards bake evenly, until the custards look firm and just tremble slightly in the middle. Allow to cool, then refrigerate at least 3 hours or up to 2 days.

To serve, sprinkle the cold custards with brown sugar, coating the tops completely. Caramelize the sugar with a kitchen torch held about an inch and a half from the surface. Alternatively, the custards can be caramelized under a broiler, although it is best to do this one at a time, so they are evenly browned. Take care that the sugar does not burn.

Allow to cool briefly so the surface crisps, then serve.

YOGURT PANNA COTTA WITH MIXED BERRY SOUP

MONTRACHET

BACK IN THE LATE 1980S, when TriBeCa was just beginning to become a dining and nightlife destination, Drew Nieporent, restaurateur extraordinaire, cobbled together a partnership and raised enough money to open Montrachet. It has never wavered from its original concept, to offer fine American food with a French accent, and French wine discoveries to accompany it, all at a reasonable price. The dining room has been enlarged, and enlivened with art, but the focus remains what is on the plate and in the glass. Though Nieporent has gone on to open other places, including Nobu and Tribeca Grill nearby, in partnership with Robert DeNiro, his heart belongs to Montrachet, his first-born.

SERVES 6

3 cups mixed berries
  (strawberries, blueberries,
  blackberries, and raspberries)

1 cup sugar

1 vanilla bean

1 tablespoon lemon juice

1¼ cups heavy cream

1 package unflavored gelatin
  (1 tablespoon)

14 ounces (1¾ cups) plain whole
  milk yogurt

> Five hours sounds like a long time to cook the berries, but what you are really doing is infusing them with sugar and vanilla.

Inniskillin Ice Wine "Vidal" 1998, Ontario, Canada, or another rich dessert wine

Combine the berries, ⅔ cup of the sugar, the vanilla bean, and 2 cups water in a metal mixing bowl. Place the bowl over a saucepan of barely simmering water, so the bottom of the bowl is not in contact with the water, and let cook for 5 hours. Yes, 5 hours. Check from time to time that there is enough water in the saucepan. At the end of the cooking time add the lemon juice and strain, but do not crush, the mixture through a sieve lined with several layers of cheesecloth into a bowl. Discard the vanilla bean. Refrigerate the juice and strained berries separately.

While the berries are cooking, mix the remaining ⅓ cup of sugar with the heavy cream in a saucepan. Bring just to a boil, remove from heat, and whisk in gelatin. Place yogurt in a mixing bowl and stir. Slowly whisk in cream mixture. Ladle mixture into 6 (4-ounce) muffin tin cups, preferably nonstick. Cover and refrigerate at least 6 hours. To serve, unmold yogurt panna cottas onto each of 6 dessert plates or shallow soup plates. Spoon some of the berry juice around each portion and some of the strained berries on top of the panna cottas.

MANGO AND PAPAYA CARPACCIO WITH CILANTRO CANDY

UNION PACIFIC

Rocco DiSpirito's notoriety has more to do with television and his mother's Italian-American cooking than with the refined, Asian-accented food for which he became known at Union Pacific. But Union Pacific, a dramatic room with soaring arches and stone paving, is where his gastronomic energy is concentrated. Elaborate tasting menus that focus on seafood and exotic flavors progress from sheer, cold tidbits to beautifully-presented main courses, to desserts, like this refreshing tropical fruit carpaccio. In this dish, the term carpaccio means thinly sliced ingredients arranged on a plate.

SERVES 4 TO 6

12 large fresh cilantro leaves

1 egg white, beaten until foamy

6 tablespoons superfine sugar

2 ripe but firm mangoes

1 ripe but firm yellow papaya

1½ packages unflavored gelatin

Zest of 1 lemon

Pinch of freshly ground white pepper

Pineapple, mango, or orange sorbet

Preheat the oven to 200 degrees. Wash the cilantro leaves and pat them dry on paper towels. Place them on a cutting board. Brush the leaves on one side with the egg white, then dust with some of the sugar. Carefully turn the leaves over, brush with egg white, and dust with sugar on the second side. Lift the leaves off the cutting board and onto a mesh baking rack or a sheet of parchment on a baking sheet. Turn the oven off and place the baking sheet in the oven. When the leaves have dried and are starting to feel stiff, after about 20 minutes, remove them from the oven and set aside to cool. Use a spatula to transfer them to a flat plate.

Place each mango flat on a surface. Cut the mangoes not quite in half from top to bottom so you slice through the fruit just above and below the pit. Peel the mango halves. Slice them very thin. Peel the center section around the pit and chop the flesh that surrounds the pit. You should have about ½ cup of the chopped mango. Quarter, seed, and peel the papaya. Slice very thin. Arrange alternating slices of mango and papaya on 4 to 6 dessert plates.

The dessert can be arranged even more dramatically on a large platter and served by cutting portions like spokes of a wheel.

Place the gelatin in a small saucepan. Add ¼ cup of warm water and stir. When the gelatin has softened after a few minutes, stir in another ¾ cup of water, the remaining sugar, the chopped mango, and the lemon zest. Bring just to a boil, stirring; transfer to a blender and puree. Strain through a fine sieve and season with pepper. Spread over the mango and papaya slices on the plates. Refrigerate until the puree is firm, 30 minutes or longer.

To serve, decorate each portion with some of the candied cilantro and add a scoop of sorbet.

Coteaux du Layon or other moderate sweet wine, even Moscato d'Asti

WHITE SESAME MOUSSE

KAI

THIS COOL GREEN AND BLACK GRANITE SECOND-FLOOR ENCLAVE over a tea shop has to be a destination. It serves lunch, tea, and, for dinner, elegant and inventive *kaiseki* Japanese menus. As with most *kaiseki* menus, exquisite presentation is the rule. And so are surprises, like a tantalizing bit of seasonal herb here, or an unusual flavor there. Delicately nutty white sesame paste gives this chilled dessert mousse a unique personality. Kai is owned by the Japanese tea company, Ito En, whose shop is downstairs.

SERVES 4 TO 6

¼ cup Japanese white sesame paste
    (sold in Asian markets)
1⅓ cups whole milk
½ cup sugar
¼ teaspoon salt
1 packet unflavored gelatin
    (1 tablespoon)
1 cup heavy cream
⅓ cup warm chocolate sauce,
    optional
1 tablespoon toasted white sesame
    seeds

Japanese sesame paste is like natural peanut butter. It separates. Before using it, stir it thoroughly to reincorporate the oil.

In a 1-quart saucepan, whisk the sesame paste into the milk until well-blended. Stir in the sugar and salt and ½ cup of water. Bring to a simmer, whisking constantly. Remove from the heat. Soften the gelatin in ½ cup of cold water in a small dish, and whisk it into the milk and sesame mixture. Return to the heat very briefly, whisk, then remove. Transfer the mixture to a medium metal bowl and set the bowl in a larger bowl of ice water so it can chill. Whisk it from time to time as it cools.

When the mixture has cooled and started to thicken, whip the cream. Gradually fold the whipped cream into the sesame mixture until it is smoothly incorporated. Spoon the mixture into 4 to 6 stemmed goblets, cover each with plastic wrap, and refrigerate at least 6 hours.

To serve, drizzle a little warm chocolate sauce on top of each portion, then sprinkle with sesame seeds. The sauce can be omitted and just the sesame seeds used, if desired.

Malvasia Passito Vigna del Volta La Stoppa 1999 or another late-harvest Malvasia

CHEESECAKE

A TOURIST MAGNET IN MIDTOWN, a Broadway icon, and a landmark of sorts, the Carnegie Deli, named for nearby Carnegie Hall, is an abiding representative of New York's Jewish culture. Known for its sandwiches piled high with corned beef and pastrami as much as for its brusque waiters, it is a place to go for the bustling scene as much as for the food. You do not need a recipe to make one of those sandwiches. You just need to buy enough sliced meat. But the classic New York cheesecake is another story. You can bake it and, as your waiter might say, "Enjoy!"

SERVES 10 TO 12

9 tablespoons soft unsalted butter

½ cup sifted confectioners' sugar,
  plus more for dusting

3 eggs

2¾ cups all-purpose flour

½ teaspoon salt

2 pounds cream cheese, softened

1¼ cups granulated sugar

1 teaspoon vanilla extract

2 tablespoons lemon juice

½ cup sour cream

 A cuppa coffee

The rather unorthodox baking
method assures that the top of
the cake and the pastry will brown
but that the cake will not crack or
sink from overbaking.

Beat the butter in an electric mixer. Beat in ½ cup of the confectioners' sugar until smooth. Beat in 1 egg. Whisk 2 cups of the flour with the salt. Stir the flour mixture into the butter mixture and beat just until a soft dough forms. Divide it in half. Roll one half into a circle to fit in the bottom of an 8-inch springform pan. Roll the remaining dough into a rectangle about 6 by 12 inches. Cut it in half lengthwise. Place the strips in the pan to line the sides, pressing the seams together. Trim to make a smooth edge on top. Prick the bottom. Refrigerate while the oven is preheating.

Preheat oven to 425 degrees.

Line the pastry-filled pan with foil and weight with dry beans or pastry weights. Place in the oven and bake about 10 minutes. Remove the foil and continue baking until the pastry has just started to color, another 6 to 8 minutes. Remove from the oven and increase the temperature to 475 degrees.

Beat the cream cheese with the granulated sugar. Beat in the remaining ¾ cup of flour, 2 eggs, the vanilla, lemon juice, and sour cream. Pour into the pastry shell, place in the oven, and bake about 20 minutes, until the top is golden. Remove cake from the oven. Lower temperature to 350 degrees. Allow the cake to sit for 20 minutes. Return the cake to the oven and continue baking it for about 25 minutes, until the top starts to puff. Set the cake aside at room temperature for about 5 hours, then refrigerate until cold.

Remove cake from refrigerator at least 1 hour before serving and sift a layer of confectioners' sugar on top.

BITTERSWEET CHOCOLATE SOUFFLÉ
PAYARD BISTRO

FRANÇOIS PAYARD, from a family of pastry chefs in Nice, France, worked in some of New York's best kitchens and made his reputation before venturing out on his own. His pastry shop–tea room–bistro on the Upper East Side has a regular following for morning croissants, light café fare, a bistro lunch at mid-day, and cocktails and dinner in the evening. The coffee and wine bar is always crowded. The shop and two-story restaurant have a traditional look, suggesting Art Nouveau. But look again. You may notice that some of the light fixtures are designed like whisks.

SERVES 8

6 tablespoons soft unsalted butter

⅓ cup plus 2 tablespoons sugar

7 ounces high-quality bittersweet chocolate, chopped

1 tablespoon crème fraîche

4 eggs, separated, at room temperature

3 egg whites, at room temperature

½ teaspoon cream of tartar

Unsweetened whipped cream, optional

Château Monbazillac, another Monbazillac, or a Sauternes

Using about 1½ tablespoons of butter, generously brush the insides of 8 (6-ounce) ramekins with butter. Place them in the freezer and chill for 15 minutes. Brush with another 1½ tablespoons of butter. (Preparing the ramekins should use 3 tablespoons of the butter.) Use the 2 tablespoons of sugar to coat the insides of the ramekins. Tap out any excess. Place the ramekins in the refrigerator.

Place remaining 3 tablespoons of butter and the chocolate in a 1-quart metal bowl over simmering water in a saucepan, or in the top of a double boiler. Melt, stirring occasionally, until smooth. Whisk in the crème fraîche. Transfer mixture to a 4-quart bowl, and set aside to cool.

Preheat the oven to 350 degrees.

Whisk the 4 egg yolks into cooled chocolate mixture. Using an electric mixer, beat the 7 egg whites at low speed until foamy. Add the cream of tartar and beat at medium speed until softly peaked. Gradually add the remaining ⅓ cup of sugar and beat at medium-high speed until stiffly peaked but still glossy. Using a large rubber spatula, fold a scoop of the beaten whites thoroughly into the chocolate mixture. Gently fold in remaining whites.

Carefully spoon the mixture into the ramekins, filling them three-quarters full. Take a piece of paper towel and wipe the exposed butter and sugar from the ramekins. Place ramekins on a baking sheet and bake about 12 minutes, until puffed. Serve hot with whipped cream if desired.

CHOCOLATE FONDANT

ONE IF BY LAND, TWO IF BY SEA

ACKNOWLEDGED TO BE ONE OF THE MOST ROMANTIC dining rooms in Manhattan, One If By Land, TIBS, as it is known, is tucked into a flower-filled, candlelit landmark carriage house—it was once owned by Aaron Burr—on a quiet Greenwich Village street. It even has a working fireplace. And it remains one of the few bastions of Continental cooking, offering elaborate special-occasion standbys like oysters, foie gras, smoked salmon, beef Wellington, and rack of lamb. And for dessert, there is plenty of chocolate: a soufflé, a tart, and these individual molten chocolate cakes, served warm.

SERVES 8

9 ounces unsalted butter
   (18 tablespoons; 2 sticks plus
   2 tablespoons)

3 tablespoons unsweetened cocoa

6 ounces bittersweet chocolate, at
   least 70% cacao solids (see tip)

½ vanilla bean, halved lengthwise
   and seeds scraped out

6 eggs, separated, at room
   temperature

⅓ cup sugar

1 tablespoon all-purpose flour

Vanilla ice cream or whipped
   cream, for serving

Many of the finer brands of semisweet and bittersweet chocolate are now sold with the percentage of cacao solids indicated on the label. The higher the percentage, the more bitter the chocolate.

Use 2 tablespoons of the butter to grease 8 (4-ounce) soufflé dishes or ramekins. Muffin tins can be used. Dust the ramekins with the cocoa.

Place the remaining 2 sticks of butter, the chocolate, and vanilla seeds in the top of a double boiler and stir over simmering water until the mixture is melted and smooth. Transfer to a large mixing bowl and set aside to cool.

Beat the egg whites until frothy, then beat until softly peaked, adding the sugar gradually. Fold the flour into the chocolate mixture. Lightly beat the egg yolks, then stir them into the chocolate mixture. Fold in the egg whites. Transfer the mixture to the prepared ramekins, cover with plastic wrap, and refrigerate overnight.

About 30 minutes before serving time, preheat the oven to 350 degrees. Place the ramekins in the oven and bake about 12 minutes. The tops of the cakes will be barely firm but the cakes will show signs of releasing around the sides. A cake tester will not come out clean. Remove the cakes from the oven, quickly run a knife around each, then invert them onto individual plates. If you have used muffin tins, place a baking sheet or a plastic cutting board over the tins to invert them all at once. Serve the cakes before they cool and start to sink, with whipped cream or ice cream alongside.

Blandy's 10-year-old Malmsey Madeira, another Madeira, or M. Cosentino 1997 Zinport Lodi from California

WARM WALNUT TART

WAYNE NISH, THE CHEF AT MARCH, has maintained his highly personal style over the years. His cooking has an Asian inflection and he excels at creating elaborate tasting menus in the multi-level town house restaurant he owns with Joseph Scalice, the wine expert and managerial side of the partnership. Nish trained in the kitchen of Barry Wine, whose Quilted Giraffe led the way in the 1980s for American chefs who sought to establish their own restaurants in the image of the finest that France had to offer. March maintains that tradition.

SERVES 8

½ cup (1 stick) unsalted butter

⅔ cup light brown sugar

2 tablespoons granulated sugar

¼ cup honey

¼ cup heavy cream

1 pound walnut pieces
   (about 3½ cups)

1 partially-baked 9-inch tart shell

Vanilla ice cream, for serving

> You'll need a sharp knife to cut the tart.

Combine the butter, brown sugar, granulated sugar, and honey in a 4-quart saucepan. Bring it all to a boil, stirring, over medium heat. Continue cooking until the mixture registers 253 degrees (hard ball stage) on a candy thermometer. Remove the pan from the heat and carefully stir in the cream and nuts.

Spoon the mixture into the tart shell, tamping it down to fill it evenly.

Preheat the oven to 325 degrees. Bake the tart for about 20 minutes, until the filling begins to bubble. Allow it to cool a bit and serve it warm with vanilla ice cream. You can let it cool completely, then rewarm it in the oven.

 Muscat de Beaumes-de-Venise

STONE FRUIT CRISP

ORIGINALLY, VERBENA WAS OWNED JUST BY DIANE FORLEY, one of New York's prominent female chef-restaurateurs. Then she married Michael Otsuka, who had been the chef at Thalia, and he joined her in her understated restaurant in a low-key corner of Manhattan, Irving Place. Otsuka's input has added some Asian touches to the food, but locally grown produce is still given a starring role, as in this seasonal Stone Fruit Crisp, strictly a summertime dessert. It can be made with apricots, peaches, nectarines, or all three, depending on what is ripe and fresh.

SERVES 8

3 pounds ripe apricots, peaches, or nectarines, or a mixture

Juice of 2 lemons

1 cup sugar

1 cup stale white bread cubes, crusts removed

¾ cup (1½ sticks) soft unsalted butter, plus butter for baking dish

¾ cup all-purpose flour

1½ cups rolled oats

¼ cup finely chopped almonds

1 teaspoon cinnamon

Apricots and nectarines do not require peeling. The dessert can also be made with unpeeled peaches. But it will have more finesse if the peaches are peeled.

Pit the fruit. If using apricots, quarter them; cut the peaches or nectarines in eighths. Place the fruit in a large bowl and toss with the lemon juice and ½ cup of the sugar. Fold in the bread.

Place the butter and the remaining ½ cup of sugar in a food processor and blend until smooth. Add the flour, oats, almonds, and cinnamon, and pulse until crumbly.

Preheat oven to 350 degrees. Butter a 2½- to 3-quart shallow baking dish. Spread the fruit mixture in the dish and cover with the oat topping. Bake 1 hour 15 minutes, until the fruit bubbles and the topping is browned. Serve while still warm.

 Muscat de Beaumes-de-Venise or Champagne

CHERRY CLAFOUTI

w d 5 o

CLINTON STREET IN THE LOWER EAST SIDE is now a bona fide Restaurant Row. Its fine, mostly small places signal the changes in this once-Jewish area that now caters to the young and trendy. Wylie Dufresne, who worked with Jean-Georges Vongerichten, first made his mark cooking inventive American fare in a closet-size kitchen at 71 Clinton Fresh Food. He then moved across the street and opened wd50, a combination of his initials and the street address. Now his creativity is working overtime, layering anchovies on blocks of foie gras, and cutting threadlike "noodles" out of squid. Sam Mason, the pastry chef, is no slouch when it comes to invention, either. His clafouti, a kind of French batter cake, is baked in a pastry shell and relies on a filling of cherries marinated with pepper and star anise.

SERVES 6 TO 8

1½ cups granulated sugar

1 cup ruby port

6 whole black peppercorns

1 piece star anise

Zest of 1 orange, grated

1 vanilla bean, halved lengthwise and seeds scraped out

1 pound cherries, pitted

¾ cup sliced almonds

1½ tablespoons plus 2 cups all-purpose flour, and more for work surface

1 cup heavy cream

3 whole eggs

3 egg yolks

9 tablespoons soft unsalted butter

½ cup sifted confectioners' sugar

½ teaspoon salt

1 tablespoon lightly toasted chopped, unsalted pistachios

Combine 1 cup of the granulated sugar with ¼ cup water in a heavy saucepan. Cook over high heat, watching carefully, until the mixture just begins to color. Stir in 1 cup very hot water and mix until the sugar has dissolved. Add the port, peppercorns, star anise, orange zest, vanilla bean, and cherries. Simmer for 10 minutes. Remove from the heat, allow to cool to room temperature, cover, and refrigerate overnight.

While the cherries are cooking, place the almonds in a dry skillet and toast. Grind very fine in a blender. Mix the ground almonds with the 1½ tablespoons flour and the remaining ½ cup of granulated sugar. Bring the cream to a boil. In a bowl, beat 2 of the whole eggs with the 3 egg yolks, and gradually beat in the cream. Whisk in the almond mixture. Cover and refrigerate overnight.

Also on the day before you bake the clafouti, make the pastry. Beat the butter with the confectioners' sugar. Slowly beat in the remaining egg. Mix the remaining 2 cups of flour with the salt and stir into the butter mixture. Beat for a minute or so to make a tender dough. Wrap in plastic and refrigerate.

Refrigerating the batter overnight allows the flavor of the almonds to intensify.

Start to assemble the clafouti about an hour before it is to be served. Preheat the oven to 425 degrees. Allow the dough to come nearly to room temperature, then roll it on a lightly floured surface and fit it into a 10-inch tart pan. Prick the surface, line it with foil, weight it with pastry weights, and bake about 10 minutes. Remove it from the oven and reduce the temperature to 350 degrees.

Drain the cherries well, discarding the whole spices and reserving the syrup. Spread the cherries on the partially-baked pastry. Whisk the almond mixture and pour it over the cherries. Place the tart pan in the oven and bake about 35 minutes, until just set. Remove from the oven. Scatter the pistachios on top and drizzle with a little of the syrup.

Serve while still warm, with more of the syrup alongside.

Coteaux du Layon Rochefort "Les Rayelles" Château Pierre Bise 1996, or a vintage port

RASPBERRY CROSTADA

Eli Zabar has been in the restaurant business about as long as he has had food markets on the Upper East Side. The café at E.A.T. on Madison Avenue feeds a well-heeled clientele looking for a place to eat near the Metropolitan Museum of Art. The upstairs café at the Vinegar Factory, on the same Yorkville block as his bread bakery, has long been a venue for brunch and parties. Taste is the most ambitious of his restaurants, a café by day and a more serious place with a wine bar in the evening. Scott Bieber, the chef, takes advantage of all the fine ingredients that come into the market. His lemon meringue cake is a signature, but these jam-filled raspberry tartlets are easier to manage at home.

SERVES 12

3 cups all-purpose flour,
   plus additional for kneading
   and rolling

½ teaspoon salt

¾ cup granulated sugar

1½ cups (3 sticks) cold unsalted
   butter, diced

3 egg yolks

1 whole egg

1½ cups good raspberry jam

1½ pints fresh raspberries

Sifted confectioners' sugar

Whipped cream or vanilla ice
   cream, optional

Place the flour, salt, and granulated sugar in a food processor. Pulse briefly to mix. Add the butter and pulse just until the mixture is crumbly. Lightly beat 2 of the egg yolks and the whole egg together. Add them to the food processor, then pulse until a dough starts to form. If the mixture is too dry to gather into a ball, sprinkle with a little cold water and pulse again. Briefly knead the dough, flatten it into a disk, wrap it in plastic, and refrigerate it at least an hour.

Roll out the dough to a thickness of ⅛-inch on a floured surface. Cut as many 5-inch-diameter circles as you can. This first pass should yield about 9 circles. Reroll your scraps and you'll be able to cut out 3 more.

Cover a large baking sheet with parchment.

Spread 2 tablespoons of the jam in the center of each pastry circle, leaving a ½-inch border. Fold the border over, pleating it as you go, so each crostada has a pastry border and a jam center. Beat the remaining egg yolk with a tablespoon of water and brush this wash on the pastry

Brachetto d'Acqui, a sparkling Italian red wine

edges. With a wide, flat spatula, arrange the crostadas on the baking sheet and refrigerate 15 minutes. Preheat the oven to 400 degrees. Place the crostadas in the oven and bake until they're golden, about 25 minutes. Transfer the pastries from the pan to a rack to cool. Arrange fresh raspberries over the jam, standing them closely at attention. Dust with confectioners' sugar and serve. Whipped cream or vanilla ice cream alongside? Why not!

VANILLA CAKE

CITARELLA WAS FIRST A FISH MARKET on the Upper West Side. Then it morphed into a fancy food shop with several branches. Now it is also a fine seafood restaurant in Rockefeller Center, in what had been Hurley's, a "real estate holdout" tavern that resisted being incorporated into the skyscraper complex. Citarella offers some of the freshest fish in the city. It also has a compelling dessert menu, thanks to Bill Yosses, its master pastry chef. His vanilla cake with vanilla syrup, which begs to be served with vanilla ice cream, is a retort to the omnipresent molten chocolate cakes. (Never mind that it's bolstered with white chocolate.) But be prepared to take out a bank loan to pay for all those vanilla beans.

SERVES 6

8 ounces white chocolate, diced

6 tablespoons unsalted butter, plus butter for greasing molds

½ cup all-purpose flour, sifted

5 eggs, separated

6 Tahitian vanilla beans, halved lengthwise and seeds scraped out

1 cup sugar

¼ teaspoon cream of tartar

2 cups sparkling mineral water

2 pieces star anise

Grated zest of ½ orange

½ teaspoon unflavored gelatin

Vanilla ice cream, for serving

Kracher Beerenauslese 2001 from Austria or another late-harvest riesling

This recipe has to be started a day in advance. And the cakes are best baked shortly before the dessert is to go on the table, so they can be served delectably tender and warm.

Place the white chocolate and butter in a medium metal bowl over a pot of simmering water. Stir frequently until the chocolate is melted and smooth. Remove from heat. Whisk in the flour, the egg yolks, and the vanilla scrapings from 4 of the beans.

Place the egg whites, 1 tablespoon of the sugar, and the cream of tartar in an electric mixer. Whip at medium speed until the whites are softly peaked, then gradually add ½ cup of the sugar, whipping all the while, until the whites are stiff. Fold in the chocolate mixture fairly thoroughly—perfection is not required. Refrigerate this batter overnight.

You can also prepare the sauce a day ahead. Bring the mineral water, the remaining sugar, the star anise, the rest of the vanilla scrapings, and the orange zest to a simmer. Whisk in the gelatin and boil the mixture about 5 minutes, whisking from time to time, until you have 1½ cups of sauce. Refrigerate the sauce, covered.

Be sure to allow the batter to rest overnight as it will be easier to bake. Otherwise the cake will be too fragile.

Also, it is important not to over-bake the cakes. They should come out of the oven before the tops are completely firm.

Since you've only used the seeds from the vanilla beans, you can get your money's worth by storing the scraped pods in sugar to make vanilla sugar, or in vodka for your own extract.

About an hour before serving time, remove the batter from the refrigerator. Preheat the oven to 350 degrees. Grease 6 (4-ounce) ramekins—big muffin tins will do the trick. Give the batter a quick whisk, then spoon it into the molds. Place in the oven and bake about 20 minutes, until the tops are puffed and golden and somewhat firm to the touch. (A cake tester will not come out perfectly clean.) Remove the cakes from the oven, allow them to cool in the pans for 15 minutes, then run a knife around the edges and invert them to remove them. To serve, place a cake on a plate with a scoop of vanilla ice cream alongside and the sauce drizzled all around.

WARM ORANGE CAKE WITH GRAND MARNIER ICE CREAM

VERITAS

V ERITAS IS AS MUCH ABOUT WINE AS IT IS ABOUT FOOD. A partner in this compact but elegant spot in the Flatiron District has a deep cellar, and supplies the restaurant with the lion's share of its wine list, especially the bottles from California and the Rhône Valley. The food is as finely crafted as the room, more subtle than splashy, and relies on the best materials at hand. This delicate orange dessert is a complex affair that is usually served with a panna cotta and some mint syrup, but home cooks can simplify it, omitting those two elements.

SERVES 8 OR 12

13 tablespoons (1½ sticks plus 1 tablespoon) soft unsalted butter

1 cup plus 3 tablespoons all-purpose flour

½ cup cake flour

2 teaspoons baking powder

1 teaspoon salt

1¼ cups sugar

Grated zest and juice of 2 oranges, plus additional orange juice if needed

2 eggs

1 cup crème fraîche

½ cup bitter orange marmalade

¼ cup Grand Marnier

1 tablespoon finely slivered mint leaves

Grand Marnier ice cream (recipe follows)

Preheat the oven to 350 degrees. Use 1 tablespoon of the butter to grease 12 (3-ounce) or 8 (4-ounce) brioche molds or cupcake tins. Dust with 1 tablespoon of the all-purpose flour and shake out the excess. Sift together the rest of the all-purpose flour, the cake flour, baking powder, and salt.

In an electric mixer, beat the remaining 12 tablespoons of butter with ¾ cup of the sugar and the orange zest. Beat in the eggs one at a time. Stir in the sifted dry ingredients, then beat in the crème fraîche. Spoon into the prepared molds, filling them no more than three-quarters full. Place in the oven and bake for 15 to 25 minutes, depending on the size of the molds, until barely beginning to brown around the edges. Remove the cakes from the oven and allow them to cool 10 minutes before unmolding.

While the cakes are baking, measure the juice of the oranges and add as much as needed to make 1 cup. Place in a saucepan with the remaining ½ cup of sugar and the marmalade. Bring to a boil, stirring, until the marmalade has dissolved and the mixture is syrupy. Stir in the Grand Marnier. Transfer this sauce to a container and refrigerate.

A Sauternes such as Château
de Rayne Vigneau

MAKES 1 QUART

4 cups half-and-half

½ cup sugar

3 egg yolks, beaten

¼ cup Grand Marnier

2 teaspoons orange flower water
(sold in fancy food shops)

The ice cream is best if prepared
a day in advance to allow it to
harden properly and for the flavors
to infuse. But be sure to remove it
from the freezer and put it in the refrigerator about a half hour before
serving to temper the texture.

To serve, preheat the oven to 250 degrees. Warm the
cakes in the oven for 10 minutes. Arrange on a plate and
top with a few threads of the mint, and place a scoop of
the ice cream alongside. Top the ice cream with a little of
the sauce.

GRAND MARNIER ICE CREAM

Combine the half-and-half and the sugar in a saucepan
and bring barely to a simmer. Remove from the heat and
gradually whisk in the egg yolks. Return to the stove and
cook, stirring constantly with a wooden spoon, until the
mixture has thickened a bit and steam just begins to rise
from the pan. Remove from the heat and add the Grand
Marnier and the orange flower water. Strain into a clean
container and chill thoroughly, at least 5 hours.

Place in an ice cream maker and churn according to the
manufacturer's directions. Spoon into a container and
freeze several hours or overnight to firm up before serving.

PINEAPPLE UPSIDE-DOWN CAKE

WASHINGTON PARK

WHEN JONATHAN WAXMAN AND MELVYN MASTER opened Jams on the Upper East Side in the early 1980s, New York certainly took notice. Jams was the first example of "California cuisine" in the city. Waxman had been the chef at the trendsetting Michael's in Santa Monica. What California contributed was a culinary ethic that demanded fresh seasonal produce above all. It might even have been considered a wake-up call. Jams eventually closed (but a New York edition of Michael's opened and is still going strong, see page 102). Which brings us to Washington Park. It's a welcome return of Jonathan Waxman to the stove in New York after a 10-year hiatus.

2 ripe organic pineapples,
 or 1 large golden pineapple

1 cup (2 sticks) unsalted butter

1 cup dark brown sugar

¼ cup dark rum

2 cups all-purpose flour

2 teaspoons baking powder

½ teaspoon salt

1 cup granulated sugar

4 eggs, separated, at room
 temperature

½ cup milk

1 teaspoon vanilla extract

If you have the patience, you can carefully arrange the pieces of pineapple in the pan in a pattern before pouring the batter over them.

Quarter the pineapples. Remove cores, slice off the peel and cut out any "eyes." Cut the pineapple in 1-inch pieces. Melt 1 stick of the butter over medium-low heat in a 12-inch cast-iron skillet. Add the brown sugar and rum. Cook for 5 minutes. Add the pineapple, baste it, and cook for 3 minutes. Set aside to cool.

Sift together the flour, baking powder, and salt and set aside. Preheat the oven to 400 degrees.

In an electric mixer, cream the remaining stick of butter with the granulated sugar until light and fluffy, at least 5 minutes. Add the egg yolks one at a time, beating well. Fold in the flour mixture alternately with the milk. Beat the egg whites until softly peaked. Add the vanilla and beat until stiff but still creamy. Fold the egg whites into the batter and spread over the pineapple in the skillet. Place in the oven and bake about 30 minutes, until the top is browned and fairly firm to the touch, and a cake tester comes out clean.

Cool the cake in the skillet on a rack for 10 minutes. Then run a knife around the edges and cover the pan with a large platter. Invert to release the cake onto the platter. Serve warm.

 Château Reynon Cadillac 1999, a sweet Bordeaux

ILONA TORTE

WITH ITS SPLENDID HOWARD CHANDLER CHRISTY PAINTINGS and warm, clubby atmosphere, Café des Artistes has long been a magnet for New Yorkers and tourists alike. And its location, a block or so from Lincoln Center, has made it something of a hangout for musicians. That's also because its co-owner, George Lang, is a violinist and a close friend of a number of the soloists and conductors on the New York concert scene. The food is continental with hints of Middle Europe, thanks to Lang, a Hungarian émigré who also owns restaurants in Budapest. The restaurant's name comes from its location, in a building called the Des Artistes, on a block where most of the buildings were constructed with duplexes and double-height windows for artist's studios. The Ilona Torte is a Hungarian confection that Lang named for his mother and for one of his daughters.

SERVES 12

Butter and all-purpose flour for pan

13 ounces semisweet chocolate, coarsely chopped

1 cup granulated sugar

26 tablespoons (3 sticks plus 2 tablespoons) soft unsalted butter

8 eggs, separated, at room temperature

8 ounces walnuts, ground (about 1¼ cups)

2 tablespoons soft white bread crumbs

Pinch of salt

3 tablespoons instant espresso powder

3 egg yolks

1 cup confectioners' sugar, sifted

2 tablespoons chopped walnuts

Preheat the oven to 375 degrees. Butter a 10-inch spring-form pan. Line the bottom with parchment. Dust the pan with flour, shaking out any excess.

Place 5 ounces of the chocolate, the granulated sugar, and ¼ cup water in a metal bowl set over a pan of simmering water. Heat, stirring, until the chocolate melts and the sugar dissolves, 5 to 6 minutes. Set aside.

In an electric mixer, beat 6 tablespoons of the soft butter until light. Beat in the 8 egg yolks one at a time until smooth and creamy. On low speed beat in the chocolate mixture, then the ground walnuts and bread crumbs.

In a separate bowl beat the 8 egg whites with salt and 1 tablespoon of ice water until stiffly peaked but still creamy. Fold the whites into the chocolate mixture. Because the chocolate mixture is quite heavy, it will be slow going at first. When it's well-blended, spoon the batter into the pan, smooth the top, and bake about 40 minutes, until the top is firm to the touch and a cake tester comes out clean. Place the cake on a rack and allow it to cool in the pan. The cake will sink; not to worry.

In order to make handling the cake easier, when you split the cake to fill and frost it, be sure that the cut sides are what will be covered with the filling and that the smooth sides form the bottom and top of the cake.

When cake is cool, place remaining 8 ounces of chocolate with the espresso powder and ½ cup boiling water in a metal bowl over simmering water. Stir to make a smooth mixture. Remove from heat and beat in the 3 egg yolks one at a time.

In an electric mixer beat the remaining 20 tablespoons of soft butter until creamy. Gradually beat in the confectioners' sugar, mixing well. Stir in the chocolate mixture.

When cake has cooled completely, remove it from the pan, invert it, and peel off the parchment. Use a large serrated knife to slice the torte horizontally into two layers. Place the top half cut side up on a platter. Frost it with 1 cup of the buttercream. Place the second layer cut side down on top. Frost top and sides with remaining buttercream. Sprinkle chopped walnuts on top and serve.

A fine, sweet Tokay Azsu, 5 or 6 puttonyos

RAVANI, ALMOND CAKE WITH CITRUS SYRUP

MOLYVOS

A RUSTIC HOME OF REGIONAL GREEK COOKING IN MIDTOWN, Molyvos is decorated with copperware, pottery, and family photos from the owners, the Livanos family, who own several restaurants in Westchester County as well as Oceana, a fine seafood establishment, in Manhattan. Molyvos is the place for traditional Greek dining, from the array of meze appetizers to the syrupy desserts. The wine list, too, offers a rich assortment of wines from the Greek mainland and the islands, which can be expertly paired with the food.

13 tablespoons (1 stick plus 5 tablespoons) soft unsalted butter

⅓ cup unblanched almonds, finely
   chopped

¾ cup all-purpose flour

1½ cups semolina flour

1½ teaspoons baking powder

1 teaspoon baking soda

4 eggs, separated, at room
   temperature

1 teaspoon vanilla extract

1½ cups sugar

Pinch salt

1 cup honey

2 teaspoons grated orange zest

2 cups whole milk yogurt,
   preferably Greek, for serving

1 orange, cut in segments,
   pith removed, for serving

When pouring the hot syrup over the cake, do it very gradually. Allow the syrup to be absorbed before adding more, so the syrup will penetrate evenly.

Preheat oven to 325 degrees. Use 1 tablespoon of the butter to grease a 6-cup loaf pan. Line the bottom with parchment paper and butter the paper.

Place the almonds, all-purpose flour, semolina flour, baking powder, and baking soda in a bowl and whisk together to combine.

Using an electric mixer on medium-high speed, beat the egg yolks, vanilla, and ¾ cup of the sugar until very thick and light. Gradually beat in remaining 12 tablespoons butter, beating until creamy. In a separate mixing bowl, beat the egg whites at medium-high speed with salt until they hold firm peaks but are still creamy.

Return the egg yolk bowl to the mixer and on low speed gradually beat in the dry ingredients. The mixture will be stiff. By hand, stir one-fourth of the beaten egg whites into the batter, then fold in the rest. Spoon the batter into the pan and smooth the top. Bake until golden and cake tester comes out clean, about 50 minutes. Remove cake from oven and place the pan on a rack to cool.

Place remaining ¾ cup of sugar with the honey, orange zest, and 3 cups water in a saucepan. Bring to a boil and simmer 5 minutes. Remove from heat. Using a thin bamboo skewer, poke down into the cake over the entire surface. Gradually pour two-thirds of the hot syrup over cake. Allow to stand at least 2 hours.

Remove the cake from the pan and slice. Serve topped with yogurt and orange segments, with remaining citrus syrup spooned over.

Moscato of Limnos, or other sweet moscato wine

DRINKS

FARMER'S LEMONADE

ROSSINI COCKTAIL

COSMOPOLITAN

MOJITO

FRRROZEN HOT CHOCOLATE

FARMER'S LEMONADE

CITY BAKERY

M AURY RUBIN'S CITY BAKERY began as a café a few steps from the Union Square Greenmarket. It has since moved to larger quarters about a block away. Now, in addition to an expanded array of fresh baked goods, it has assorted food buffets for breakfast, lunch, and dinner, a soda fountain that serves homemade ice cream and root beer floats, and a "chocolate room," an alcove lined with chocolate confections. Rubin also throws "block parties" in his restaurant to celebrate the harvest.

SERVES 6

Juice of 15 large lemons
½ cup sugar
½ cup heavy cream

Place the lemon juice in a large bowl or 2-quart pitcher. Whisk in the sugar and add 4 cups cold water. Whisk until the sugar has dissolved. Whisk in the heavy cream. Pour over ice and serve.

When mixing in the sugar and water, it helps to use your hands to rub the sugar so it will dissolve faster.

240 | DRINKS

ROSSINI COCKTAIL

HARRY CIPRIANI

THERE IS NO HARRY'S BAR IN NEW YORK, but nonetheless there is a major
Cipriani presence. Harry Cipriani, the first of the collection to open, remains the flagship. It has a menu that is a close copy of the original in Venice,
with carpaccio, risottos, simple pastas, fish and meat, and sumptuous desserts.
The furnishings are lower than normal, another signature of the Cipriani style.
The SoHo restaurant called Downtown, Cipriani Dolci in Grand Central Terminal, the Rainbow Room and Rainbow Grill, and Cipriani 42nd Street, a vast
catering hall in the former Bowery Saving Bank building, constitute the rest of
the Cipriani group. Their signature drink is the Bellini, a combination of fresh
white peach puree and sparkling prosecco created by Arrigo Cipriani in Venice.
But everyone serves Bellinis these days. The Rossini is a variation, made only
when good fresh strawberries are available.

SERVES 4

1 pint fresh strawberries
2 teaspoons sugar, or to taste
1 bottle prosecco, chilled

If you forego refills you will
have enough to serve 8.

Trim the strawberries, reserving 4 nice ones for garnish.
Puree the rest in a blender until very smooth. If the puree
is very tart, sweeten it lightly–it should not be very sweet.
Chill the puree.

To serve, spoon about 1½ tablespoons of the puree into
each of 4 Champagne flutes. Slowly pour in the prosecco.
Garnish each drink with a strawberry perched on the rim
of the glass. You should have enough of the puree and
wine for a second round of drinks.

COSMOPOLITAN

ARDI'S REMAINS THE PLACE OF CHOICE for pre- and post-theater drinks, dining, and celebrations, as it has been since Vincent Sardi opened it in 1921. The stars are immortalized in caricatures that cover the walls of the restaurant. Sardi's is famous for its opening night parties, often held on the restaurant's second floor, removed from the public dining room, so the first reviews could be read to cheers or tears. Rather than actually dining on the restaurant's famous lasagna or cannelloni on these occasions, most Broadway denizens just prefer a drink.

SERVES 2

½ ounce dry vermouth
2½ ounces Cointreau
6 ounces vodka
½ cup cranberry juice
Juice of ½ lime

Combine the vermouth, Cointreau, vodka, and cranberry juice with ice cubes in a cocktail shaker. Shake to blend. Add the lime juice, stir, and strain into chilled martini glasses.

MOJITO

IN RECENT YEARS, Latin food has given a hot new beat to New York dining, and put mint-infused mojitos on the drink list. Caribbean and South American cooking was always a presence in neighborhoods in the Bronx and Queens and on the Upper West Side, but it has now become a mainstream cuisine. Calle Ocho, named for the Cuban boulevard in Miami, is an Upper West Side example of this new wave, in a part of the city where bodegas and diners that offer Cuban-Criolla rice and beans still survive, untouched by trends. Calle Ocho is part of an eclectic restaurant collection that includes Rain, serving Southeast Asian food; Django in Midtown, where Mediterranean touches prevail; and the highly regarded Union Pacific in the Flatiron district. At Calle Ocho, Douglas Rodriguez, who brought high-end Latin food to New York from Miami, is now shaping the menu.

SERVES 4

1 bunch mint
¼ cup fresh lime juice
4 ounces light rum
1 lime, cut in 4 wedges
3 cups ice cubes
2½ cups sparkling water or
    club soda, approximately

If you have a nice large cocktail shaker, now is the time to take it out. Place half the mint in it, add the lime juice, and bruise the mint with a muddler or wooden spoon. Add the rum.

Divide the remaining mint among 4 large old-fashioned glasses, lightly squeeze in the lime wedges, and drop them in. Add about ½ cup of ice to each of the glasses. Add the remaining ice to the cocktail shaker and shake well. Strain the mixture into the glasses, fill each with sparkling water, and serve.

This mojito is made without sugar, but for a slightly sweeter drink, a tablespoon of simple syrup can be stirred in with the lime and mint. Make the simple syrup by simmering two parts sugar to one of water until the sugar dissolves, then cool.

FRRROZEN HOT CHOCOLATE

SERENDIPITY 3

SERENDIPITY OPENED IN THE PRE-PSYCHEDELIC 1950S, in a basement on East 58th Street, with a collection of mismatched furniture, funky accessories, and a menu of amusing specialties like foot-long hot dogs, Aunt Buba's Sand Tarts, rhubarb omelets, and Frrrozen Hot Chocolate—all of which are now classics. In 1958, the three owners (the "3" of the name, though they look more like the Magi on the logo) moved the restaurant to its present quarters on East 60th Street. Access to the dining room with its Tiffany lamps is through a boutique selling tchotchkes and souvenirs. New Yorkers who flocked to Serendipity as teenagers now bring their children and maybe even their grandchildren for birthday parties. Serendipity 3 sells a mix for making their famous frozen hot chocolate at home—in both chocolate and coffee flavors.

SERVES 6

6 ounces semisweet chocolate, preferably a mixture of brands, in small chunks

1½ tablespoons unsweetened cocoa

3 tablespoons sugar

2½ cups cold milk

1 cup heavy cream

6 cups ice cubes

3 tablespoons semisweet chocolate shavings

> There are a lot of good brands of chocolate available now. At Serendipity 3, they like to mix more than one brand in a recipe.

Place the 6 ounces of chocolate in the top of a double boiler and allow it to melt over boiling water. Your other options are to put it in a heavy saucepan over low heat and watch it *very* carefully, or to melt it in the microwave. Whisk the melted chocolate until it's smooth, then whisk in the cocoa and sugar. Gradually whisk in the milk. Now you have the basis for the recipe. Place it in a pitcher or container, cover it, and chill it.

While the chocolate mixture is chilling, put 6 (8-ounce) goblets in the refrigerator to chill so they'll be nice and cold when you're ready to dish out the confection. Whip the heavy cream for the topping and refrigerate it.

Minutes before you're going to serve, place half the chocolate mixture in a blender with half the ice. Blend until it's thick and smooth, and spoon it into 3 of the chilled goblets. Repeat with the remaining chocolate mixture and ice. Top each serving with whipped cream and chocolate shavings, and serve at once.

WINE IN NEW YORK RESTAURANTS

KEVIN ZRALY

New York is, unquestionably, the wine capital of the world. With access to more wine at every level of quality and price than any other city—6,000 labels, in fact—New Yorkers can pick and choose wines from some of the most sophisticated lists in the world. Wines of every conceivable variety can be found from virtually every country, and almost every producer.

Nearly 20,000 restaurants spread across five boroughs present wine lists that mirror the New York population—diverse and staggering—ranging from a single selection "house pour" wine to exhaustive inventories boasting 3,000 selections. The lists offer wines from the city's backyard, the Hudson Valley and Long Island, and from such far-flung regions as New Zealand, South Africa, Chile, and Croatia.

This is a development of fairly recent vintage, just in the past 25 years. My own personal collection of wine lists includes one from the '21' Club dating from the 1950s. It is long, 70 pages. The first 50 list French wines only, primarily from Bordeaux and Burgundy. These are followed by 15 pages of German wines, leaving the last five for a sparse inventory of Italian, Spanish, and California wines. In those days, when the cocktail was more important than wine, a list like that was the exception.

Today, New York's savvy restaurateurs and their clients know that a great restaurant is in no small part defined by the quality of its wine list. That fine wines and good food are at the heart of a memorable meal seems obvious. The wine director and the wine list are decisive in defining whether a restaurant is merely good or truly great. Diners judge restaurants as much by their wine lists as by their menus, service, and decor. Many restaurateurs report that more than 40% of their revenue is from wine sales, and some of them wisely use their wine list as a promotional vehicle.

When Windows on the World opened on top of One World Trade Center in 1976, the owner, Joe Baum, instructed me to "create the best wine list that New York has ever seen." Windows immediately became known as having one of the finest wine lists in the country, one that was a pioneer in recognizing what California had to offer. It also ended up with the highest wine sales for any restaurant in the world. Another benefit of the great wine list was that it attracted many wine enthusiasts to the restaurant and to the downtown area.

The same year that Windows opened, The Four Seasons, another of Joe Baum's inspirations, held its first California barrel tasting dinner. It featured the 1975 vintage of 18 wineries, as yet unbottled, all the wines paired with a gala menu. The event was meant as a promotion for the wines, not for the restaurant, but it served both purposes. The annual tradition lasted for 10 years, by which time New York had become a solid wine-drinking city and The Four Seasons had become one of the best-known venues for wines and wine dinners.

Alan Stillman, the president of the Smith & Wollensky Restaurant Group, is another restaurateur who has cleverly used wine to help promote his restaurants, by creating a Wine Week, during which customers are treated with an array of wines freely poured at any of his restaurants during lunch. The owners, winemakers, or representatives of the wineries are there to answer questions.

Most of the wine-friendly restaurants in New York City have a sommelier or wine director. When Le Cirque 2000 opened at a new location in 1997, for the first time ever owner Sirio Maccioni hired a wine director, Ralph Hersom, to run his wine program. Other notable wine directors include Karen King at Gramercy Tavern, Roger Dagorn at Chanterelle, Jean-Luc Le Dû at Daniel, Michael Greenlee at Gotham Bar & Grill, Richard Shipley at '21' Club, and Matthew McCartney at Craft.

Drew Nieporent, owner of Montrachet, Tribeca Grill, and Nobu, has not only created some of New York's most innovative restaurants, but also has two of the top wine directors, Daniel Johnnes at Montrachet and David Gordon at Tribeca Grill. Danny Meyer, the owner of Gramercy Tavern and Union Square Cafe, two of New York's most popular restaurants, involves his staff in the wine list selection process.

There are so many great steak restaurants in New York—how does an owner make his restaurant stand out from the herd? The late Pat Cetta, owner of Sparks, created a fantastic wine list at outrageously low prices to attract customers to his restaurant. Other steakhouses such as Morton's and Del Frisco's have followed his example and offer great wine lists.

Some of the classic French restaurants such as La Caravelle, La Côte Basque, and Lutèce still maintain great wine cellars as do relative newcomers like Alain Ducasse, Jean Georges, and Le Bernardin. In New York, great wine lists are also a given in Italian restaurants. Felidia has it all when it comes to food and wine with one of the greatest selections of Italian wines in the country. Babbo, Barolo, Barbetta, and San Domenico NY are my other favorite Italian wine restaurants.

New Yorkers take their Chinese food seriously, so don't be surprised when you are presented a wine list at one of the great Chinese restaurants. Not in Chinatown, mind you, but in uptown places like Chin Chin. To pair with the newly popular tapas, restaurants offer sherries and deep collections of fine Spanish wines. And now sake lists are showing up, and not only in Japanese restaurants.

New York has even started to rediscover the wines of Austria and Germany, those very wines which were so prominent on my old '21' Club list, but out of fashion for decades since. They are available on more and more lists, to the delight of an increasingly sophisticated wine-drinking public, and not merely in the obvious places such as Wallsé and Danube.

Wine service has also changed, becoming less stuffy and haughty, and more accommodating, relaxed, and matter-of-fact. The quality of stemware is the best that it has ever been. The Internet even allows wine connoisseurs to peruse a restaurant's list in advance and order a serious wine to be left upright to diminish sediment, or to be properly chilled, or decanted so it is ready to drink when the party arrives at the restaurant. Elaborate wine cellars double as popular private dining rooms in many restaurants.

Some wine collectors have partnered with chefs to open their own restaurants, giving us Veritas and Washington Park where the wines may be rare and otherwise unavailable in today's market. Even one of the most famous New York wine retailers, Morrell & Co., has opened up a café next to their wine store, as well as a wine-oriented restaurant.

And it is not just a Manhattan phenomenon. Across the Brooklyn Bridge there are others. At the River Cafe, wine director Joe DeLissio has a superb list. In fact, these days it is hard to find a good restaurant that does not have a solid selection of wines, designed to complement the food, in a range of prices. And, this being New York, order a pepperoni pizza somewhere and it would not be surprising to be handed a wine list so you can choose a nice bottle of red to go with it!

DESIGN IN NEW YORK RESTAURANTS

DAVID ROCKWELL

W HEN THE RUSSIAN IMPRESARIO SERGEI DIAGHILEV wanted Jean Cocteau to create a libretto for his dance company, he presented the 23-year-old Parisian literary sensation with the two-word artistic challenge: "Astonish me."

The same demand inevitably punctuates the conversation whenever a member of New York City's intrepid band of restaurateurs approaches a designer with the idea for a potential project. Restaurateurs function in a supercharged, highly competitive, make-or-break atmosphere, and their lust for astonishment reflects the fact that restaurant openings have become as significant a cultural and social event as the premiere of the latest Broadway extravaganza.

It is no surprise then that the restaurant community replicates the rituals commonly associated with the theater. In common with a Broadway production, a new restaurant goes out of its way to generate anticipatory publicity. As the opening approaches, the restaurant stages a series of dress rehearsals with friends cast in the roles of patrons. A demanding assortment of critics, fellow restaurateurs, opinion makers, and food savvy patrons fills the tables as soon as the curtain officially rings up. Immediately afterwards, they unhesitatingly deliver public proclamations revealing how much astonishment they experienced—or didn't.

In this context, it is no wonder that a restaurateur must function as choreographer, director, and conductor all in one, producing the dining experience as if it were a three-act play. Yet the marriage of dining and showmanship is not new: It has been with us since March 1830, when the Swiss-born brothers, John and Peter Delmonico, expanded their confectionery shop into New York's first restaurant. After the brothers instituted their first menu, they went on to compile a list of 340 entrées, stock their cellar with 16,000 bottles of the best French wine, and in 1861, hire the first celebrity chef, Charles Ranhofer. Show business obviously coursed through the brothers' bloodstreams.

In 1968, at the age of 11, I dined with two of my older brothers at our first New York restaurant, a branch of the now-legendary Schrafft's chain. Although we were boisterous youths, the refined atmosphere so overwhelmed us that we automatically sat up straight and dropped our voices to whispers. Schrafft's served moderately priced food, and when our waitress (who wore a pastel handkerchief in her hair!) served my cheeseburger and fries, her benign smile expressed the dignified restraint that usually accompanies the arrival of haute cuisine.

In retrospect, every design element at Schrafft's was calculated to allow middle-class patrons to believe that they had been enveloped by the same understated atmosphere ordinarily reserved for people of wealth. Little did I know then that I had experienced my first example of dining as theater, and that the experience had been superbly produced.

In common with design for the theater, restaurant design encompasses the journey from an abstract idea to a physical reality. Unlike the theater, though, where the playwright supplies the concrete framework (a script), the restaurateur and chef—often the acknowledged star of the production—ordinarily provide only a concept, accompanied by suggestions about the prospective mood and atmosphere of their project. Drawing on imagination and a hefty dose of research, the designer then sets out to transform their concept into a specific vision.

When I had the privilege of designing Nobu for Nobuyuki Matsuhisa, I understood from the get-go that I had to depict Nobu's genius for blending the finest foods and techniques of traditional Japanese cookery with those of the West, particularly South America. It was my job to create the visual equivalent of Nobu's highly sophisticated, minimalist culinary wonders.

No matter the final result, be it a fantasy world, a Jungian dream come to life, or a loving evocation of the past, the design must have the power to immerse diners into a world that is as unexpected as it is inimitable. Balthazar, Pastis, and Odeon plunge diners into worlds that suggest Belle Époque Parisian brasseries with enormous success. David Bouley's Danube evokes late nineteenth-century Vienna through explicit visual references so effective that patrons feel they are actually dining inside a Gustav Klimt painting.

Designers know that every space is inherently dramatic. When a restaurant occupies a space originally created for a diametrically different purpose, the element of surprise produces an especially dramatic result. Heading the list is the wonderfully exuberant spectacle of Le Cirque 2000, which resides within one of McKim, Mead and White's distinguished quartet of Gilded Age mansions that form the base of the Palace Hotel in Midtown.

Another example, the American brasserie, Guastavino, occupies the towering, cathedral-like tiled vaults under the Queensboro Bridge that were originally designed as an open air market. A visit to Grand Central Terminal demonstrates that the cool modernism of Metrazur and the romantic scenography of Michael Jordan's The Steakhouse co-exist comfortably within the Beaux Arts masterpiece. Head downtown and you will discover that the East Village people-watchers' hangout, B Bar and Grill (a.k.a. Bowery Bar) occupies a former gas station. Further south on the

Bowery, Capitale, a recent addition to New York City's portfolio of grander-than-grand dining rooms, makes its home in Stanford White's marbled and cavernous Bowery Savings Bank.

In his classic essay, "Here is New York," E. B. White chooses an old willow tree in Turtle Bay to symbolize life in our city. The tree represents "life under difficulties, growth against odds, sap rise in the midst of concrete and steady reaching for the sun." Those qualities are inherently dramatic, but then everything in New York is dramatic. Like the multitudes before me and the multitudes to come, New York City is my Emerald City. I feel honored to be a participant in our shared drama of astonishment.

Noche, see recipe, page 180

AFTERWORD

TIM ZAGAT

For two weeks each year, something magical happens here in New York. The city's halls of haute cuisine are transformed into bastions of democracy, where everyone from students to the corporate elite can be found sampling some of the most expertly prepared food in the world for prices more appropriate to a small town than a great dining capital.

These two weeks are called, quite simply, Restaurant Week, and what began as a simple idea has grown to involve hundreds of the best restaurants on the planet. Along the way, it has also played an important role in fortifying New York's now thriving restaurant scene and spawned countless imitators throughout the world.

And it came about, like a surprising number of treasured institutions, quite by accident. During the summer of 1992, New York was busy gearing up to welcome the Democratic National Convention. Modern political conventions being what they are, Bill Clinton had already sewn up the nomination and the prospects of any real news coming out of the four-day festivities were slim. Of course, despite this fact, the press was descending on New York in larger numbers than ever before—a total of 15,000 reporters from around the country and the world.

The New York City Convention Host Committee recognized this tailor-made promotional opportunity for a city that, at the time, was in the middle of a recession and in desperate need of some positive PR. The Host Committee identified New Yorkers in highly visible industries to coordinate initiatives showing off key aspects of the city's cultural organizations, theaters, retailers, and restaurants.

The late, great Joe Baum (creator of inter alia, The Four Seasons, Windows on the World, and the renovated Rainbow Room) and I were asked to cochair the Restaurant Subcommittee. And the idea we developed was simple.

New York City was home to some of the world's finest restaurants. But apart from the occasional expense-account interview, the thousands of journalists who were set to stream into town would never see the inside of a single one of these culinary palaces, let alone taste their wonders. Unless we invited them.

So Joe and I gathered the city's top restaurateurs and proposed that for one week, the week of the 1992 convention, they serve three-course prix-fixe lunches for the price of the year—then a very reasonable $19.92. The idea was that the resulting publicity would far outweigh what we assumed would be a money-losing proposition for the restaurants.

What Joe and I failed to realize was that hundreds of thousands of New Yorkers and vacationers would jump at the opportunity to sample these wonderful restaurants. Suddenly, the city's high-end eateries, some of which had been struggling due to the poor economy, were full. The phones were ringing off the hook, with the *New York Times* reporting that restaurants like Le Cirque, Bouley, and the Quilted Giraffe were getting 5,000 reservation calls a day. And since these new customers were treating these lunches as a special occasion, they were ordering wines and specials that normal customers did not—and spending roughly as much as the non–Restaurant Week regulars. The $19.92 prix-fixe was a win-win for everyone.

The program was so successful that the restaurant community requested that we do it again the following summer. And that's exactly what we did. Thus, New York City gained a new institution, Restaurant Week. In the years since, inflation of the prix-fixe menus has been one penny a year, making, economists tell me, each successive program a better deal than the year before. Several years ago we responded to popular demand—from both restaurant-goers and restaurateurs—and added a second January component to the traditional week in June. It has continued to be so successful that many restaurants extend the special menus for months or even all year long. And we now boast almost 200 restaurants who clamor to participate.

People are drawn to Restaurant Week because it's a good deal. It also gives those who never imagined they could afford a fine restaurant the chance to try one. Restaurateurs in turn enjoy many benefits. They are able to reach out to a clientele that might otherwise feel somewhat intimidated by their famous name or flashy decor—and demonstrate to them the warmth and hospitality that places New York's restaurants a cut above the rest. They fill their restaurants during periods that are typically extremely slow. And they have the opportunity to give back to the city and the people who support them all year long.

Restaurant Week is an interesting—and rare—example of how a product sometimes transcends its own publicity. Restaurant Week's incredible success and longevity have nothing to do with marketing. They are a reflection of the quality and diversity of New York City's restaurants and how this community of hardworking and imaginative men and women are constantly creating and reinventing the city's fine dining scene.

This book is a delicious tribute to the wonderful spirit of these restaurants, and to everyone from the dishwashers to the cooks, chefs, and restaurateurs who make the restaurants possible.

SOURCES

Not only is New York's restaurant landscape rich and diverse, it is matched by the markets that provide the ingredients necessary for preparing everything from a simple, top-notch broiled steak or a perfect Caesar salad, to glassy Korean noodles infused with soy sauce, tender okra needing an Indian spice cabinet, or a Mexican salsa made with the right blend of fresh and dried chiles. At one time, it took a trip to an ethnic neighborhood to find some of these exotic seasonings and vegetables. It still may be the case but increasingly a wide range of Asian, Hispanic, and Middle Eastern products are sold in the big food halls and even in supermarkets.

FOOD HALLS

The well-stocked food halls scattered throughout the city can be the one-stop shopping resource needed for most recipes. They sell packaged groceries, spices, and condiments as well as produce, meats, game, and seafood. Some, like Dean & DeLuca and Zabar's, have well-stocked housewares departments.

AGATA & VALENTINA, 1505 First Avenue (79th Street), Manhattan, 212-452-0690.

AMISH MARKET, 731 Ninth Avenue (49th Street), Manhattan, 212-245-2360; 240 East 45th Street, Manhattan, 212-370-1761; 17 Battery Park Place, Manhattan, 212-871-6300.

BALDUCCI'S, 155 West 66th Street, Manhattan, 212-653-8320, www.suttongourmet.com.

A. L. BAZZINI, 339 Greenwich Street (Jay Street), Manhattan, 212-334-1280.

CITARELLA, 2135 Broadway (75th Street), Manhattan, 212-874-0383; 1313 Third Avenue (75th Street), Manhattan, 212-874-0383; 424 Avenue of the Americas (9th Street), Manhattan, 212-332-1599; www.citarella.com.

DEAN & DELUCA, 560 Broadway (Prince Street), Manhattan, 212-431-1691, www.deandeluca.com.

ELI'S MANHATTAN AND THE VINEGAR FACTORY, 1411 Third Avenue (80th Street), Manhattan, 212-717-8100; 431 East 91st Street, Manhattan, 212-987-0885; www.elizabar.com.

FAIRWAY, 2328 12th Avenue (132nd Street), Manhattan, 212-234-3883; 2127 Broadway (74th Street), Manhattan, 212-595-1888.

GARDEN OF EDEN, 7 East 14th Street, Manhattan, 212-255-4200; 310 Third Avenue (23rd Street), Manhattan, 212-228-4681; 162 West 23rd Street, Manhattan, 212-675-6300; 180 Montague Street (Court Street), Brooklyn, 718-222-1515; www.gardenofedengourmet.com.

GOURMET GARAGE, 117 Seventh Avenue (West 10th Street), Manhattan, 212-699-5980; 453 Broome Street (Mercer Street), Manhattan, 212-941-5850; 301 East 64th Street, Manhattan, 212-535-6271; 2567 Broadway (96th Street), 212-663-0656; www.gourmetgarage.com.

GRACE'S MARKETPLACE, 1237 Third Avenue (71st Street), Manhattan, 212-737-0600, www.gracesmarketplace.com.

SAHADI, 187 Atlantic Avenue (Court Street), Brooklyn, 718-624-4550, www.sahadis.com.

TODARO BROS., 555 Second Avenue (30th Street), Manhattan, 212-532-0633, www.todarobros.com.

WHOLE FOODS, 250 Seventh Avenue, (24th Street), Manhattan, 212-924-5969, www.wholefoodsmarket.com.

ZABAR'S, 2245 Broadway (80th Street), Manhattan, 212-787-2000.

ETHNIC MARKETS

Where the big, generalized food halls may fall short, certain ethnic markets take over to stock the pantry with exotic ingredients.

BANGKOK CENTER GROCERY, 104 Mosco Street (Mott Street), Manhattan, 212-349-1979. *Asian*

DESPAÑA BRAND FOODS, 86-17 Northern Boulevard, Queens, 718-779-4971. *Spanish*

FOODS OF INDIA, 121 Lexington Avenue (28th Street), Manhattan, 212-683-4419. *Indian*

HAN AH REUM MARKET, 25 West 32nd Street, Manhattan, 212-695-3283; 29-02 Union Street, Queens, 718-445-5656. *Korean*

HONG KONG SUPERMARKET, 109 East Broadway (Pike Street), Manhattan, 212-227-3388; 6023 Eighth Avenue, Brooklyn, 718-438-2288; 82-02 45th Avenue (Broadway), Queens, 718-651-3838; 37-11 Main Street, Queens, 718-539-6868. *Chinese*

KALUSTYAN'S, 123 Lexington Avenue (28th Street), Manhattan, 212-685-3451, www.kalustyans.com. *Middle Eastern, Indian*

KAM MAN, 200 Canal Street (Mott Street), Manhattan, 212-571-0330. *Chinese*

KATAGIRI, 224 East 59th Street, Manhattan, 212-755-3566, www.katagiri.com. *Japanese*

KITCHEN MARKET, 218 Eighth Avenue (21st Street), Manhattan, 212-243-4433, www.kitchenmarket.com. *Mexican, Asian*

M2M, 200 East 11th Street, Manhattan, 212-353-2698. *Japanese*

PACIFIC SUPERMARKET, 75-01 Broadway (75th Street), Queens, 718-507-8181. *Asian*

PATEL BROTHERS, 37-27 74th Street (Northern Boulevard), Queens, 718-898-3445; 42-79C and 42-92 Main Street, Queens, 718-661-1112; www.patelbrothersusa.com. *Indian*

SAM BOK GROCERIES, 127 West 43rd Street, Manhattan, 212-582-4730. *Korean, Japanese*

SUNRISE MART, 4 Stuyvesant Street (9th Street and Third Avenue), Manhattan, 212-598-3040. *Japanese*

HERBS AND SPICES

There are some markets that specialize in spices, seasonings, and condiments from every corner of the planet. *See also Ethnic Markets.*

ADRIANA'S CARAVAN, Grand Central Market, Lexington Avenue and 43rd Street, Manhattan, 212-972-8804, www.adrianascaravan.com.

ANGELICA'S HERBS, SPICES AND OILS, 147 First Avenue (9th Street), Manhattan, 212-677-1549.

APHRODISIA, 264 Bleecker Street (Seventh Avenue), Manhattan, 212-989-6440.

PRODUCE

Locally grown, seasonal produce is the stock-in-trade of the Greenmarket system, which has been in business since 1977. Farmers, cheese makers, fishermen, bakers, and other artisanal food producers from the surrounding region bring their products to sell on a regular schedule to all five boroughs, some throughout the year, others on a more limited basis. The Union Square Greenmarket, open on Mondays, Wednesdays, Fridays, and Saturdays, is the flagship. Information and schedules are available from 212-477-3220, www.cenyc.org. *See also Food Halls, Ethnic Markets.*

GREENWICH PRODUCE, Grand Central Market, Lexington Avenue and 43rd Street, Manhattan, 212-490-4444.

MANHATTAN FRUIT EXCHANGE, Chelsea Market, 75 Ninth Avenue (16th Street), Manhattan, 212-989-2444.

SEAFOOD, MEAT, POULTRY, AND GAME

Most of the food halls have well-stocked seafood, meat, and poultry departments, but there are also many specialty stores.

SEAFOOD

CENTRAL FISH, 527 Ninth Avenue (39th Street), Manhattan, 212-279-2317.

PISACANE MIDTOWN, 940 First Avenue (51st Street), Manhattan, 212-752-7560.

RANDAZZO'S SEAFOOD, 2327 Arthur Avenue (187th Street), Bronx, 718-367-4139.

SEA BREEZE, 541 Ninth Avenue (40th Street), Manhattan, 212-563-7537; 8500 18th Avenue (85th Street), Brooklyn, 718-259-9693.

TAN MY MY, 249 Grand Street (Chrystie Street), Manhattan, 212-966-7878.

WILD EDIBLES, Grand Central Market, Lexington Avenue and 43rd Street, Manhattan, 212-687-4255; 535 Third Avenue (35th Street), Manhattan, 212-213-8552; *see also Oppenheimer Prime Meats.*

MEAT, POULTRY, AND GAME

D'ARTAGNAN, 152 East 46th Street, Manhattan, 212-687-0300, 800-327-8246, www.dartagnan.com.

FAICCO'S PORK STORE, 260 Bleecker Street (Seventh Avenue), Manhattan, 212-243-1974; 6511 11th Avenue, Brooklyn, 718-236-0119.

KUROWYCKY, 124 First Avenue (7th Street), Manhattan, 212-477-0344.

LOBEL'S PRIME MEATS, 1096 Madison Avenue (82nd Street), Manhattan, 212-737-1373, 800-556-2357, www.lobels.com.

OPPENHEIMER PRIME MEATS, 2606 Broadway (99th Street), Manhattan, 212-662-0246.

SCHALLER & WEBER, 1654 Second Avenue (86th Street), Manhattan, 212-879-3047, 800-847-4115, www.schallerweber.com.

TARTARE, 653 Ninth Avenue (46th Street), Manhattan, 212-333-5300.

MUSHROOMS AND TRUFFLES

For fresh white and black truffles, and also for mushroom products, prices are sometimes a trifle lower at specialty wholesale-retail markets than in the food halls.

DA ROSARIO, 29-24 40th Avenue, Queens, 718-392-5050, www.shopdarosario.com.

D'ARTAGNAN, *see Meats.*

TRUFFETTE, 96 Avenue B (6th Street), Manhattan, 212-505-5813.

PASTA

A few pasta-makers have been in business for generations.

BORGATTI'S RAVIOLI, 632 East 187th Street, Bronx, 718-367-3799.

RAFFETO'S, 144 West Houston Street (Sullivan Street), Manhattan, 212-777-1261.

CHEESE

Some of the best cheese assortments are sold at markets like Fairway, Zabar's, and Dean & DeLuca. In addition, there are several excellent cheese purveyors in the city.

ARTISANAL, 2 Park Avenue (32nd Street), Manhattan, 212-532-4033.

DIPALO FINE FOODS, 200 Grand Street (Mott Street), Manhattan, 212-226-1033.

MURRAY'S CHEESE SHOP, 257 Bleecker Street (Cornelia Street), Manhattan, 212-243-3289; Grand Central Market, Lexington Avenue and 43rd Street, Manhattan, 212-922-1540; also 888-692-4339, www.murrayscheese.com.

COOKWARE

A number of shops have well-edited cookware inventories.

THE ART OF COOKING, 555 Hudson Street (West 11th Street), Manhattan, 212-414-4940.

BRIDGE KITCHENWARE, 214 East 52nd Street, Manhattan, 212-688-4220, 800-274-3435, www.bridgekitchenware.com.

BROADWAY PANHANDLER, 477 Broome Street (Greene Street), Manhattan, 212-966-3434, 866-266-5927, www.broadwaypanhandler.com.

DEAN & DELUCA, *see Food Halls.*

GRACIOUS HOME, 1217 and 1220 Third Avenue (70th Street), Manhattan, 212-517-6300; 1992 Broadway (67th Street), Manhattan, 212-579-9957; www.gracioushome.com.

New York Cake and Bake Supply, 56 West 22nd Street, Manhattan, 212-675-2253, 800-942-2539.

Twin Supply Inc., 1201 Castleton Avenue (Roe Street), Staten Island, 718-442-1010, www.twinsupply.com.

Williams-Sonoma, 121 East 59th Street, Manhattan, 917-369-1131; 1175 Madison Avenue (86th Street), Manhattan, 212-289-6832; 110 Seventh Avenue (17th Street), Manhattan, 212-633-2203; also 800-541-2233, www.williams-sonoma.com.

Zabar's, *see Food Halls.*

WINE AND LIQUOR

Every neighborhood has wine shops and, given the world-wide selection that lines their shelves, it is hard NOT to find an acceptable wine for dinner. Here are some of the more outstanding examples.

Acker Merrall & Condit Co., 160 West 72nd Street, Manhattan, 212-787-1700, www.ackerwines.com.

Astor Wines & Spirits, 12 Astor Place (Lafayette Street), Manhattan, 212-674-7500, www.astoruncorked.com.

Best Cellars, 1291 Lexington Avenue (87th Street), Manhattan, 212-426-4200, www.bestcellars.com.

Burgundy Wine Co., 143 West 26th Street, Manhattan, 212-691-9092, www.burgundywinecompany.com.

Chambers St. Wines, 160 Chambers Street (Greenwich Street), Manhattan, 212-227-1434, www.chambersstwines.com.

Italian Wine Merchants, 108 East 16th Street, Manhattan, 212-473-2323, www.italianwinemerchant.com.

Morrell & Co., 1 Rockefeller Plaza (49th Street), Manhattan, 212-688-9370, 800-969-4637, www.morrellwine.com.

Park Avenue Liquor Shop, 292 Madison Avenue (40th Street), Manhattan, 212-685-2442, www.parkaveliquor.com.

Pet Wines and Spirits, 415 East 91st Street, Manhattan, 212-987-7600.

PJ Liquor Warehouse, 4898 Broadway (204th Street), Manhattan, 212-567-5500, www.pjwine.com.

Red White & Bubbly, 211 Fifth Avenue (Union Street), Brooklyn, 718-636-9463, www.redwhiteandbubbly.com.

Sherry-Lehmann, 679 Madison Avenue (61st Street), Manhattan, 212-838-7500, www.sherry-lehmann.com.

Skyview Discount Wines & Liquors, 5681 Riverdale Avenue (259th Street), Bronx, 718-601-8222.

Union Square Wines & Spirits, 33 Union Square West (16th Street), Manhattan, 212-675-8100, www.unionsquarewines.com.

Wine & Spirit Co. of Forest Hills, 108-50 Queens Boulevard (72nd Avenue), Queens, 718-575-2700.

BIBLIOGRAPHY

Many of the restaurants and chefs included in this book have cookbooks of their own, which are worth consulting for more recipes and background. Some have more than one book, but only the most recently published book has been listed.

ALAIN DUCASSE
Ducasse, Alain. *Spoon: Food & Wine*. Woodbury, Conn.: Ici La Press, 2003.

AN AMERICAN PLACE
Forgione, Larry. *Heart-Healthy Cooking for All Seasons*. New York: Pocketstar, 1996.

AQUAVIT
Samuelsson, Marcus. *Aquavit: And the New Scandinavian Cuisine*. Boston: Houghton Mifflin, 2003.

AUREOLE
Palmer, Charlie with Judith Choate. *The Art of Aureole*. Berkeley: Ten Speed Press, 2003.

BABBO
Batali, Mario. *The Babbo Cookbook*. New York: Clarkson N. Potter, 2002.

BALDORIA
Pellegrino, Frank. *Rao's Cookbook*. New York: Random House, 1998.

BALTHAZAR
McNally, Keith, and Riad Nasr, Lee Hanson, and Kathryn Kellinger. *The Balthazar Cookbook*. New York: Clarkson N. Potter, 2003.

BEACON
Malouf, Waldy and Melissa Clark. *High Heat*. New York: Broadway Books, 2003.

BEPPE
Casella, Cesare and Eileen Daspin. *The Diary of a Tuscan Chef*. New York: Doubleday, 1998.

BOLO
Flay, Bobby and Julia Moskin. *Bobby Flay Cooks American*. New York: Hyperion, 2001.

BOULEY
Bouley, David and Melissa Clark. *East of Paris*. Hopewell, New Jersey: Ecco, 2003.

CAFÉ DES ARTISTES
Ferretti, Fred. *Café des Artistes*. New York: Lebhar-Friedman, 2000.

CALLE OCHO
Rodriguez, Douglas. *Great Ceviche Book*. Berkeley: Ten Speed Press, 2003.

CHANTERELLE
Waltuck, David and Melicia Phillips. *Staff Meals from Chanterelle*. New York: Workman Publishing Company, 2000.

CITARELLA
Miller, Bryan and Bill Yosses. *Desserts for Dummies*. New York: John Wiley & Sons, 1997.

CITY BAKERY
Rubin, Maury. *Book of Tarts*. New York: William Morrow, 1995.

CRAFT
Colicchio, Tom. *Craft of Cooking*. New York: Clarkson N. Potter, 2003.

DANIEL
Boulud, Daniel. *Daniel's Dish*. Paris: Filipacchi Books, 2003.

D'ARTAGNAN ROTISSERIE
Daguin, Ariane, George Faison, and Joanna Preuss. *D'Artagnan's Glorious Game Cookbook*. Boston: Little Brown and Company, 1999.

DO HWA
Kwak, Jenny and Liz Fried. *Dok Suni: Recipes from My Mother's Korean Kitchen*. New York: St. Martin's Press, 1998.

FELIDIA
Bastianich, Lidia. *Lidia's Italian-American Kitchen*. New York: Alfred A. Knopf, 2001.

THE FOUR SEASONS
Mariani, John with Alex Von Bidder. *The Four Seasons*. New York: Crown Publishers, 1994.

FRESCO BY SCOTTO
Scotto Family. *Italian Comfort Food*. New York: Regan Books, 2002.

GOTHAM BAR & GRILL
Portale, Alfred. *Alfred Portale's 12 Seasons Cookbook*. New York: Broadway Books, 2000.

GUASTAVINO
Orr, Daniel. *Daniel Orr Real Food*. New York: Rizzoli, 1997.

HARRY CIPRIANI
Cipriani, Arrigo. *The Harry's Bar Cookbook*. New York: Bantam Books, 1991.

JEAN GEORGES
Vongerichten, Jean-Georges and Mark Bittman. *Simple to Spectacular*. New York: Broadway Books, 2000.

LE BERNARDIN
Ripert, Eric and Michael Ruhlman. *A Return to Cooking*. New York: Artisan Publishers, 2002.

LE MADRI
Luongo, Pino. *La Mia Cucina Toscana*. New York: Broadway Books, 2003.

LUTÈCE
Soltner, André with Seymour Britchky. *The Lutèce Cookbook*. New York: Alfred A. Knopf, 1995.

MARCH
Nish, Wayne and Ellen Greaves. *Simple Menus for the Bento Box.* New York: William Morrow, 1998.

MOLYVOS
Kremezi, Aglaia. *The Foods of the Greek Islands, with Recipes from Molyvos Restaurant.* Boston: Houghton Mifflin, 2000.

NOBU
Matsuhisa, Nobuyuki. *Nobu: The Cookbook.* Translated by Laura Holland. New York: Kodansha International, 2001.

OLIVES
English, Todd and Sally Sampson. *The Figs Table.* New York: Simon & Schuster, 1998.

OUEST
Valenti, Tom and Andrew Friedman. *Soups, Stews, and One-Pot Meals.* New York: Scribner, 2003.

OYSTER BAR
Grand Central Oyster Bar Restaurant and Sandy Ingber. *The Grand Central Oyster Bar and Restaurant Complete Seafood Cookbook.* New York: Stewart, Tabori & Chang, 1999.

PALM
Binns, Brigit Legere. *The Palm Restaurant Cookbook.* Philadelphia: Running Press, 2003.

PAMPANO
Sandoval, Richard, David Ricketts and Ignacio Urquiza. *Modern Mexican Flavors.* New York: Stewart, Tabori & Chang, 2002.

PATSY'S
Scognamillo, Sal and Nancy Sinatra. *Patsy's Cookbook.* New York: Clarkson N. Potter, 2002.

PAYARD BISTRO
Payard, François. *Simply Sensational Desserts.* New York: Broadway Books, 1999.

PEARL OYSTER BAR
Charles, Rebecca and Deborah Di Clementi. *Lobster Rolls and Blueberry Pie.* New York: Regan Books, 2003.

REMI
Antonucci, Francesco and Adam Tihany. *Venetian Taste.* Text by Florence Fabricant. New York: Abbeville Press, 1994.

RIVER CAFE
DeLissio, Joseph. *The River Cafe Wine Primer.* Boston: Little Brown and Company, 2000.

ROSA MEXICANO
Howard, Josefina. *Rosa Mexicano.* New York: Viking, 1998.

ROY'S NEW YORK
Yamaguchi, Roy with Joan Namkoong. *Hawaii Cooks*. Berkeley: Ten Speed Press, 2003.

SAN DOMENICO
May, Tony. *Italian Cooking—Basic Cooking Techniques*. New York: Tony May Group, 2001.

SARDI'S
Sardi, Vincent and George Shea. *Sardi's Bar Guide*. New York: Ballantine Books, 1992.

SECOND AVENUE DELI
Lebewohl, Sharon and Jack, Rena Bulkin and Second Avenue Deli. *The 2nd Avenue Deli Cookbook*. New York: Villard, 1999.

SERENDIPITY 3
Miller, Pat and Serendipity Restaurant. *The Serendipity Cookbook*. New York: Citadel Press, 1994.

TERRE
Delouvrier, Christian. *Mastering Simplicity: A Life in the Kitchen*. New York: John Wiley & Sons, 2003.

'21' CLUB
Lomonaco, Michael with Donna Forsman. *The '21' Cookbook*. New York: Doubleday, 1995.

UNION PACIFIC
DiSpirito, Rocco. *Flavor*. New York: Hyperion, 2003.

UNION SQUARE CAFE
Meyer, Danny and Michael Romano. *Second Helpings from Union Square Cafe Cookbook*. New York: HarperCollins, 2001.

VERBENA
Forley, Diane with Catherine Young. *The Anatomy of a Dish*. New York: Artisan Publishers, 2002

ZARELA
Martinez, Zarela. *Zarela's Veracruz*. Boston: Houghton Mifflin, 2001.

ACKNOWLEDGMENTS

THIS IS THE SECOND TIME I have collaborated on a cookbook with my daughter, Patricia Fabricant, a gifted graphic designer. Working with her is always a pleasure. It was largely thanks to her that the job of writing this book landed in my lap. It had to be completed in just a few months, which would not have been possible but for Cristyne Nicholas, Natasha Caba, and especially, Laura Herrera and her staff at NYC & Company, including Tara San Filippo, who were there for me, literally night and day, accomplishing miracles in obtaining the necessary material from the restaurants and their chefs. At Rizzoli, Charles Miers and Christopher Steighner cracked the whip when I doubted that the deadlines could be met, and somehow, it all came together in record time.

—FLORENCE FABRICANT

WE WOULD LIKE TO ACKNOWLEDGE the following key individuals for their support: Phillip Baltz, Jane Dystel, Scott Feldman, Frank Giallorenzo, Anthony Giglio, Evan Korn, Buzzy O'Keeffe, Sheryl Shade, Jeffrey Stewart, Jonathan M. Tisch, Commissioner Iris Weinshall, Clark Wolf, Keith Yazmir, Melanie Young, and Jenny Zinman.

A special thank you to the NYC & Company restaurant committee and book contributors who enthusiastically provided their insight about New York City dining: Stephen Hanson, Rita Jammet, Alan Kurtz, Tony May, Danny Meyer, Tracy Nieporent, David Rockwell, Tim Zagat, and Kevin Zraly.

Lastly, we extend our appreciation and gratitude to the participating restaurants that have made this endeavor possible.

—NYC & COMPANY

INDEX OF RESTAURANTS

CITARELLA (228)
1240 Sixth Avenue
212-332-1515

CITY BAKERY (240)
3 West 18th Street
212-366-1414

CITY HALL (171)
131 Duane Street
212-227-7777

CRAFT (72)
43 East 19th Street
212-780-0880

DANIEL (174)
60 East 65th Street
212-288-0033

D'ARTAGNAN ROTISSERIE
(54)
152 East 46th Street
212-687-0300

DO HWA (34)
55 Carmine Street
212-414-1224

ESTIATORIO MILOS (123)
125 West 55th Street
212-245-7400

FAIRWAY STEAKHOUSE (198)
2127 Broadway, 2nd Floor
212-595-1888

FELIDIA (86)
243 East 58th Street
212-758-1479

FIAMMA OSTERIA (84)
206 Spring Street
212-653-0100

FIREBIRD (197)
365 West 46th Street
212-586-0244

THE FOUR SEASONS (156)
99 East 52nd Street
212-754-9494

FRESCO BY SCOTTO (83)
34 East 52nd Street
212-935-3434

GOTHAM BAR & GRILL (66)
12 East 12th Street
212-620-4020

GUASTAVINO (130)
409 East 59th Street
212-980-2455

HANGAWI (89)
12 East 32nd Street
212-213-0077

HARRY CIPRIANI (241)
Sherry Netherland
781 Fifth Avenue
212-753-5566

JEAN GEORGES (30)
Trump International Hotel
1 Central Park West
212-299-3900

JEWEL BAKO (27)
239 East 5th Street
212-979-1012

JIMMY'S UPTOWN (196)
2207 Seventh Avenue
212-491-4000

KAI (215)
Ito-En
822 Madison Avenue
212-988-7277

KIN KHAO (153)
171 Spring Street
212-966-3939

L'ABSINTHE (33)
227 East 67th Street
212-794-4950

LA CARAVELLE (124)
33 West 55th Street
212-586-4252

LA CÔTE BASQUE (187)
60 West 55th Street
212-688-6525

LE BERNARDIN (132)
155 West 51st Street
212-554-1515

LE CIRQUE 2000 (208)
NY Palace Hotel
455 Madison Avenue
212-303-7788

LE COLONIAL (74)
149 East 57th Street
212-752-0808

LE MADRI (106)
168 West 18th Street
212-727-8022

LE PAIN QUOTIDIEN (113)
100 Grand Street
212-625-9009
1131 Madison Avenue
212-327-4900
1336 First Avenue
212-717-4800
833 Lexington Avenue
212-755-5810
50 West 72nd Street
212-712-9700
38 East 19th Street
212-673-7900

LE PÉRIGORD (164)
405 East 52nd Street
212-755-6244

L'IMPERO (78)
45 Tudor City Place
212-599-5045

LUTÈCE (142)
249 East 50th Street
212-752-2225

MARCH (222)
405 East 58th Street
212-754-6272

MARIO'S (82)
2342 Arthur Avenue
718-584-1188 (Bronx)

MARSEILLE (160)
630 Ninth Avenue
212-333-2323

MICHAEL'S (102)
24 West 55th Street
212-767-0555

MOLYVOS (236)
871 Seventh Avenue
212-582-7500

MONTRACHET (210)
239 West Broadway
212-219-2777

NAM (205)
110 Reade Street
212-267-1777

NOBU (128)
105 Hudson Street
212-219-0500

NOCHE (180)
1604 Broadway
212-541-7070

OLIVES (60)
W Union Square Hotel
201 Park Avenue South
212-353-8345

ONE IF BY LAND,
TWO IF BY SEA (220)
17 Barrow Street
212-228-0822

OUEST (28)
2315 Broadway
212-580-8700

OYSTER BAR (59)
Grand Central Terminal
212-490-6650

PALM (71)
837 Second Avenue
212-687-2953

PAMPANO (40)
209 East 49th Street
212-751-4545

PATSY'S (138)
236 West 56th Street
212-247-3491

PAYARD BISTRO (218)
1032 Lexington Avenue
212-717-5252

PEARL OYSTER BAR (110)
18 Cornelia Street
212-691-8211

PEARSON'S TEXAS
BBQ (103)
71-04 35th Avenue
718-779-7715 (Queens)
170 East 81st Street
212-288-2700

PETER LUGER STEAK
HOUSE (192)
178 Broadway
718-387-7400 (Brooklyn)

PETROSSIAN (94)
182 West 58th Street
212-245-2214

RED CAT (200)
227 Tenth Avenue
212-242-1122

RELISH (68)
225 Wythe Avenue
718-963-4546 (Brooklyn)

REMI (93)
145 West 53rd Street
212-581-4242

RIVER CAFE (118)
1 Water Street
718-522-5200 (Brooklyn)

RM (136)
33 East 60th Street
212-319-3800

ROSA MEXICANO (162)
61 Columbus Avenue
212-977-7700
1063 First Avenue
212-753-7407

ROY'S NEW YORK (120)
Marriott Financial Center
130 Washington Street
212-266-6262

SAN DOMENICO NY (172)
240 Central Park South
212-265-5959

SAPORI D'ISCHIA (104)
55-13 37th Avenue
718-446-1500 (Queens)

SARDI'S (243)
234 West 44th Street
212-221-8440

SAVOY (203)
70 Prince Street
212-219-8570

SECOND AVENUE DELI (52)
156 Second Avenue
212-677-0606

SERENDIPITY 3 (247)
225 East 60th Street
212-838-3531

SHUN LEE PALACE (179)
155 East 55th Street
212-371-8844

SMITH & WOLLENSKY (176)
797 Third Avenue
212-753-1530

STRIP HOUSE (194)
13 East 12th Street
212-328-0000

TAMARIND (204)
41-43 East 22nd Street
212-674-7400

TASTE (226)
1413 Third Avenue
212-717-9798

TAVERN ON THE GREEN (64)
Central Park West at
67th Street
212-873-3200

TERRE (46)
430 West 14th Street
212-243-3328

TOWN (50)
Chambers Hotel
15 West 56th Street
212-582-4445

TRATTORIA DELL'ARTE (44)
900 Seventh Avenue
212-245-9800

'21' CLUB (38)
21 West 52nd Street
212-582-7200

UNION PACIFIC (212)
111 East 22nd Street
212-995-8500

UNION SQUARE CAFE (116)
21 East 16th Street
212-243-4020

VERBENA (223)
54 Irving Place
212-260-5454

VERITAS (230)
43 East 20th Street
212-353-3700

VINE (36)
25 Broad Street
212-344-8463

WALLSÉ (168)
344 West 11th Street
212-352-2300

WASHINGTON PARK (232)
24 Fifth Avenue
212-529-4400

wd50 (224)
50 Clinton Street
212-477-2900

ZARELA (146)
953 Second Avenue
212-644-6740

ZITOUNE (150)
46 Gansevoort Street
212-675-5224

INDEX OF RESTAURANTS BY LOCATION

INDEX

M

PHOTOGRAPHY CREDITS

© 2003 Barbara Alper: page 216; Quentin Bacon: 227; Emmanuel Bastien: 146; Linda Campbell: 98; Kenneth Chen: 143; Citysearch: 136; © Thomas Dallal: 2, 5, 24, 34, 37, 50, 54, 56, 61, 73, 80, 87, 90, 101, 129, 160, 163, 168, 174, 193, 229, 243, 245; Tracey David: 152; © Envision Stock Photography, Inc. / Workbookstock.com: 28, 211; Patricia Fabricant: 150; Jean-Pierre Gabriel: 112, 113; Richard Gilbert: 202; Gayle Gleason: 42; Gotham Bar & Grill: 66; Mick Hales: 235; Anne Hall: 180; Fransisco Herrera: 107; Michelle Hood: 95; Warren Jager: 236; Paul Johnson: 92; Michael Katz: 23; L'Absinthe: 33; Eric Langiel: 84; Le Cirque Archives: 208; John Lei: 167; Le Perigord: 164; Henry Leutwyler: 213; Beckett Logan: 45; Lou Manna: 177; © Peter Medilek / ClausNY: 20, 58, 70, 104, 109, 138, 144, 198, back cover; Michael Mundy: 74; Fumiko Nozawa: 220; Octopus Press: 130; Robert Polidori: 225; Thomas Schauer: 190; Frank Schramm: 125; © Liz Steger, www.lizsteger.com: 31, 157, 184, 219, 246; Steph Graphics: 126; Buff Strickland: 26, 111, 232; Joseph Tabacca: 40; Michael Tongt: 178; '21' Club: 39; Union Square Cafe: 116; Paul Warchol/Rockwell Group: 195; Vincent Wolf: 79.